Pressing Tasks of China's Economic Transition

By Chi Fulin

FOREIGN LANGUAGES PRESS   BEIJING

First Edition 1996

The project is aided by
(Hainan) China Foundation for Reform and Development Research.

Translated by Yin Zhongyi and others
English text edited by Paul White

ISBN 7-119-01967-8

Published by Foreign Languages Press
24 Baiwanzhuang Road, Beijing 100037, China

Distributed by China International Book Trading Corporation
35 Chegongzhuang Xilu, Beijing 100044, China
P.O. Box 399, Beijing, China

Printed in the People's Republic of China

Preface

Having entered a key period in the overall transformation of her economic system on the basis of the successful and progressive reform policy, China plans to accomplish the strategic task of transforming the traditional planned economy system into a market economy one in the next 15 years. However, there still exist a series of problems calling for prompt solutions if China is to quicken the pace of her economic reform and smoothly push forward the transition towards a market economy system taking into account her concrete conditions.

Although the overall goal of China's economic reform has been quite explicitly decided upon, all important reform programs call for in-depth studies and explorations before they are implemented. This is because overall economic transformation involves many extremely complicated and deep-rooted problems, and almost all important reform programs have varying degrees of complexity and involve deep-seated contradictions.

This book presents some tentative explorations into some of the major theoretical and practical issues arising in China's transition from the the traditional planned economy system toward a market economy one.

The theory and practice of China's economic system transformation would require a huge volume for a relatively thorough discussion and exploration. Besides, many issues have barely been touched upon until now. So I am willing to continue to exert my own efforts to contribute to the debate. For this purpose, comments and suggestions on the present book will be sincerely appreciated.

My heartfelt gratitude goes to the German Technical Cooperation Corporation, which sponsored the publication of this book, to my colleagues and friends at the China Foreign Languages Press, who gave their all-out support during the whole process of its preparation, and especially to Mr. Yin Zhongyi who completed the initial translation of a large part of the English-language version.

Chi Fulin
June 4, 1996

Contents

Restructuring China's Macro Economy: History and Development

It has been 15 years since China began to restructure her economic system. The magnificent achievements scored in this period have attracted worldwide attention. The overall economic structure has undergone tremendous changes and the GNP has been increasing at an average of nine percent annually. The traditional economic system has basically been revamped and the elements of the new system have been constantly developing. In 1992 China set the goal of establishing a socialist market economy, which signified that the overall economic restructuring had entered an entirely new stage. In the process of restructuring, major breakthroughs have been made in the transformation of the macro economy. At present, in moving toward a market economy, the series of reform measures in the macro economy sphere will greatly accelerate the pace of transition.

I. The Historical Process of Restructuring China's Macro Economy

Before 1978 the economic system in China was a highly centralized planned one, a system that incorporated the macro mechanism with the micro mechanism into one. The role of the government was not only to regulate the aggregate GNP, but also to be directly involved in the management of production and operation. The major production sectors were brought into line with state planning, and the fiscal management was to have all incomes from state-owned enterprises turned over to the central treasury department; in return, all necessary expenditures were disbursed by the department. The management of materials was

1

based on centralized allocation, transfer and rationing, and likewise fiscal management was based on centralized allocation in accordance with planning. Administration was carried out hierarchically by means of promulgating decrees and orders. This special characteristic of the administrative structure determined that a special approach had to be adopted in restructuring the country's macro economy. By giving more autonomy to the lower levels, with the expansion of enterprise autonomy and the development of the market, the restructuring of the macro economy in China has progressively unfolded. This restructuring since 1978 has basically undergone three stages, involving constant in-depth reform of the macro economy.

The first stage: December 1978 to October 1984

In late 1978, at the 3rd Plenary Session of the 11th Central Committee of the Communist Party of China, a decision was made to shift the priority of the Party's central task to economic construction, and the historic mission of restructuring the economic system was put before the nation. During this period, the disadvantages of the incumbent economic system were pointed out as being excessive centralization of power in administration, the inappopriateness of merging governmental administration with enterprise management and the misguided economic egalitarianism in allocation. Hence the reform was oriented toward "transferring power to the lower levels and maximizing subordinates' interests" and toward following and utilizing the law of value and giving full play to the function of economic levers.

The restructuring of the economy in China was initiated in the rural areas. This brought about miraculous changes in a short time and accelerated the transformation of the traditional small-scale peasant economy into a commodity economy. The rural reform drive has enabled China's 800 million peasants to shake off poverty, to have adequate food and clothing and to approach a "comfortably well-off living standard."

Rural reform was carried out mainly in three areas. First was the implementation of the "household contract responsibility system." This was a departure from the highly centralized system practiced by the people's communes. By allocating collectively-owned land to each peasant household on a contract basis operations are carried out in a decentralized manner, while the collective still retains the ownership of the land. This reform has not only transformed the former operational system in the rural areas, it has also, to a great extent, altered the former property relations due to the fact that it has brought about local accumulation of capital and ensuing benefits. Statistics show that, by the end of 1991 the average fixed assets of each peasant household equaled 1,497.09 yuan, Thus, the peasant household has not only become a production unit and a consumer unit, but also an investment and accumulation unit.

Second was the transformation of the purchasing and sales system as well as the reform of the pricing system for agricultural by-products. Rationed purchase was implemented on a contract basis, and prices for most agricultural and side-line products were regulated by the market.

Third was the adjustment and transformation of the rural economic structure and the emergence of township and village enterprises, which have become the most important factors in the restructuring of the rural economy. The value of production of township and village enterprises in China exceeded 1,000 billion yuan in 1991, comprising 59.2% of the total production value in the rural area. The township and village enterprises have become the most dynamic force in the economic development of the rural economy. They have also increased the incomes of the rural population.

Areas outside the rural economy have likewise initiated reform experiments in several aspects. The experiments focus on the following: expanding the autonomy of enterprises in production and operation; actively developing diversified economic modes; transforming the circulation mechanism for commodities between urban and rural areas; giving full play to the economic function of metropolises; implementing the policies of opening up to external markets and establishing special economic zones; and opening the coastal cities for the expansion of international cooperation in economy and technology.

In this stage, in conjunction with the practice of expanding the autonomy of enterprises, some adjustments were made in the macro economy in terms of reforming the urban economic system through delegating decision-making powers to the lower levels of administration and modifying managerial approaches. Major measures introduced during this period included gradually delineating income and expenditure, letting each level take responsibility for itself at the provincial, municipal and autonomous regional levels, and abolishing the practice of submitting all the profits of state-owned enterprises to the state and putting in its place a system of taxation. In the domain of finance, since 1979, specialized banks have either been restored or newly established, a central banking system has been set up and conditions have been created for the transition of direct control of loans toward indirect control. Centrally directed planning for agricultural production in rural areas has been minimized. In fact, by 1985 such planning for agricultural production has been basically terminated. At the same time steps have been taken to rely less and less on material goods which are subject to unified egalitarian allocation by the state.

The second stage: October 1984 to 1992

In October 1984, at the 3rd Plenary Session of the 12th Central Committee of the CPC, a document titled *Decision of the Central Committee of the CPC Concerning the Restructuring of the Economy* was adopted. It explicitly postulated that the socialist economy was a planned commodity economy based upon market regulation, and thus established the orientation of the economic restructuring in China. Through a deep-going understanding of the flaws manifested in the traditional economic system, more and more people have begun to realize that, apart from the excessive concentration of power, other impediments inherent in the old structure included resistance to the market and the rigid allocation of resources. The idea of delegating more decision-making power to lower levels of administration while letting them retain a proportion of profits was scrutinized once again as a rationale for economic restructuring. In 1987 a basic concept of the new economic structure was being ascertained. This included three major aspects: enterprises with autonomous power in business operation which bear responsibility for their own profits and losses; a sound market system; and a macro-control mechanism based mainly upon indirect guidance.

The strategy during this stage was to carry out the economic restructuring in the urban areas and the central link in the economic restructuring was to do a good job of revitalizing enterprises. The main contents of the restructuring of the macro economy during this stage included the following: planning, investment, finance, taxation, pricing, material sources, commerce and foreign trade. The number of items listed in mandatory plans and covered by the state's unified pricing was gradually reduced. Prices were gradually freed through the adoption of a "dual pricing" system. In addition, tax categories and tax rates were regulated. Adjustments were made on several occasions to the fiscal responsibility system. During the late 1980s and early 1990s experiments were carried out with regard to "divided taxation" and "divergence of taxes and profits." With the waning of direct state control, a series of reforms have also been carried out in finance, resulting in a rapid development of the finance and capital markets. With the strengthening of the implementation of economic policies and the functioning of economic levers to regulate the macro economy, the economic functions of pricing, rate of interest, rate of taxation and rate of exchange have all been constantly reinforced. Such a reform has brought about a great change in state administration, which used to call for administrative decrees and directives based upon hierarchical relationships. The role of finance as a means of indirect regulation has also been gradually strengthened in the steady progress toward indirect administration.

In this stage, with the constant eradication of the elements of the old economic administrative system and the gradual increase in market components, the regulatory role of the market has been greatly strengthened. However, the new economic relationship and the new pattern of profits formed during the process of economic restructuring are, on the one hand, a driving force that impels economic development and serves as a major force that keeps at bay the traditional economic system at a time when two systems co-exist. On the other hand, in some areas the new vested interests and the old economic system are together an inhibitive force that runs counter to the tide of reform as well as to the newly established mechanism for macro economic administration. It is worth noting that the joint operation program of reform started in 1986, with regard to the reform of pricing, taxation and finance, was eventually proved to be a miscarriage due to immature conditions and various inhibitive forces. Therefore, during this stage, in which the macro economic administrative system was undergoing transformation, the sluggishness in the establishment of the new administrative system left much to be desired, though remarkable achievements have been accomplished in terms of making breakthroughs in the traditional system.

The third stage: since 1992

In October 1992 the 14th National Congress of the CPC confirmed explicitly that the target of economic restructuring in China was to set up a socialist market economic model. Such a model would ensure the fundamental role of the market in distributing resources under macro economic regulation and control. To shift from a traditional planned economy to a planned commodity economy, and eventually to a market economy, represents a major development in the target model and guiding ideology for the economic restructuring of China. The economic reform will be unfolded in an all-round manner in accordance with the requirements for the establishment of the new socialist market economy system.

In the wake of the new round of overheating in the economy in the first half of 1993, which shook the economic order and introduced increasingly unstable factors in the macro economy, the central government exerted great efforts to regulate and control economic growth. The fluctuation in the national economy, the problems exposed in its operation as well as the practice of the state's macro-economic regulation and control have repeatedly demonstrated that China is short of means and levers for indirect regulation and control on the one hand, and lacks a macro system that allows flexibility in their application on the other. The development of economy calls for the acceleration of economic restructuring, especially the speedy establishment of macro-economic regulation and control system that mainly depends on indirect yet effective means of regulation. The purpose is to strengthen the capacity of the state in its indirect regulation and control of market economy operations, and eventually help the national economy embark on a track of sound circulation, and healthy and speedy development. To this end, great efforts have been made in term of preparation. A series of major reform measures were introduced in 1994 with regard to finance, taxation, investment, foreign trade and foreign exchange, state-owned assets management and the institutional reform of enterprises. All these vital reform measures aim at the establishment of a basic framework for the state's macro-economic regulation and control in the socialist market economy system.

II. Historical Achievements in Restructuring the Macro Economy in China

1. Restructuring the planned economy system

(1) The background to restructuring the planned economy and its progress

Before the implementation of the policies of reform and opening up, China practised a highly centralized planned economy system which took shape during the first Five-Year Plan period (1953-1957). At that time, when China's economy was still underdeveloped, such a system played a great role in mobilizing limited resources for the initial establishment of a relatively intact industrial setup. But with the development of the economy serious drawbacks inherent in this system were gradually brought to light. From the 1950s to the 1970s several major measures of reform and adjustment were carried out to remedy these drawbacks. However, the measures were limited to adjusting the administrative jurisdiction between the central and the local and

7

between the departmental and the regional administrations, and the result was never-ending haggling over the issues of delegating or removing responsibilities. Since 1978 a better understanding has been gained in regard to the drawbacks inherent in the planned system, of which the major ones are: too centralized control in the state's planning; excessively rigid control exercised over enterprises; and a tendency to relying upon administrative means to distribute resources while ignoring the roles of the law of value and the market mechanism. A series of measures have been adopted to remedy these drawbacks.

In the first stage of reform (1979-1984), which was the preparatory stage as well as a stage for limited adjustment for the restructuring of the planned economy system, a target model was sought. At this stage, a new understanding of the role of the law of value and the supplementary role of market regulation was achieved. The outcome of this new understanding was the consideration and utilization of the law of value in formulating plans, which resulted in reducing the amount of state planning in the forms of directive targets for agricultural and industrial production, etc.

In the second stage (1984-1992), a stage which saw an all-round unfolding of the restructuring of the planned economy system, the key to the restructuring was to gradually reduce the scope of directive planning, to delegate administrative responsibilities for planning to lower levels, to stress the application of economic regulatory means and economic policies, to give full play to the market mechanism, to carry out different forms of the planned contract responsibility system, and to intensify the adjustment and orientation of the industrial setup through the formulation of the industrial policies. In reforming the management and operations of investment, responsibility was delegated to the lower levels of administration for the examination and approval of projects related to investment in fixed assets; at the same time, the scope for investment under the control of state planning was narrowed. In reforming finance, restructuring has been carried out to stop the utilization of construction capital without compensation; and, beginning in 1981, financial allocation has been replaced by bank loans in terms of investment for replaced by bank loans in terms of investment for basic construction. In 1985 major developments were made in this transformation, followed by some other adjustments. The year 1988 saw the establishment of a central funding system for basic construction, which brought about the founding of specialized investment companies, etc. In the fiscal management of investment project, since 1984 a projects investment responsibility system has been introduced, in which the proprietor is responsible for the preparatory planning, fund raising and designing, followed by construction, production, operation and debt paying. He is also responsible for the value maintenance of state-owned assets.

In the third stage (since 1992) a new calculation system has been implemented, which has brought about an improvement in the economic evaluation index, further reduced the number of items included in directive production planning and developed a planning system based upon the market. Guided planning was introduced as a major means to accelerate the transformation of the role of the departments in charge of planning, and, to this end, advisory and information services were intensified. As regards investment, a risk-bearing responsibility system for bank loans and corporate investment will be gradually introduced; a system of project registration will replace the system of project application examination and approval; and a new planning system will be established in accordance with the requirements of the market economy.

(2) Major achievements and changes in the course of the restructuring of the planned economy

a. Reduction of plans with the nature of directives, narrowing down the scope of direct administration; utilization of plans with the nature of guidelines and fully displaying the role of market regulation.

—Abolishing all directive plans for agricultural production and the system of assigned purchasing of agricultural by-products. Before 1979, some 25 items of major agricultural products were covered by state directive planning. Also included in the directive plans for agricultural production were the plantation areas for 25 kinds of crops and the total yield of crops based on different regions. Such directive plans were basically abolished in the first stage of economic restructuring, and, beginning in 1985, unified purchasing and assigned purchasing of agricultural by-products were gradually abolished, being replaced by contract purchasing and market purchasing.

　—Reducing directive plans for industrial production. In 1987 there were 120 items listed in the directive plans for industrial production formulated by the State Planning Commission, comprising 40% of the nation's total value of industrial production. This would reach around 90% if an additional 1,900 kinds of industrial items covered by the directive planning of other industrial departments, provinces and cities were included. The number of products covered by the directive plans of the State Planning Commission was reduced to 80 in 1987 and to 50 in 1988, comprising 17% of the nation's total industrial output value in 1987, 11.6% in 1991 and 6.8% in 1993, respectively. It is estimated that the percentage would drop to 4% in 1994, accompanied by a wide-margin decrease in the number of items covered by directive plans delegated by each province and city.

　—Reduction of the variety and quantity of goods covered by the unified distribution plan and goods under the control of ministry while developing the market for means of production. The State Planning Commission is responsible for regulation in this respect. Goods under the unified distribution plan numbered 256 kinds in 1979. Now the value of goods under the unified distribution plan comprises less than 20% of the social demand. There has been a continual decline in proportion with regard to the total of major goods under the unified distribution plan, such as steel, timber, cement and coal, etc. In 1988 measures were taken to make an inventory of goods under the administration of each department, and for the management of goods, different forms were employed, such as guideline-based planning, contract purchasing, linking demand with production, and free purchasing and selling, etc.

　—Transforming the practice of single prices resulting from the centralized price-fixing system. In 1978 the proportion of the total amount of agricultural by-products covered by the centralized price-fixing system was 94.4%. This was reduced to 60% in 1987, and further to around 15% by the end of 1992. This means that the total value of goods under market regulation or the state's indirect regulation approached 90%.

b. Expanding the power of local administration and enterprises in investment and implementing the utilization of capital with compensation by gradually employing economic means to regulate investment activities, so as to bring about a new pattern of diversified investment and funding for investment sourcing from different channels.

—Delegating power for the examination and approval of investment projects and simplifying the process of formalities. The ceiling on funds to be examined and approved by the State Planning Commission with regard to production construction projects and technological transformation projects related to industries such as energy, communications and raw materials has increased from the 10 million yuan set in 1984 to 50 million yuan; for industries other than the above, the ceiling has been increased from 10 million yuan to 30 million yuan. In addition, non-production construction projects are, in principle, to be examined and approved by departments, provinces or cities, provided that the conditions of the applicant meet the standard of investment. The power of regional and departmental administrations has been expanded in the examination and approval of construction projects that utilize foreign capital. Furthermore, formalities for the examination and approval of projects have been simplified, and the State Planning Commission will examine and approve only projects of large and medium size. Formerly, documents like project proposals, feasibility reports, project designing, applications for initial designing and commencement of construction, etc, had all to be submitted for examination and approval, but after the simplification of formalities was completed, only project proposals and design assignment reports are required to be examined and approved. With the gradual expansion of the power in investment matters of regional and enterprise administrations, instead of having only the central authorities

11

responsible for decision making, now the decision-making power related to investment projects has been extended to all levels of administration, from the central government to regional governments and to enterprise management.

—Reducing the proportion and scope of investment covered by the state's centralized planning so as to bring about a pattern of diversified investment through multi-channels for the development of resources. In 1978, among the various financial resources in fixed assets investment in the society as a whole, the proportion of the centralized financial allocation accounted for 62.2%, and the proportion of internal loans was 1.7%, foreign capital 4.2%, and funds raised by local administrations and enterprises accounted for 31%. However, in 1990 these proportions were gradually lowered to 8.7%, 19.6%, 6.3% and 52.4%, respectively. In recent years, there has been a continuous decline in the proportion of the state budgetary investment, while the proportions of domestic loans, foreign capital and self-raised funds have increased further. The sources of investment have developed from the major form of centralized financial allocation into several forms of investment made through various channels, which include state financing, bank loans, foreign capital and funds from regional administrations and enterprises. The main body of investment has also developed from the former investment made mostly by state-owned enterprises into a new pattern of diversified investments made by the public, collectives, individual households and foreign business entities.

To date, investment from the non-state-owned economy accounts for one third of the total investment.

c. Employing economic levers to promote the realization of the planned objectives.

With the delegation of administrative power to the lower levels of administration and the strengthening of the role of the market, the work of planning has gradually shifted towards employing economic levers to regulate economic activities. The major measures taken are as follows: gradually regulating and releasing price controls by stages to bring about rational pricing by remedying price differences between industrial and agricultural products; transforming the irrationality of internal price parities among industrial products; carrying out utilization of investment with compensation, except for those projects related to public welfare, and allowing differences in the rates of interest related to loans and discounts for basic construction; taxing construction and investment in fixed assets; and undertaking several experiments in employing economic means to put the scale of investment under control and readjust the investment structure.

    d. Improving methods of planning.

In planning, emphasis has been laid on the integration of economy, science and technology, and social development. Additional areas have also been covered in planning, namely, the development of science and technology, control of population, the people's livelihood, construction of apartment buildings, and environmental protection, etc. The planning system has been improved and the focus of attention has been shifted toward mid-term and long-term development projects. The general planning index has been improved and a new calculation system for the national economy has been put into operation. The modes of planning have also been updated, and forecasts for the national economy and social development have been improved. A national network for economic information has also been set up.

2. Restructuring the finance system

    (1) Background to the reform

Before 1978 the financial system practiced in China was one that was compatible with the highly centralized system of planning. The major flaws in such a system were as follows: with no distinction between government administration and enterprise management, the functions of government were merged with those of enterprises; a misguided kind of economic egalitarianism was practiced in which the localities depended heavily upon the central government, while the enterprises relied upon the state without bearing any risks themselves. Such a practice inhibited the initiative of the local administrations and enterprises, resulting in a lack of vigor in economic operation. The binding mechan-

13

ism of the financial budget was weak, bringing about low efficiency in the utilization of capital and low returns on investment, which made it almost impossible to give play to the regulative role of financial policies.

(2) The main features of financial restructuring

In the first stage of restructuring the economy, the focus of reform was on allowing greater autonomy to enterprises and on adjusting the financial relationships between the central and local governments.

—In conjunction with the reform carried out in enterprises, methods of profit allocation were modified between the state and the enterprises. Since 1978 the enterprise foundation system has been introduced successively to all state-owned enterprises. This policy allows the retaining of a proportion of the profit by the enterprise instead of turning over all of it to the state. The aim is to allow the enterprise to have power over its own finances, to motive it to make more profit and to link the performance of an enterprise with the material benefits of its employees, helping to set up a profit-motivation mechanism in the enterprise. To standardize the profit-sharing relationship between the state and enterprises a major reform measure was introduced in June 1983 to levy income tax on state-owned enterprises, and various methods were employed for the allocation of profits after tax. At the same time, some enterprises and department still practiced the contract system based on the contractor being responsible for all profits and losses.

—Since 1978, based upon the newly adjusted power relations between the central government and regional governments concerning the scope of revenue and expenditure, an investigation with regard to the reform of the financial management system has been pursued. In 1980 a new fiscal system dividing budgets into fixed income, fixed proportional income based on percentage allotment and regulative income was introduced. Expenditure is divided into recurrent expenditure delineated in accordance with the hierarchical relationships for enterprises and institutions and expenditure for special items transferred by the central financial institutions as specialized funds. In accordance with the guidelines for income and expenditure at each administrative level, and taking the estimated revenue and expenditure for 1979 as the base, a proportion is set for each region either for the amount of profit to be turned over to the state, for the amount of income to be regulated or for a fixed amount of grant-in-aid to be allocated by the central government. Responsibility for profits and losses is assigned to each administrative level in the echelon for a period of five years. The original motive for the promotion of the responsibility-sharing fiscal system was to alleviate fiscal difficulties through the expansion of regional fiscal responsibility and the stimulation of initiative for increasing income while economizing on expenditure. However, the motivating mechanism based upon the form of responsibility system has also brought about many new problems.

—In line with the needs of opening up to the global market, beginning in 1980, income tax on Sino-foreign joint ventures, individual income tax and foreign enterprise income tax were levied. Consequently, other taxes required of export-oriented enterprises were also levied, and basically a tax collection system related to export-oriented enterprises was set up.

In the second stage of restructuring (October 1984 to 1992) further expansion was continuously made in the reform of the fiscal system based upon the results of the first stage.

—To further regulate the allocation relationship between the state and enterprises, and to ensure increases in the state fiscal income, beginning in October 1984, the second-stage program for the transforming of profit collection into tax collection was introduced. The program made further modifications in terms of income tax and regulative tax.

—In the second stage a major transformation took place with regard to the former unitary industrial and commercial taxation, in which taxation was classified into four types, i.e., product tax, value-added tax, salt tax and business tax. Other taxes introduced in the same period were resources tax, municipal construction and maintenance tax, real estate tax, land-use tax, vehicle tax, and others. This reform basically established a tax collection system based on circulation tax and income tax as its mainstays.

—Based on the results of the second step, in 1985 a fiscal management system was introduced for the local administrations based upon delineating the kinds of taxes, checking and ratifying income and expenditure, and profit and responsibility sharing by each administrative level. This fiscal management system basically preserved the characteristics of the responsibility system at the first stage, while some modifications were made to readjust the delineation of budgetary income for governments at each level based upon the tax type established in the second step. This measure has begun to transform the former method of income delineation based upon a hierarchical relationship in enterprises and institutions.

—Proceeding from "tax collection instead of profit collection," an overall promotion of the contract responsibility system was made. The introduction of taxes replacing profit surrender did not bring about the anticipated results, as enterprises were continuously suffering from a decline in profits. Therefore, beginning in 1987 an overall promotion of the contract responsibility system was carried out in enterprises. The main characteristics of the contract responsibility system are summed up as: Contracting based on definite terms and ensuring the allocated percentage of profit to be turned over—the excessive income to be retained and the deficient portion to be borne by the contractor. This contract system not only delegates responsibility to the contractor for the turnover of profits, but also for income tax, and even circulation tax. This practice stimulated enterprises for a certain period, yet it also brought about many problems.

—Standardizing again the allocation relationship between the state and enterprises. To counter the problems cropping up in the contract responsibility system, in 1988 a pilot experiment was conducted to make clear the distinction between taxes and profits, and ensure that taxes are paid before debts and contracts are undertaken after tax. Though the orientation was a correct one, yet the results of the experiment have left much to be desired.

—Based on the contract responsibility system promoted in the state-owned enterprises, a large-scale responsibility system for fiscal operations was introduced to stabilize the fiscal relationship between the central and local areas. Based upon the fiscal system of 1988 the new fiscal system made some adjustments and modifications with regard to the measures adopted by different regions for fiscal responsibility, with the starting point being to acknowledge the appropriate adjustment with regard to the increase of fiscal income.

In the third stage of reform (since 1992) a new experiment is being carried out with regard to the fiscal responsibility system and the standardization of the fiscal budgetary system. In addition, a further step has been taken to reform taxation. Beginning in 1992, to overcome the problems that accompanied the implementation of the large-scale fiscal responsibility system, a "separate tax and responsibility system" has been carried out on a trial basis in nine provinces and municipalities. The main idea is to delineate the revenues of the central government and the local government based on tax categories and to introduce a big proportion of mutually shared tax. In expenditure, the former base for expenditure remains unchanged. But this experiment has not brought about the anticipated results. In 1992 the state budget began to be based on compound budget drafting, which combines recurrent budget and compound budget.

With the development of the economy, the fiscal responsibility system can no longer adapt itself to market demands. Beginning in 1993, there was much discussion about introducing a new round of reform in taxation and practicing a new "separate tax system."

(3) Some major changes since the restructuring of the financial system

a. Changes in the profit allocation relationship between the state and enterprises. According to official statistics, in profit allocation the percentage of profits shared by the state was around 90% in 1979 and declined to around 40% in 1991. The enterprises began to retain greater shares of profits and thus created conditions for them to be able to bear the responsibility for their own profits and losses. However, it is noteworthy that investigations have shown that, due to the many inherent problems still existent in the mechanism of state-owned enterprises, such as the lack of funds, heavy debts accruing from fixed assets investment, and the not yet clearly defined role of government administration and enterprise management, the power to manage finances on the part of enterprises is very limited. Furthermore, the system of state revenue which mainly relies upon state-owned enterprises has not been fundamentally changed—the proportion of state revenue coming from state-owned enterprise is around 80%. Also, the proportion of the state-owned economy in the GNP accounted for 80% in 1978 and has declined to less than 50% at present.

b. Great changes in the proportion of the state's fiscal revenue. In 1978 the state's fiscal revenue (not including liabilities income) comprised 31.8% of the GNP, and 1985 it had declined to 20.8%, and later to 14.7% in 1992. During the same period the proportion of fiscal revenue (with liabilities income included) in the GNP was: 31.2% in 1978, 21.8% in 1985 and 17.5% in 1992. Great changes also occurred in the proportion of central fiscal income in the total fiscal revenue. Before the restructuring, the proportion of central fiscal income in the total fiscal revenue was set at more than 60%, but in 1992 the proportion (liabilities income included) dropped to around 40%. The proportion of central fiscal expenditure in the total fiscal expenditure was 53.9% in 1980, 45.3% in 1985 and 38% in 1990.

c. Rapid increase in extra-budgetary income. Extra-budgetary income refers to that which is not included in the state budgetary estimate. It is raised in accordance with the scope delineated by the state to be used by localities, departments, enterprises, institutions and administrative organs. In 1978 the extra-budgetary income comprised 30% of the budgetary income, in 1985 it increased to 83%, in 1989 to 95% and to 100% at present. In extra-budgetary income, that allocated to the central government accounts for over one third. The extra-budgetary income of state-run enterprises and the department in charge of them accounts for about 3/4 of the total, and the rest goes to the local financial departments and administrative departments. The increase in extra-budgetary income is a manifestation of the outcome of delegating responsibilities to lower levels of authority

and of maximizing local benefits. It also reveals the problems that exist in budget management and in the role of the government.
   d. Great changes in tax collection system. Through introducing income tax and by transforming the circulation tax, a foreign-related tax system was set up. The measures include introducing special regulative tax categories including tax categories for regulating differential income. The new system, which represents a shift from unitary taxation to compound taxation depending upon circulation tax and income tax as the major resources complemented by other tax categories, is composed of several layers and several linkages. The proportion of tax revenue in the state's fiscal revenue has risen from about 50% in 1978 to about 90% in recent years.

3. Restructuring the monetary system

   (1) Background and progress of reform
   The monetary system in China was formed in the 1950s. To adapt to the highly centralized planned economy all domestic monetary institutions were incorporated under the People's Bank of China, which was, on the one hand, a state mechanism for monetary management and currency issuance, and on the other, an economic organization that operated all the financial business across the nation in unified manner. Many credit instruments, inter-enterprise credit and commercial credit were abandoned; instead, all credit was brought under the centralized control of the national bank. The People's Bank of China established a vertical mode of management for the planning of credits and loans, and fund handling.
   The major flaw in the former monetary system lay in the supply system of fund allocation and its misguided economic egalitarianism. The malfunction of the monetary system was manifested in the following: rigidly allocating funds in accordance with state plans while ignoring economic benefits; employing administrative means to operate banks and consequently inhibiting the development of banking institutions and other monetary establishments. Banking institutions had long degenerated to the status of mere accountants and tellers incapable of

financing and utilizing financial resources effectively. The much-needed capital for social productive activities depended mainly upon the state fiscal revenue. In 1978 the amount of funds furnished by banks for economic activities comprised only one third of the total fiscal investment.

During the first stage of restructuring, monetary reform started by expanding the credit domain and featuring savings, followed by the trial of reform of the fiscal organization, money system, financial market, and management of foreign exchange and insurance. All these preliminary trials of reform imply that in the fiscal system of state financial allocation and utilization, a breakthrough was made in the traditional pattern, which mainly relied upon unified income and expenditure. In monetary policies, the focus was directed to the application of multi-functioning of monetary policies.

In 1985 a proposal was made with regard to the establishment of a highly efficient fiscal system that was full of vigor and was self-regulating. Subsequently, a series of reform measures were adopted aiming at developing the financial market, establishing a mechanism of macro regulation and control, reshaping the bank interest rate system, opening up the financial market and improving the management of foreign exchange.

With the progress of the reform, monetary reform has become more and more important in the national economy. In 1979 savings in various categories in banks totaled only 133.91 billion yuan, but by the end of 1991 the amount had reached 1,488.16 billion yuan, an increase of 11.11 times. The financial situation and the application of monetary policies have become critical factors in the development and operation of the national economy. In the summer of 1993 a series of monetary policies were employed which greatly improved the chaotic financial order. Since this adjustment, totally new requirements have been put forth with regard to the further deepening of the reform of the monetary system.

(2) The major aspects of the restructuring of the monetary system

a. Setting up and developing the fiscal system

The goal for the 1980s was to set up a fiscal system led by the central bank, with the state specialized banks as the main bodies and with the support of various kinds of fiscal organs. In this connection, the following tasks were carried out:

(a) Establishing a central banking system

In September 1983 the government of China decided to set up a national banking system. The People's Bank of China is authorized to carry out the function of the central bank. The main responsibilities of the People's Bank of China were as follows: to conduct research and to formulate the principles, policies, decrees, and basic rules for monetary activities, to take effect upon examination and approval by the higher authorities; to undertake the reform of currency and regulate the flow of money; to exercise unified management of RMB savings and rates of exchange; to draft the state credit plan and exercise centralized management of credit funds; to manage the national foreign exchange reserves and gold reserve; to examine and approve on behalf of the state treasury applications for the establishment of financial institutions; to coordinate and audit routine business for all financial institutions; to manage the financial market; and to participate on behalf of the Chinese government in international financial activities.

(b) The revival and establishment of specialized and general banks

—In 1979 the Agricultural Bank of China was revived as a specialized bank in charge of rural financial affairs.

—In 1980 the Bank of China under the People's Bank of China was established as an independent banking institution which was officially designated as a specialized bank in charge of the state's foreign exchange reserves in 1991.

—In 1983 the Industrial and Commercial Bank of China was set up to handle business related to industrial and commercial credit and savings, which had been handled as part of the business of the People's Bank of China, and in 1984 the Industrial and Commercial Bank of China became an independent specialized bank in charge of urban financial affairs.

—In 1983 the Construction Bank of China was reorganized as a national specialized bank and an independent accounting unit in charge of the management of investment related to basic construction. To facilitate the utilization of credit from international financial organizations, in 1981 the China Investment Bank was established. Under the People's Bank of China, it is a specialized bank designated by the state to raise funds from abroad and to handle business related to investment and credit.

—In 1986 the Communications Bank was re-established, and in 1987 the Zhongxin Industrial Bank was established, both as national comprehensive banking institutions involved in raising and handling domestic and overseas funds as well as all kinds of financial business related to the RMB and foreign exchange.

—Several local banks have also been established, most of which are incorporated banks responsible for handling savings in RMB or foreign currencies and other business in areas approved by the higher banking authorities.

(c) The revival and establishment of other financial institutions

—The domestic insurance business of the People's Insurance Company of China was restored.

—The development of municipal credit cooperatives.

Municipal credit cooperatives have been set up in large and medium-sized cities as public financial organizations composed of shares from medium-sized and small enterprises and individuals.

—Transformation of rural credit cooperatives.

Rural credit cooperatives are collective financial organizations in rural areas. Authorized by the People's Bank of China, the Agricultural Bank of China exercises leadership and management over rural credit cooperatives.

—The development of all kinds of financial business companies, including trust and investment companies, corporate finance companies, finance and leasing companies and securities companies.

—Development of joint Chinese and foreign financial institutions, overseas Chinese-funded or foreign-funded financial institutions.

b. Initial establishment of a macro regulation and control mechanism under the central bank

The objective in the 1980s was to establish a financial regulation and control mechanism which would be flexible in exercising the functions of macro regulation and control.

(a) Monetary policies: Proceeding from the dual objectives of developing the economy and stabilizing the monetary situation, in 1993, based upon the summing up of experience related to the application of monetary policies, the government of China put forth the stabilization of the monetary situation as the major target for the central bank.

(b) Development of instruments for monetary policies to bring about the transformation of direct regulation and control to indirect regulation and control.

—Planned management has all along been one of the most important instruments in the monetary policies of China.

Planned management is divided into three strata: the state comprehensive credit plan, credit plan of the People's Bank of China, and credit plan of specialized banks. Through the means of planning, the central bank defines the scope of credit, the amount of currency to be issued and the amount of loans to be extended by the central bank to the specialized banks.

—Preparatory means for savings.

Since 1983 reserves for savings have been set up, and after several adjustments the proportion of savings reserve per bank was set at 12% in 1987.

—Means for loan re-financing and re-discount of the central bank.

Re-discount has been introduced since 1988.

—Means of regulating rates of interest.

In China, the rates of loan re-financing, re-discount and interest for credit, and personal and corporate savings in specialized banks and other financial institutions are, with certain exceptions, set by the central bank and put into effect upon examination and approval by the State Council. From 1979 to 1991, based on the need for macro regulation and control, the central bank has on 11 occasions adjusted the standards and structures of rates of interest for different categories and thus strengthened the regulatory role played by rates of interest over economic activities.

—Means of handling foreign exchange and foreign debt.

Centralized management has been exercised over revenue and expenditure in the area of foreign exchange, and the exchange rate has been applied for the regulation of supply and demand in foreign exchange and import and export trade. Since 1981 the government of China has progressively adjusted the exchange rate of the RMB to narrow the difference between the official exchange rate and the market exchange rate, creating conditions for the realization of a fluctuating exchange rate.

—Means of handling the monetary market.

Through managing the short-term financial market the People's Bank of China has introduced inter-bank financing among financial institutions to spur the horizontal flow of cash.

In the course of macro regulation and control monetary policies have become the most important means for the regulation and control of the aggregate demand. However, to date, as far as the methods of regulation and control are concerned, the major method adopted is still the one of controlling the scope of loans.

(c) Reform of the mechanism of the management of credit funds.

In the traditional banking system, bank savings at all levels were turned over to the central bank, while loans were based upon allocated quotas under the directive plan issued by the central bank. The system of credit was based on centralized savings and loans.

—In 1980 the credit system of centralized savings and loans was transformed into a system of balance control. The quota management system imposed by the central bank for the aggregate savings and loans at local banks was replaced by credit balance management, releasing control over the aggregate credit at the local banks while maintaining the control of the balance of loans.

—In 1985, in managing credit funds, the People's Bank of

China took control of loans and savings under centralized planning.

Major changes were: The self-raised capital and other credit funds of the specialized banks were checked and ratified by the central bank before the specialized banks could use them as operating funds based on autonomous operation as independent accounting units; the central bank and specialized banks keep separate accounts to ensure cash flow based on separate business accounting; regulations for savings reserves have been established; and financial leasing has been introduced in inter-bank and inter-financial institutions. Such a reform has met the needs of the new monetary system, modifying the traditional practice of making funding available only to those projects listed in the centralized plans. It is required that all specialized banks determine the application of funds in accordance with the source of funding, thus bringing about the transformation of the traditional system that was based on administrative fund allocation. The establishment of this financial relationship has provided conditions for the central bank to exercise its role of indirect regulation and control. However, in essence, it is still a blending of direct and indirect modes of regulation and control, and it is still a form of management based primarily on centralized planning.

—In 1988, taking into consideration the economic overheating and inflation, the People's Bank of China exercised a ceiling management over credit funds and required that loans issued by all specialized bank and all regions were to conform strictly to this ceiling, except with special approval. Such a mode of management is still a directive one. The economic situation in 1992 and the first half of 1993 demonstrated that, with the changes in the economy, the use of direct credit scales and loan ceilings had already become less effective, while many flaws in management were manifested in the meantime. Therefore it was imperative to institute reforms to bring about a transition toward indirect management.

b. Establishment and development of the monetary market

The traditional mode of financial structure was unitary, and credit was monopolized by the central bank. Commercial credit was rejected while all sorts of direct financing activities were prohibited. But, with the short-term market spurring on the long-term market, the reform has brought about the development of a financial market composed of a long-term financing market based mainly on bonds of all kinds and a short-term financing market mainly featuring inter-bank financing and leasing.

(a) Development of the short-term financing market

—Since 1985 a market for inter-bank financing and leasing has been established, which is a short-term capital market that allows monetary facilities to conduct financing and leasing. The rate of interest for financing and leasing between banks fluctuates in accordance with the tightening and easing of the money supply, which is also an indication of supply and demand in the money market.

—In 1985 commercial bill acceptance business was put into operation across the nation. In 1986 rediscount business was introduced for discount bills in specialized banks, and thus a discount market for bills began to take shape.

—In 1987 individual enterprises began to issue short-term bonds on a trial basis, and in 1989 a short-term financing market for enterprises was officially established across the nation.

(b) Establishment of a long-term monetary market

—Bond issuing market

From 1981 bonds of all kinds began to emerge as the times required, and the amount issued increased year by year. By the end of 1992 the accumulated value of bonds of all kinds totaled more than 300 billion yuan. The major bonds are: national bonds of all kinds, which include treasury bonds (issued once a year, the accumulated value since 1981 totals over 100 billion yuan); investment bonds for key construction and financial bonds issued by the Ministry of Finance; basic construction bonds issued by national specialized investment companies, value-preservation bonds, special bonds, monetary bonds, enterprise bonds, etc.

—Stock market

Shenzhen issued stock for the first time in the nation in 1983. By the end of 1984 China had begun setting up pilot enterprises for stock issuance on a trial basis. By the end of 1992 the total amount of stock issued to the public had reached 10.9 billion yuan-worth.

—Securities circulation market

From 1981 to 1992 the amount of securities of all kinds issued totaled 381.7 billion yuan-worth. Beginning in 1986, a securities circulation market began to take shape with the trading of national bonds as the main activity. The Shanghai Securities Exchange was set up in 1990, and 1991 saw the official establishment of the Shenzhen Securities Exchange.

III. Program for the Restructuring of the Macro Economy for the Transition to a Market Economy

To keep in line with the demand for the transition to a market economy and in view of the existing problems and contradictions in the prevailing economic system, China has accelerated its pace in carrying out some major reforms in restructuring the macro economy.

1. Major problems existing in the current macro economy

In 1993, in connection with overheating in the economy and confusion in economic activities, measures of macro-economic regulation and control were employed which have brought about fairly satisfactory results due to the utilization of economic levers as the major instruments. However, the harsh realities indicate that in the context of the current system the measures adopted can by no means effect a radical cure; the root causes of the violent fluctuations in the economy still remain. From a short-term point of view, the fundamental measures to be adopted are to accelerate the restructuring of the macro economy and enterprises; to adjust the benefit-stimulating mechanism between enterprises and governmental departments at all levels; to strengthen the risk-binding mechanism and to provide policies exercising effective indirect regulation and control; and eventually to establish a macro structure which can accomplish the goals defined in the policies.

The major problems existing in the prevailing macro-economic structure are as follows:

(1) Irrational taxation. The irrational taxation is reflected mainly through the tax base being too small and overdependence upon the processing industry. Because of the changes that occur in the various economic elements, irrational taxation can no longer adapt to the changing financial resources, resulting in instability in financial revenue. The categories of circulation tax, taxable items and tax rate were primarily established during the period of the fixed pricing system, and though some adjustments have been attempted, yet they have been overly directed at adjusting the structure of industries and the functions of enterprises under different ownerships. The overly inclination to tax policy resulting in too many taxable items, and complex grading and disparities in taxation; this makes it hardly possible to achieve the aims of the policies; on the contrary, it hinders the standardization and unification of the tax system, and creates loopholes for tax evasion.

(2) The current "fiscal responsibility system" cannot provide an institutional base for the regularization of the fiscal allocation relations between the central and local administrations. First of all, the delineation of fiscal revenue is not immune from the administrative hierarchical relationship, which is detrimental to the separation of government administration and enterprise management. Second, in local fiscal revenue, the proportion of circulation tax which has a considerable impact on the economic structure is found to be unduly high, resulting in duplication in construction and unrealistically scrambling for high speed, which in turn aggravates the extent of fluctuation and regional segregation. Third, in implementing the fiscal responsibility system the practice of bargaining a quota or contracting on a fixed figure have resulted in a continuous drain on the fiscal revenue of the central government. The result is that fiscal revenue records slow growth in spite of the rapid growth in the economy as a whole.

(3) Lack of clarity in terms of objectives and functions in the monetary system has led to stagnation in operation.

First, the central bank has a dual objective in monetary policy—aiming at economic growth and maintaining monetary stability while giving priority to economic growth. This has resulted in frequent conflicts with the stability of currency. Second, the central bank has undertaken too heavy a responsibility in exercising the function of adjusting the economic structure and in operating derivative businesses, which generally runs contrary to the objective of aggregate demand management. Third, the central bank mainly relies upon administrative means for the regulation and control of the money supply, lacking indirect regulatory means of monetary policy, and making it difficult to regulate aggregate demand in a flexible manner. Fourth, the operation mechanism of specialized banks is still administrative in character, resulting in a lack of vigor. Suspended accounts and bad debts of the central bank have risen as high as several hundred billion yuan-worth, which has led to a further deterioration of the value of state assets. Therefore, when there is excessive inflation in aggregate demand, and a lack of both an effective monetary policy as an instrument and a monetary system that is conducive to accomplishing the objective defined in the monetary policy, the solution is, without exception, to resort to administrative and directive means to control aggregate demand. The outcome represents, on the one hand, an inability to control monetary behavior not covered by centralized planning, and on the other, a hindrance to the key construction projects listed in the central plans.

(4) The scope of direct interference by the centralized planning system in economic activities has been narrowed considerably, but an effective mode for displaying the guiding role of the state in the market economy has yet to be established. The tripartite relationship in terms of economy and administration among planning, finance, and monetary policy has not been straightened out, and ineptitude is obvious in utilizing the levers of macro-economic policy to carry out comprehensive regulation. In planning, the former administrative method, which employed a static approach in planning and aimed at achieving a misguided egalitarianism, remains basically unchanged. Moreover, the plan-

ning system has not yet thoroughly freed itself from the administration of micro-economic activities.

(5) Decision-making power with regard to investment is still mostly dominated by governmental departments at all levels. Policy is carried out based on administrative means, on scope control and on examining and approving project applications. The most striking problem is the dissociation of linkages among decision making for investment projects, fund raising, construction, production, operation and loan repayment, lacking a well-defined binding mechanism for responsibility and risk in investment activities.

With the further freeing of prices, in actual economic operations, especially in the operation of enterprises, the pace of marketization will certainly be speeded up. But with the restructuring of the macro economy falling behind, the friction between the current administrative system on the one hand and enterprises and the market on the other will certainly become more and more aggravated. Therefore, intensification of the restructuring of macro-economic regulation and control has become an urgent need for the establishment of a market economy mechanism and for ensuring stable and rapid economic growth.

2. Basic framework of the new mechanism for state macro-economic regulation and control

(1) The major targets of state macro economic regulation and control are: to maintain a basic balance in economic aggregate, promote economic stability and growth, remedy the deficiencies in the market mechanism, provide society with services and commodities, regulate revenue distribution to ensure social fairness and promote the even development of the regions, and adopt appropriate industrial policies to spur the optimization of the industrial structure so as to increase the capacity of overall supply.

(2) Pattern of division of functions for the macro policy: regulation of the aggregate demand based mainly on monetary policies, moderate adjustment of the economic structure based mainly on financial means, and industrial policies based mainly

on functional policies avoiding adopting tendentious policies that allow a wide margin in application. All these are aimed at the upgrading and transformation of the economic structure. Through a comprehensive utilization of monetary and financial policies it is essential to regulate overall demand and, in combination with industrial policies, to accomplish the objective of macro-economic regulation and control.

Such a pattern and a corresponding and compatible macro-economic restructuring should include the following:

First, the main function of the tax collection system is to provide the government with a stable income base and to create a fair environment for market competition. The function of tax collection policies is to regulate allocation of income. The objective should be to gradually transform the practice of using tendentious policies in allocating resources into an impartial tax system. Therefore, the establishment of a new tax system should be characterized by an extensive tax base, by fairness in taxation, and efficient tax collection and management. The new tax system should reform the circulation tax and promote a standard value-added tax. The former product tax and consolidated industrial and commercial taxes should be replaced by a value-added tax so as to set up a circulation tax system with value-added tax as the mainstay. On top of the value-added tax levied on some special consumer goods a consumption tax should be levied.

Consolidated corporate income tax and individual income tax will unify the domestic corporate income tax systems and modify the former practice of levying different standards of income tax on enterprises based upon their differences in ownership. This should be accompanied by the abolition of the regulative tax on state-owned enterprises. Consolidated income tax with the same tax rate as for individuals will be levied regardless of nationality, and the collection and management of individual income tax should be made more efficient.

Second, the major function of the fiscal system is to provide for public infrastructure and social services to promote the even development of the regions through the re-allocation of fiscal revenue and the application of funds; to maintain the long-term stability of the economy and its stable growth; and at the same time to regulate the overall demand through financial policies in conjunction with monetary policies. To perform such a function it is necessary to implement a tax-divergent financial system based upon the rational delineation of power among the central and local administrations.

In accordance with the delineation of power among the central and local governments, the central treasures will primarily bear all the needed expenditure for national security, foreign affairs and the operation of the central state organs. It will also bear all the expenditure incurred in the adjustment of the national economic structure, and in the coordination of regional development. Expenditure incurred in implementing macro-economic regulation and control and in developing undertakings directly under the central government will also be borne by the central treasury. The regional financial bodies will be mainly responsible for the expenditure for the operation of local government organs and other expenses needed for the development of regional economies and undertakings. In accordance with the respective authority vested in the central and local governments, it is necessary to delineate the scope of their income. Categories of tax that are related to safeguarding state interests and rights and that are related to exercising macro-economic regulation and control are to be defined as central tax; likewise, tax categories closely related to the development of regional economies and undertakings, and those that it is appropriate for the regional tax offices to levy should be defined as local tax. Tax shared by central and local bodies will be decided in accordance with the actual conditions.

In coordination with the implementation of the tax divergence system, two separate organs for tax collection and management will be set up: i.e. the Bureau of State Taxation and the Bureau of Local Taxation. The former will be responsible for the collection of central and shared taxes, of which the revenue from the central shared tax will be divided between the central and local bodies in accordance with the proportion agreed upon; the Bureau of Local Taxation will be responsible for collecting local taxes.

Third, one of the goals of restructuring the monetary system is to establish a central bank directly under the State Council vested with the authority to independently implement monetary policies. It should be capable of macro-economic regulation and control. A monetary system should be set up that separates policy-oriented finance from commercial finance, with the state-owned commercial banks as the main body and a variety of financial institutions co-existed. In addition, an open monetary market system characterized by orderly competition and strict management is necessary to accomplish the above tasks.

The central bank takes a critical position in the monetary system. To deepen the reform of the monetary system, the primary task is to operate the People's Bank of China as an authentic central bank. The major responsibilities of the People's Bank of China are to formulate and implement monetary policies so as to maintain monetary stability and to ensure strict efficiency in financial operations. The monetary policies of the central bank are important levers for macro-economic regulation and control. The ultimate goal of monetary policies is to maintain the monetary stability for the promotion of economic growth. The intermediary goal and the operational target of monetary policies are directed at the supply of currency, the total amount of credit, inter-bank financing and leasing rate, and the rate of bank reserve funds. The central bank should supervise and monitor the other banks and maintain financial order. However, it should not interfere with the business of specialized banks, let alone directly handle business that belongs to specialized banks. The central bank will no longer employ policy-oriented loans to exercise direct regulation of the economic structure.

Policy-oriented banks should be set up to bring about the separation between policy-oriented financial business and commercial financial business. Policy-oriented banks will be backed by state credit to attract long-term funds for infrastructure facilities and the construction of fundamental industries for which return on investment is long-term. Under the guidance of the state's industrial policies and planning, policy-oriented banks will exercise autonomous operation based on independent risk bearing. They will preserve capital with minimal profits and follow the principle of conducting no financial business commercial in nature. Policy-oriented banks include the State Development Bank, Import and Export Credit Bank and Agricultural Development Bank of China. These banking institutions have developed an integrated policy-oriented investment and financing system undertaking policy-oriented investment and financing business in different economic sectors.

The remaining state-owned specialized banks, that is the Industrial and Commercial Bank of China, Agricultural Bank of China, Bank of China and Construction Bank of China, will all be transformed into commercial banks. In the meantime, based upon the current urban and rural credit cooperatives, it is necessary to actively and steadily develop a cooperative banking system, establish rural cooperative banks and set up urban cooperative banks on a trial basis. The main task of the cooperative banks is to handle the business of commercial banks, providing services to medium and small enterprises and agriculture, and for the development of regional economies.

We must continue to develop and improve the monetary market with bank financing as its foundation, actively develop standard inter-bank financing and leasing, open up the market for bill discounting and strengthen the management of the monetary market. To rationalize the rate of savings, and smooth the relationships between loan and securities rates, all money rates should indicate the validity period and the difference between cost and risk, to maintain a rational difference in interest reflecting the relationship between supply and demand.

We must continue to develop and improve the securities market. This involves continuing to expand step by step the scope of bond issuance and to set up bond-issuancing organs and bond credit grading institutions to promote the healthy development of the bond market. We must continue to expand progressively the scope of stock issuance, to develop and improve the secondary market for stocks and securities, to develop by stages a batch of cooperative investment foundations, to undertake securities investment at the entrustment of medium and small investors, to engage in securities investment and to reduce the related risks. We must also strengthen the management of the stock markets.

Fourth, we must deepen the reform of the management mechanism in foreign trade and foreign exchange, and open up wider to the global market.

Autonomy in business operations for enterprises involved in foreign trade should be implemented in an all-round manner. In accordance with the requirements of modern enterprises, regulations must be enacted to develop an export-oriented enterprise management mechanism and simplify administrative formalities. The coordination between commercial organizations and the economic means for regulation and control must be improved and regulations concerning quotas, public bidding and auctioning should be enacted gradually. To speed up the legislation of foreign trade and set up comparatively systematic rules and regulations for international trade are also important steps.

Restructuring foreign trade management and striving for coordination between foreign exchange policies and monetary policies. The long-term objective for the restructuring of the management of foreign trade is to bring about the convertibility of the RMB. The unification of the rates of foreign exchange and the setting up of a unitary, manageable RMB fluctuation exchange rate system based on the market exchange rate were achieved in 1994. The practice of retaining a proportion of foreign exchange on enterprises is to be abolished and replaced by the practice of foreign exchange settlement. Examination and approval procedures for foreign exchange requests will be abolished to bring about routine foreign currency conversion for the RMB, and a national unified interbank foreign exchange transaction market will be set up to replace the current foreign exchange center. Strictly forbid foreign currency price marking and circulation.

To take advantage of the opportunity for further opening to the market both in width and in depth, the stress will be upon doing a good job of continually opening up the coastal regions, regions along major rivers and border areas. Further opening-up should be enforced in regions along the main communications arteries, and should be extended to tertiary industry. These steps should be taken gradually. Active efforts must be made to attract foreign capital and enforce the necessary policies for the speedy development of tertiary industry, and gradually shift the focus of attracting foreign investment from granting preferential policies to offering an excellent investment environment and legal safeguards while continuing to pay attention to attracting direct foreign investment and obtaining foreign loans. It is also necessary to focus on the expansion of equity and securities financing, and take a further step to simplify the procedures for the examination and approval of foreign investment projects.

Fifth, the main function of the centralized planning system is to conduct research for a long-term development strategy, to put forward mid- and long-term plans, formulate industrial policy, and do a good job of forecasting for economic development to bring about an overall economic balance.

State planning should be based on the market. On the whole, it should be a guiding plan, giving priority to micro-economic strategy and policy, laying stress on long-term planning and exercising comprehensive coordination between economic policies and economic levers. Yearly plans should include those quotas that need to be preserved, including some necessary quotas added for the macro aggregate index. Directive plans in the domains of production, circulation and allocation should be further reduced and the nation's goods ordering system should be gradually developed and improved.

To further carry out reform in the investment structure, a risk-bearing responsibility system is needed in bank credit and corporate investment. Proceeding from this foundation, it is imperative to eventually push all competitive investment and financing projects onto the market, where enterprises will independently make their own decisions and be responsible for their own risks. We must introduce the practice of project registration instead of project proposal submitted for examination and approval. We must also expand the financing and investment channels for basic projects and key construction projects, and set up a central policy-based financing and investment system, encouraging investment from all sides. It is imperative to actively promote the corporate responsibility system with regard to new projects and projects already under construction.

Sixth, in step with the in-depth reform in the macro-economic system, it is imperative to effect the transformation of state-owned enterprises, the market system, social security, etc. State-owned enterprises are the principal part of the market economy. The transformation of state-owned enterprises involves not only recreating their micro foundation, but is also a major issue of the macro economy. It is an issue that in essence touches upon the overall macro management mechanism and the related setup of government organs as well as the mode of governmental behavior. The reform of state-owned enterprises is oriented toward the speedy establishment of regulations for modern enterprises. At present, the breakthrough is to be made via the transformation of the system of property rights and efforts to find a way to bring about the marketization of state-owned assets so as to speed up the transition of state-owned enterprises into state capital organs. The state-owned large and medium-sized enterprises with sole investment may be reorganized into solely-funded companies in accordance with the regulations; those with several investment partners may be reorganized in accordance with the regulations into limited or incorporated companies. The existent national general companies of different industries may be gradually transformed into national holding companies. All state assets are the property of the state, but governments at all levels may exercise supervision and administration over them. While enterprises engage in independent operations, governmental functions should be separated from social economic administration, although the government is the assets' proprietor. It is necessary to find a rational mode for the operation and management of state-owned assets.

For invigorating the flow of capital, the emphasis should be on establishing a transaction market for property rights, to speed up the cultivation and development of a market for factors of production, remove the barriers and blockades between regions and departments, and create a proper environment for fair competition. Consolidating the opening efforts will create an excellent market environment for the reform of the macro-economic mechanism and for the implementation of regulation and control. It is necessary to accelerate the reform of pricing and to establish a mechanism that basically relies upon the market to set prices. Maintaining a relatively stable price level as a prerequisite, it is obligatory to free prices for competitive commodities and for services, abolish the double-track system in the pricing of means of production and speed up the process of the marketization of prices related to the factors of production. The money market, labor market, real estate market, technology market, information market and other markets of production must be actively cultivated and developed.

The reform of the social security system should be accelerated and a stratified social security system be set up to meet the needs of the market economy. The social security system includes social insurance, social relief and social welfare, settlement of demobilized soldiers, mutual aid and personal savings accumulation guarantee. Policies concerning social security should be unified and management should be law-governed. It is necessary to set up a unified social administrative organ. Priority should be given to improving the retirement and unemployment insurance systems, smoothing the functions of social services and alleviating the burdens on enterprises in this respect. Premiums for retirement pensions and medical insurance should be jointly borne by the employing unit and the individual employee in cities and townships. Unified social and individual will become standard. It is imperative to further perfect the unemployment insurance system. Premiums will be collected from both enterprises and individual employees based on certain proportions and the total amount of salaries. Mutual aid should be encouraged and commercial insurance business should be developed as a supplement to social insurance.

Major achievements have been won over the past 15 years since the restructuring of the macro economy started. At present, a series of reform measures in this respect, some of which have already been issued and some are about to be announced, will certainly spur on China in its transition toward a market economy. The task now is to speed up the restructuring.

(Read at the *Inaugural Meeting of the UN Asia-Pacific Network for Strengthening Cooperation in Macro-Economic Management for Sustainable Development*, in Haikou, February 24, 1994.)

Effectively Curbing Inflation While Guaranteeing Rapid Economic Growth

The current inflation in China is mainly due to the fact that the restructuring of the economy has not been completed, the economy is still at a backward stage and the economic structure is seriously irrational. Therefore, we must control inflation effectively in the process of speeding up reform and promoting development.

I. Assuring the Increase of Efficient Investment and Speeding Up Economic Development So As to Fundamentally Solve the Problem of Inflation

At present and for the immediate future, the rapid growth of China's economy to a large extent relies on the increase of investment. It is documented that from 1981 to 1993 the correlative coefficient between the rate of investment increase and that of economic growth was 0.63. That is to say, 60% of the economic growth in China depends on the increase of investment. This clearly shows that large-scale investment will inevitably bring about rapid economic growth. So China should attach great importance to investment while laying stress on economic efficiency. At present, the major problem is the low efficiency of large investment in the state-owned sector. The key to this problem is not whether to invest or not, but how to solve the problem of low-efficiency investment through speeding up reform while assuring the increase of investment. In this way, high output from large investment will be guaranteed.

The increase of investment does not necessarily unavoidably lead to inflation. What is essential is that the investment system and its corresponding financial system should be in accord with the requirements of the market economy. At the same time, guidance concerning the structure of investment demand and the sources and areas of investment must be provided whenever necessary.

1. The total amount and scope of direct investment by the state must be rigidly restricted, and investment from all walks of life in society must be encouraged and supported to form a multi-dimensional investment setup.

2. Consumption funds must be converted into investment funds.

(1) Housing reform should be speeded up, centering on selling publicly owned housing at cost price.

(2) Employees should be encouraged to buy shares in their enterprises.

(3) The scope of investment for investment companies should be gradually widened so as to guide the financial resources of the whole society into investment in key projects.

3. The investment in agriculture by different sectors should be gradually increased.

The investment in agriculture is seriously insufficient. This is one of the important reasons for the weak basis of agriculture, the insufficient supply of agricultural and sideline products, and consequently the soaring of prices. The major reason for insufficient investment in agriculture is the fact that such investment is relatively inefficient. So, we should enlarge the investment in agriculture by raising the efficiency of investment in the light of the rural economic reforms, particularly the land property rights system reform and the pricing reform in the countryside.

II. Accelerating the Process of Marketization to Enhance Economic Development and Control Inflation

1. The marketization of prices cannot be controlled by administrative means and should not violate the principles of the market economy.

(1) We must do everything possible to encourage the formulation of rational price levels through competition and reduce as much as we can the non-market factors. Only through sufficient competition can a rational pricing system be formed.

(2) The macroscopic management of prices must be based on sufficient competition and price-marketization. Only in this way can we keep prices stable.

(3) We must prevent all kinds of artificial factors and anticipatory psychology having an adverse impact on prices.

2. Greater impetus must be given to property rights transactions and we must carry forward readjustment of the capital structure and the optimization of distribution of social resources in the process of the marketization of property rights so as to make social capital, particularly state capital, more efficient, and thus advance economic growth.

3. In the process of marketization, the restructuring and optimization of distribution of state-owned property should be taken as the decisive means for solving the problem of inflation by means of restructuring state-owned property.

III. Expanding the Scope of Utilization of Foreign Capital to Promote Steady Development of China's Economy and Effectively Check Inflation

1. More direct foreign investment should be sought.

During the period between 1975 and 1984 direct investment by foreign businesses in Singapore accounted for 97.7% of the total net capital in that nation. Hong Kong also took the measure of utilizing foreign capital through direct investment and South

Korea began to steadily increase the percentage of direct investment by foreigners. This indicates that encouraging direct investment is a successful practice that we can make use of in utilizing foreign capital.

Indirect foreign investment (such as government loans) involves the problem of requiring some domestic currency to operate, which will, to a certain degree, increase the total amount of money supply. On the other hand, direct investment will reduce the pressure of domestic currency requirement. Therefore, we should be more open and more courageous in encouraging the introduction of foreign capital, especially direct investment by foreign businesses.

2. The number of areas in which foreign businesses can invest should be enlarged and we should make better use of more foreign capital.

We should also offer more guidance to foreign investors as regards which industries most need investment, and combine the structure of foreign investment with the restructuring of industries and the strategy for long-term development of the national economy. We must follow diverse preferential policies. Foreign-invested projects in basic industries, in infrastuctury and high-tech industries should enjoy more preferential policies in such respects as credit loan, taxation, and so on. In particular, restrictions on foreign investment in energy and communications projects must be further relaxed.

3. Export-oriented foreign-invested projects should be encouraged and supported.

One of the major objectives of utilizing foreign capital is to enhance the development of foreign trade. But the practical choice of developing foreign trade is based on the utilization of relative advantage so as to obtain relative profits. However, from the requirements of long-term development, the consolidation of trade profits must be based on the continuous restructuring of relative advantage. Only by adhering to the strategy of encouraging export-oriented foreign-invested projects can we be sure to strengthen the competitiveness of our products on international markets, thus helping the steady development of

China's national economy.

IV. In View of the Regional Imbalances in Terms of Economic Development, Different Policies for Curbing Inflation Should Be Formulated for Different Regions

China is a large country, and regional imbalance in economic development is a problem of long standing. To curb inflation we must start from China's specific characteristics, give different treatment to different regions and formulate regional policies.

1. Regional imbalance in economic development is an objective problem, and inflation varies from region to region. Therefore, we must take different measures in different situations.

The level of development varies from region to region and so do the degree of inflation and people's psychological endurance. Therefore, how to solve the problem of contradiction between the unified monetary and credit policy and the disparities in economic growth deserves serious study.

2. In order to study and solve the problem of regional inflation, permission must be given to regional governments to formulate policies for curbing inflation in keeping with the actual situations which they face.

The reality is that the impact of inflation on the economy differs from region to region. So, we must start from the facts and apply different remedies. Macro-economic policy must be capable of benefiting both inflation control throughout the country and steady economic development in all regions. The problem must be solved in the course of economic development because only development is the touchstone of truth.

In brief, we must start from not only the general interests of the country's macro-economic development but also from the reality of different regions. We must stick to principles and have some flexibility as well. And finally, we must guarantee that the policies of the central government are carried out and at the same time protect the rapid and healthy development of local economies.

(Paper read at the *International Symposium on Rapid Economic Growth and Sustainable Development in the Asia-Pacific Region*, in Haikou, Nov. 21, 1994.)

Some Issues Concerning the Reform of China's Commercial Banking System

China is now speeding up its transition to a market economy in a comprehensive way. Against this background it promulgated the *Law of the People's Bank of China* and the *Commercial Bank Law* last year, and its enterprise reform has entered a crucial stage. As far as we can judge, the time and conditions for carrying out the reform of the commercial banking system are now ripe. Moreover, the macro-economic situation also requires banking commercialization to make substantial progress.

The reform of China's commercial banking system has now become a key factor in its transition to a market economy. This reform will greatly influence the overall economic situation. Therefore, besides dealing with the system and operating mechanism of commercial banks, the focus will also be on the relationship between the reform of state-owned commercial banks and the reform of state-owned enterprises as well as the relationship between the reform of state-owned commercial banks and the change of the functions of the government. We hold that all these are important practical issues directly related to the commercial banking system reform in our country.

The commercialization of China's banks is still at the beginning stage. It is a complex and complicated issue which will involve a long-term process of continuous study. How to reform China's commercial banking system on the basis of China's actual situation and the experience of other countries in this respect is an important issue calling for in-depth research and discussion.

I. How to Evaluate the Roles and Functions of the Reform of China's Commercial Banking System in Stabilizing Its Overall Macro-economic Situation

The reform of China's commercial banking system is a strategic issue involving the overall economy. At present, it is critical to push forward the commercialization of the state-owned banks because this will have an overall influence on both the macro- and micro-economic reforms, and will determine to a large extent their ultimate success. The commercial banking system has become a bottleneck in the overall macro-economic reform. Without commercialization of the banking industry it would be difficult to promote the related macro-economic reform and realize the marketization of state-owned asserts, and the reform of state-owned enterprises would lack the most important precondition. As the reform of state-owned banks and the reform of the state-owned enterprises twine around each other, every move to deepen the reform is extremely difficult. If a commercial banking system is not established as soon as possible, there can be no overall marketization of China's economy, no socialist market economy system in the real sense and no solid foundation for effective macro control and regulation.

To steadily push forward the reform of the commercial banking system is a key factor in maintaining macro-economic stability. If the problem of an enormous amount of bad debts is not solved, there are sure to be risky credit crises for state-owned specialized banks which are being transformed into commercial banks that will have to assume sole responsibility for their profits or losses. State-owned enterprises are now heavily burdened with debts. If their debt-burden gets heavier and heavier it is inevitable that they will land in debt crises sooner or later and find it impossible to continue production. This may in turn bring about serious economic and social problems. The complexity of the problem also lies in the fact that bank loans to enterprises have come from the savings deposits of individuals and bad loans total RMB 800 billion. So we are now confronted with a difficult

47

choice: If we speed up the commercialization of our banking industry there will be an unbearable impact on state-owned enterprises, which are already beset with many difficulties. Moreover, such an impact may cause social instability. However, if we slow down the rate of commercialization, although we may keep up the macro-economic equilibrium for some time we may lose the opportunity to complete the reform, worsen the potential bank credit crisis and have to sacrifice much more for the reform in the future.

Therefore, the core issue we have to deal with is not whether we should maintain macro-economic stability or carry out the market-oriented commercial banking reform. We are facing a much more complex problem: How to make breakthroughs in the commercialization of the banking industry while maintaining macro-economic stability in a situation in which the problems of the banking industry and those of the state-owned enterprises are intertwined and economic problems and social problems exist side by side.

II. How to Promote the Reform of the Commercial Banks in Circumstances in Which State-owned Enterprises Are Burdened with Heavy Debts

How to solve the problem of the debt burden of state-owned enterprises is the key to the reform of state-owned banks and state-owned enterprises in the Ninth Five-Year Plan period. So far as China's actual situation is concerned, the elimination of the debt problem bedeviling both state-owned banks and state-owned enterprises and the building up of a normal relationship between them are decisive for the clarification of all kinds of economic relationships in China.

The assets-to-liabilities ratios of state-owned enterprises have been running very high. According to the results of an assessment of the assets of 20,000 state-owned enterprises conducted toward the end of 1994, the average liabilities ratio had risen from 18.7% in 1980 to 79%, with the production funds of almost all state-owned enterprises coming from bank loans. In the same year it was also found that the debts recorded in the books of 27.6% of the 124,000 state-owned enterprises were larger than their total assets. As for another 21.5% of the enterprises, if their assets were used to pay their debts they would become "hollow shells."

For this worrying situation there are a number of reasons, including the following: Financial allocations for capital construction to state-owned enterprises have been changed to loans; financial allocations to them as working capital have decreased by such large margins that they have to mainly depend on bank loans; and they are unable to pay back the money they have borrowed from banks because of poor management.

Clearing up the debtor-creditor relationship between state-owned enterprises and state-owned banks, and solving the problem of enterprises being overburdened with debt and the existence of a large number of bad debts are not only matters to be tackled in the reform of state-owned enterprises but also problems that must be solved in transformation of state-owned banks into commercial banks. Only by clearing up debts is it possible for banks to have a normal mechanism for managing their assets and creditor's rights, and for a normal creditor-debtor relationship between banks and enterprises to come into existence.

There are a lot of difficulties in the way of clearing up the creditor-debtor relationship between banks and enterprises. First of all, banks do not have enough reserves to write off loans. They have to use part of their principal capital to write them off, thus affecting the sufficiency of their capital. Then how can their capital be replenished? Since it is difficult for the government to allocate money for this purpose, is it possible to replenish the capital of state-owned banks by issuing shares? Is it feasible to transform solely state-funded banks into shareholding banks?

Second, though some loans have not been defaulted on they can not be called in because they have in fact become the operating capital stock of enterprises. Some of them are already part of the fixed assets of enterprises while others have become part of the regular working capital of enterprises. Though in essence they are all part of the operating capital stock of enterprises, they belong to banks. Therefore, the solution might be to turn part of the loans from creditor's rights to stock rights. However, according to the *Commercial Bank Law* promulgated last year, banks are not allowed to become holding companies of enterprises. Therefore, there need to be medium organizations to see the stock rights transformed from creditor's rights on the capital market so as to enable banks to call in their loans. To do this also requires careful study of how to combine liabilities reorganization, capital reorganization and property rights reorganization to solve the problem of enterprises being overburdened with debts in the process of the reform of state-owned enterprises.

Third, even after the problem of old debts is solved, new abnormal liabilities may continue to crop up under the present economic conditions. Without promoting enterprise reform and banking system reform simultaneously there can be no fundamental solution to this problem.

We have put forward the idea that liabilities trusteeship organizations be established to solve the problem of bad loans. We hold that the present creditor-debtor relationship between specialized Chinese banks and state-owned enterprises cries out for a highly authoritative liabilities trusteeship organization to be established by the government. This organization should be solely responsible for operating, managing and dealing with the existing bad loans of the commercial banks within three to five years so as to promote the reorganization of state-owned enterprises.

This liabilities trusteeship organization should mainly have the following two duties:

(1) To take over bad debts from commercial banks so as to enable them to operate normally and to make real progress in their commercialization. From then on, commercial banks should not be required to offer policy loans. They should be allowed to provide loans completely in accordance with the principle of commercialization.

(2) To participate in enterprise restructuring by buying and owning creditors' rights related to enterprises so as to promote the comprehensive market-oriented reform of enterprises. They should help to restructure enterprises through reorganization of their debts, strengthen their management and improve their overall economic performance.

When the liabilities trusteeship organization takes over bad creditors' rights with enterprises, banks, enterprises and the government all should make contributions to the reorganization of liabilities by taking the following five actions:

(1) Specialized banks as creditors should offer highly attractive discounts to the liabilities trusteeship organization when entrusting their creditors' rights to the latter. These discounts should be borne by the reserve for bad accounts and part of the principal capital.

(2) It is necessary for the government to inject some capital into the liabilities trusteeship organization to enable it to buy bad creditors' rights from banks. This capital injection should be shared by both the central and local governments.

(3) The trusteeship organization can also raise funds from both domestic and overseas investors through different channels to buy from banks bad creditors' rights with relevant enterprises.

(4) After trusteeship organizations have taken over bad creditors' rights, they can dissolve part of them by changing them into shares, attracting investment, leasing, transferring or auctioning.

(5) To make part of the bad debts good again, liabilities trusteeship organizations can sign agreements with relevant enterprises to pay their debts.

Further studies should be made as to whether the above five solutions are feasible or not, how big a role each of the measures can play in dissolving bad debts and what can be the percentage of the bad debts that can be dissolved through these five measures. In this way, the idea of liabilities trusteeship organizations may be developed into an operational program.

In short, the large amount of bad debts enterprises owe to banks is a serious hindrance to both banking commercialization and the reform of state-owned enterprises. It blocks the relationship between state-owned enterprises and commercial banks and is an insurmountable barrier to the transformation of specialized banks into commercial banks. At present there are lots of ideas about how to solve this problem. For instance, some people think that banks could own the stock rights of enterprises, while others hold that creditors' rights should be allowed to be transferred among banks, enterprises and public finance. But it seems that each of these ideas has both advantages and disadvantages. The problem we are confronted with is how to develop an operational program which will enable both banks and enterprises to survive and further develop.

III. How to Realize the Transformation of State-owned Banks into Share-holding Commercial Banks with Public Shares as the Mainstay

China's present banking system is roughly made up of two types of banks. One type consists of the original four specialized banks, which are all solely state-funded. The other type is composed of the newly established commercial banks, which are all share-holding banks. Among all the newly established commercial banks, only the Shenzhen Development Bank has private subscriptions and is a listed company. The rest are all share-holding banks of public ownership. Their shares are owned by the central government, local public finance bodies, and public corporate and institutional legal persons.

The ownership of the stock rights of the new commercial banks is pluralistic. The reciprocal inhibition among the pluralistic owners is helpful in weakening the improper intervention in banks' utilization of their money by the responsible administrative departments. At the same time, the establishment of such governing organizations as share-holders' conferences, boards of directors and management has realized the separation of the ultimate ownership from the legal person ownership, which not only offers enough autonomy to the managers but also enables the ultimate owner to exert effective constraints on their property rights and effective supervision over the managers.

All the presidents of the original four specialized banks are appointed by the government. They are actual managers. But are they also the representatives of the state stock rights? If not, who represents the state in holding the shares of the state banks as solely state-funded companies? Therefore, during the process of the commercialization of the four specialized banks there also exists the problem of clarifying the ownership of their property rights.

How should the four specialized banks be transformed into commercial banks? Should they remain as solely state-funded banks as they are now? Or would it be better to change them into share-holding banks with public shares as the mainstay? If they remain as they are now, what type of enterprise-administration structure should be established? If they are to be transformed into commercial banks with public shares as the mainstay, what stock rights structure should be established? And how can favorable conditions be created to encourage the holding of more private and public shares (including foreign shares) to participate in the reform of the finance industry. These are all extremely difficult problems that need the attention of experts from all walks of life in order to make exact and proper judgments and develop feasible operational programs.

IV. Creating a Climate for Fair Competition to Speed Up the Commercialization of Banks

The creation of a climate for fair competition is another outstanding problem in the marketization-oriented reform of commercial banks.

As a corporate legal person with the right of independent management, a commercial bank has its own economic interests, and standardizes its economic activities and behavior in accordance with the principle of interest maximization. As the fundamental objective of commercial banks' management, profit maximization is realized through competition in the market. Fair competition is an objective requirement of a market economy and a basic condition for the development of commercial banks. As far as fair competition is concerned, there is a long list of issues worth careful exploration:

(1) First of all, how to accelerate marketization of interest rates: As the price of the use of capital, interest rate is a reflection of the fundamental and essential relationship between capital demand and supply. In the case of a mature market economy, marketization of interest rates is one of the most important conditions for people to participate in fair competition and enjoy economic independence. However, in the reality of the transitional stage in China's economy, this basic condition is distorted. State-owned specialized banks offer the official loan interest rate to state-owned enterprises while asking for the market loan interest rate from non-state-owned enterprises. This "double-track" interest rate charging practice violates the principle of fair competition of the market economy and accounts for the distorted capital market. It is the fundamental source of rent-seeking which is a common occurrence, though it has long been prohibited.

The non-market condition of interest rates has been a vexing obstacle in the process of the reform of China's commercial banking system. In order to accelerate the marketization of the operating mechanism of China's commercial banking system and in order to create a climate for fair competition in the finance industry, interest rates have to be deregulated sooner or later. Over this there will not be a big difference of opinion. The questions are: When will be the most favorable time to deregulate them? Will there be larger costs if all interest rates are deregulated at one time or will there be more problems if interest rates are deregulated step by step? How large exactly will the impact be on the inefficient state-owned enterprises? And what measures and procedures should be taken to deregulate interest rates without chaos resulting?

(2) How can the monopoly of state-owned banks be eliminated? This monopoly, which developed under the influence of the traditional planned economy system, is a major obstacle that cannot be evaded but has to be removed. Over a long period of

time, on the principle of "guaranteeing the capital needed by key national economic construction projects," the central bank has been giving priority to providing loans for state-owned specialized banks, creating monopoly profits for them without them being constrained by risks. Even at present, when actions are being taken to reform the assets-to-liabilities ratio, state-owned specialized banks can still ask the central bank for large loans by flaunting the banner of "insufficiency of capital needed by key projects." This phenomenon of continuing to strengthen the monopoly profits of state-owned specialized banks shows that there is a long way to go before fair competition can materialize in the financial market. Second, after many years of development, the enormous state-owned banking system has monopolized 75% of the savings and lending business of the whole society. Moreover, this monopoly is closely combined with the regionalism of China's economic development. It has a strong tinge of bureaucratic business because it involves all kinds of administrative intervention. The difficulty of solving the problem resulting from this distorted combination of economic and political monopoly is self-evident. To break down this monopoly requires a thorough restructuring of the organizational system of the specialized banks.

How should the organization setup of the specialized banks be adjusted and restructured? What type of organizational setup of the specialized banks will exactly suit the marketization of interest rates and be most favorable for fair competition? All these questions remain to be answered through extensive and in-depth exploration and discussion.

(3) How can the problem of the entry of private and foreign banks into the financial market be solved? Only with the existence of a diversified commercial banking system can an internal operating mechanism full of vitality be created through competition and can the marketization of the operating mechanism of China's commercial banking system be realized. Therefore, how to develop private banks and how to create the required conditions for foreign banks to participate in the competition in China's finance industry are both questions for

urgent study.

V. What Effective Role Can the Government Play in Promoting the Commercialization of Banks?

The traditional procedures and administrative means developed under the conditions of the planned economy for administering and controlling state-owned banks are getting more and more inappropriate for the transformation of the specialized banks into commercial ones. Therefore, to eliminate unnecessary administrative interference in banks is an important external condition for this transformation. Only when the role of the government is thoroughly changed, only when the administration and management of banks are really separated, and only when the government no longer intervenes in the operations of banks, can banks autonomously manage themselves, bear risks by themselves and assume sole responsibility for their profits and losses.

In the course of the present transition the government cannot allocate the resources of the whole society as it did in the old planned economic system through formulation and implementation of directive plans. On the other hand, it must pinpoint a clearly defined objective for each reform program and develop specific, explicit and feasible means to this end, and give impetus to and adjust economic operations so as to provide the requisite conditions for macro-economic stability. As far as the practice of the reform of China's commercial banking system is concerned, the government on the one hand must give up unnecessary interference in the banking industry so as to create an active financial climate, while on the other it must stick to necessary and strict administration and supervision over the banking industry to keep it in order, but allowing vitality through diversified and non-planned administrative and supervisory means. Therefore, how to reduce administrative interference and strengthen administration and supervision in the process of commercialization and how to correctly handle the relationship between public and private finance are all difficult questions that remain to be answered.

(Paper read at the *International Symposium on the System Restructuring of Commercial Banks in China*, in Haikou, Nov. 15, 1995.)

Restructuring China's Commercial Banks to Promote Marketization

Note: *The restructuring of China's commercial banks has a bearing on the overall economic transition. An urgent task at present is to accelerate the commercialization of the banking system.*

Over the past 17 years of reform the economic system of China has undergone tremendous changes, and the commercialization of the banking system has made some progress. First, through restoring specialized banks and the establishment of their branches, under the leadership of the People's Bank of China, a banking system composed of the Industrial and Commercial Bank of China, the Agricultural Bank of China, the Bank of China and the Construction Bank of China has taken shape. Second, a number of commercial banks have come to be set up, such as the Bank of Communications, the CITIC Industrial Bank, the Guangdong Development Bank, etc., as joint stock banks. Some individual banks have allowed private shareholding and have been listed on the stock market. They are solely responsible for their own profits and losses and consequently have greatly promoted inter-bank competition. Third, the three newly-established policy banks—the State Development Bank, the Agricultural Bank of China and the Import and Export Bank of China—have taken over all policy-related business of the former four state-owned specialized banks, and consequently created important conditions for the transformation of specialized banks into commercial banks. The promulgation and enforcement of the *Commercial Bank Law of the People's Republic of China* indicates that China has entered a new stage of overall institutional restructuring of its financial system.

In the process of transition from the traditional planned economy to a market economy, the reform of state-owned specialized banks is intertwined with the restructuring of state-owned enterprises (SOEs), and this has become a bottleneck in carrying out in-depth reform in China. At present, it is of the utmost importance to go ahead with the commercialization of banks, because without this it will be impossible to bring about the overall marketization of China's economy. The reform of state-owned commercial banks will have a significant effect on the overall situation of the economic restructuring of China.

At present, in promoting the commercialization of the banking system, the complexity and intensity of the problems and contradictions are mainly as follows:

The high debt rate of the state-owned enterprises and their low returns are still the greatest barriers to the commercialization of specialized banks. As for the SOEs whose assets account for a profit ratio of only 6% to 7% while their assets liability ratio is as high as 75%, a considerable number of SOEs are unable to carry on normal operations and consequently they welsh on their debts by shifting the losses to the banks. However, the status quo of SOEs has gravely affected the factors of fluidity and availability of credit, which in turn fundamentally constrains the commercialization of state-owned banks.

Other barriers to the commercialization of banks are unclear property rights and administrative intervention. The property rights of specialized banks which are undergoing economic transition are still realized through administrative authorization. Consequently, in bringing about their transformation into commercial banks, specialized banks are still unable to rid themselves of unnecessary control and intervention by the government. Under such circumstances it is impossible for state-owned banks to realize genuine autonomous management and sole responsibility for profits, losses and risks based on the principles of economic efficiency. A market environment which lacks fair competition can likewise hamper the commercialization of state-owned banks. As the state-owned specialized banks are overly large in scale and unduly small in quantity, and, what is more, the marketization of interest rates has made little progress, as a result a fair competition environment in the banking sector has not yet been established. It has become a more and more pressing task to reform the interest rate structure to accelerate the marketization of banking operations.

At present the opportunities and conditions for the overall promotion of commercialization of the banking system are basically available, as can be seen from the following: In the dimension of the macro economy the establishment of the three major policy banks had been accomplished by 1994 and they had gone into operation; the promulgation of the *Law on the People's Bank of China* and the *Bank Law of the People's Republic of China* greatly improved the legal environment for the commercialization of specialized banks; the further conversion of the mode of monetary regulation and control by the central bank along with the subsequent development of the securities market, the commercial bills and discount market will, to a large extent, improve the market environment for the commercialization of state-owned banks. In the dimension of the micro economy the priority of reform for 1995 was the reform of SOEs. The strategy of invigorating the whole state-owned economy will spur the increase and improvement of the overall benefits of enterprises, which will be conducive to improving the quality of current credit assets and consequently creating beneficial external conditions for the improvement of newly-added credit assets and facilitating the acceleration of the commercialization of specialized banks.

We hold that it is necessary to proceed from the realities of the situation in China and to seize the opportunity to promote the institutional restructuring of the commercial banking system with a view to promoting the process of marketization. The major tasks are: (1) to discharge the load of liabilities for both banks and enterprises by means of liabilities trusts, to set up a new type of relationship between banks and enterprises; (2) to reform the current banking system which is oriented toward multiplicity of property rights in order to gradually bring about a stockholding banking system with public ownership playing the principal role;

(3) with the marketization of interest rates as the starting point, to bring about the marketization of the banks' operational mechanism so as to speed up the process of the creation of a financial market environment based on fair competition; and (4) to give priority to standardizing governmental actions for the purpose of separating governmental administration and banking management in order to make significant preparations for the commercialization of state-owned banks.

I. Speeding Up the Reform of State-owned Banks Based Mainly on Liabilities Trusts to Remedy Banks' Assets Liabilities

1. The principal task for the commercialization of the banking system is to find an effective way to remedy bad debts

(1) The debts between banks and enterprises are a problem that has so far defied solution and has seriously perplexed both banks and enterprises in their respective efforts to bring about reform and which has become an insurmountable obstacle to the transformation of the state-owned banks into commercial banks.

The debt ratio of China's SOEs is somewhat on the high side. A study made by the State-Owned Assets Administration of 20,000 SOEs indicated that the debt ratio of SOEs rose from 18.7% to 79% from 1980 to the end of 1994 and that the circulating funds of enterprises are derived mostly from loans. Since the beginning of 1995 the financial situation has become even worse, with the budgetary debt ratio of SOEs in the first half of 1995 as high as 95.1%, the total assets of China's state-owned economy RMB 4,130 billion yuan and the total liabilities amounting to 3,100 billion yuan. The assets liability rate reached 75.1%.

The statistics speak for themselves: At present the profit rate of assets of SOEs is only 6% to 7%, while the average loan interest rate is 12%. With such a sharp contrast between profit rate and interest rate, the SOEs have incurred serious losses and have landed themselves in a predicament. The SOEs have no alternative but to shift their losses onto the banks. According to relevant statistics, the principal and interest of 20% of the total bank loans are uncollectable, while interest other than the principal of the loans that comprise 30% of the bank loans may be called in, together comprising 50% of the total amount of bank loans. The proportion of bad loans among bank assets has been rising, with the rate of bad loans of the specialized banks reaching as high as around 30%. At present the total amount of bad asset liabilities is estimated at about 800 billion yuan, which is a direct cause of the low profitability of the banking business and which poses a serious threat to its growth and development.

(2) Failure to solve the problem of bad loans will eventually lead both banks and enterprises into a cul-de-sac. It is necessary to find a new solution that is both advantageous to the commercialization of banks and to the speedy settlement of liabilities related to the reform of SOEs.

The issue of liability has become a vicious circle in terms of the relationship between banks and enterprises. Banks may tighten their management and press for repayment, and become cautious in considering applications for new loans. Enterprises which are unable to repay their debts will be unable to obtain new loans to develop production. Left untreated, the problem of the huge amount of bad loans of the SOEs will further deteriorate the quality of bank assets and increase the risk to assets. The excessive amount of bad assets poses a serious threat to the effective management of banking business, resulting in a continuing decline in economic benefits. Increase in bad assets and insufficiency in the fluidity of capital will in turn increase the financial risks to the central bank. At the same time, the banks have to infuse new loans into debt-ridden enterprises, which in turn does serious harm to the credit mechanism and results in defaults in both principal and interest. The bank income shrinks. This damages the credit standing of banks and eventually leads to their bankruptcy through the accumulation of bad debts and uncollectable accounts. In fact, crisis of payments occurred several times in 1985, 1988 and 1993. Private banks would have long been closed down under such circumstances. Hence, with the problems of debt unsolved, the banks will inevitably undergo a dangerous credit crisis. Enterprises with heavy debt burdens have been experiencing a hard time in terms of production and operation —the greater the burden of debt, the harder it is for them to survive. Such debt-ridden enterprises will unavoidably undergo financial crises which could lead to grave economic and social problems.

The liquidation of claim debt is an issue of urgency related to both enterprises and banks, and it is necessary to find effective ways and means of settling such problems. Even though the settlement of debt issues cannot untangle all the problems related to the relations between enterprises and banks, nevertheless, without extricating enterprises from debts it will be hard for them to carry out reform, and it will be likewise impossible to bring about the commercialization of banks.

Several proposals have been put forth with regard to the settlement of debt issues. One prominent proposal is to bring about the conversion of creditors' right of the banks to stock ownership of enterprises. The advantages of such a proposal are obvious, such as that it will not increase the financial burden or lead to the expansion of the total amount of credit; as an economic lever it will modify the relations between enterprises and banks. Upon the conversion of creditors' right to stock ownership, the bank may assist enterprises in carrying out rectification and reorganization, which will be conducive to improving the relations between enterprises and banks. However, owing to the present conditions in China and the provisions in the *Commercial Bank Law*, commercial banks are not entitled to directly hold the stocks of SOEs, which bars the direct conversion of creditors right to stock right between banks and enterprises. And the state-owned banks have not yet been transformed into genuine commercial banks, and the laws and regulations that restrain the operational behavior of banks have much to be improved. Moreover, the conversion of creditors' right to stock right may give rise to the flow of loans being biased toward the enterprises whole stocks are held by the banks, which would be harmful to the effective allocation of social funds and to the risk management of bank assets. Particularly the reform of the current banking system is lagging behind, in addition to the many problems that have surfaced in operation, while the banks are not equipped with the conditions to hold large amounts of equity right of enterprises. Therefore, it is necessary to find new ways of settling problems of liabilities.

2. The establishment of a debt trusteeship agency is a viable choice for solving the problem of banks' weak assets

Proceeding from the realities of the specialized banks in China and the status quo of creditors' right and debts, it is necessary for the government to set up an authoritative trusteeship agency to take overall charge of the management, operation and handling of the current bad assets of the state-owned commercial banks so as to promote the re-organization of SOEs. It is necessary for such an agency to strive to fulfil its historical mission in three to five years.

There are two major tasks for the agency:

First, it should take over all the bad debts of SOEs from the state-owned banks so as to extricate the latter from their predicament and to ensure the normal operation of banking business. The banks will no longer undertake any mandatory order to provide any policy-related loan and will provide loans based solely on the principle of commercialization.

Second, the agency should participate in the reorganization of enterprises and promote their overall marketization reform. Through reorganizing the creditors' right of enterprises and adjusting their structure, it is possible to speed up the circulation of property rights of SOEs, especially those of small and medium-sized enterprises, and to strengthen the operation and management of enterprises in order to increase the economic benefits of the overall economy.

The issue of indebtedness of SOEs in China is one of a special nature. The operation of a debt trusteeship agency should fully consider the coordination of the many-faceted interests among the state, enterprises, banks, etc. In fact, there is only one creditor, that is the state-owned bank. Since the creditor and debtor (SOE) are in essence identical (the state), in principle, the checking and writing off of liabilities can be accomplished at one stroke. However, under the same nominal ownership (of the state) there are three departments as major interested parties in terms of the indebtedness of enterprises: the SOEs as one party hope for cancelation, deduction or exemption of their debts, the more the better; while the state bank as the second party is against such solutions unless the banking system is able to obtain sufficient compensation; and the financial department as the third party is reluctant to use more financial revenue to re-infuse capital into enterprises, resulting in financial retrenchment and aggravated deficits. Therefore the key to the smooth implementation of the plan for the establishment of a debt trusteeship lies in all creditors and debtors making some sort of sacrifice to bring about an equilibrium of interests for all parties.

Meanwhile, how to scientifically and rationally define the bad credit assets at a particular moment and extricate them from the total amount of bank loans so as to hand them over directly to the trusteeship agency is an operational issue that merits earnest study. One tentative plan is to allow the grassroots offices and branches of specialized banks to register each bad loan item with its grade being specified, which occurred prior to the implementation of the *Commercial Bank Law*. After being sanctioned by the local branch of the People's Bank and the departments in charge of finance, auditing and enterprises, the registration should be submitted to the superior bank level. The bad debt should then be handed over to the trusteeship agency after being screened.

3. With a trusteeship agency taking over bad debts, banks, enterprises and governmental departments should likewise make contributions to the reorganization of liabilities

(1) The bank, as the creditor, should waive its claim for the reorganization of liabilities. In the process of liabilities consignment it is necessary to offer attractive discounts for the transfer of creditors' right to the trusteeship agency.

Such discounts should derive from the bank's reserves for doubtful debts and from a certain amount of principal. In stripping liabilities it is worthwhile for the creditor to make some necessary concessions. Even though the bank would have to significantly reduce its principal, this would be conducive to invigorating state-owned assets and further strengthening debt restriction.

(2) It is necessary for the government to infuse an appropriate amount of capital into the trusteeship agency. In addition, the central and local financial authorities may jointly invest a certain amount of capital to enable the trusteeship agency to take over the bad debts of the banks.

Thus, the agency would not only alleviate the debt burden of the banks, but also improve the quality of bank assets and promote their fluidity, effectively adjusting the credit structure. In his explanation of *The Proposal of the Central Committee of the Communist Party of China Concerning the Formulation of the Ninth Five-Year Plan and the Long-Term Target for 2010*, Premier Li Peng pointed out, "As to those state enterprises which bear heavy burdens left over from the past and from the society and, at the same time, occupy important positions in the national economy, the state will put in a sum of money. We hold that if the money promised is put into a trusteeship agency which takes the overall situation into account and solves the debts of the SOEs of all descriptions, one can anticipate a better outcome."

(3) The agency may raise funds through various channels to purchase creditors' right.

The trusteeship agency may adopt methods such as bond flotation, the establishment of a debt reorganization funds, etc., to raise funds from national or international investors for the purchase of bad credit assets of SOEs from the specialized banks concerned so as to gain creditors' right over SOEs that are in debt to the specialized banks.

(4) Obtaining partial compensation through reorganizing enterprises.

Upon taking over a bad debt, the agency should speed up the reorganization of enterprises by adopting relevant measures according to specific conditions so as to activate the stock of capital. It is also possible to dissolve a bad debt through share transfer, investment invitation, leasing, assigning, auctioning, etc.

(5) Transforming part of the bad debt into a collectable debt. In the process of debt entrustment, it is necessary to strictly differentiate between debts and handle them accordingly. Some enterprises, though ridden with heavy deficits still turn out marketable products and have bright prospects. So it is necessary to adopt different methods to deal with their debts, such as interest exemption or deferring the schedule for the repayment of principal for the purpose of supporting their development out of the red. It is necessary for the trusteeship agency to enter into new agreements with regard to the repayment of debts, thus converting part of the bad debt into a collectable debt.

4. Upon taking over a bad debt from a bank, the agency should reorganize the relevant enterprise, adopt various means to dissolve the bad debt and enhance the competitiveness of the enterprise along market economy lines

Property rights in the process of converting creditors' right into stock right. The root of the current issue of SOE debt is nothing but the issue of property rights, including indistinguishable property rights, irregular ownership, lack of property rights restraint and financial pressure in the management of enterprises. Without solving these problems it will be difficult to fundamentally solve the problems of liabilities. Consequently, the trusteeship agency should, after taking over creditors' right from a bank, carry out corporatization reform in enterprises and bring about the reorganization of property rights so as to accomplish the objective of alleviating the debt burden of enterprises. In handling the problem of liabilities, the strategy of "grasping the major and letting go the minor" also applies. As to the large-sized SOE which are of strategic significance to the national economy and people's livelihood, it is necessary for the trusteeship agency to convert all bad debts into stock rights of the enterprises, and thus the trusteeship agency will become an investor rather than a creditor and will be able to participate in the management of the enterprise in the capacity of a shareholder. As to the large and medium-sized SOEs that are not important for the national economy and people's livelihood, the trusteeship agency may attract foreign and private domestic capital so as to turn the SOEs with sole ownership into ones with mixed ownership, thus dissolving part of the liabilities. At the same time, some of the enterprises may settle their debts though assigning part of the assets to repay the debts.

The trusteeship agency may convert part of the property rights of SOEs into bonds. Upon taking over bad debts from the banks, the agency may convert creditors' rights into bonds which may be transferred to other investment banks, non-banking financial institutions or other enterprises in the circulation market for SOEs' liabilities. These methods may be used to alleviate the burden of liabilities of enterprises and to call in part of the capital so as to make up for the loss incurred by the banks. Needless to say, it is necessary to cultivate the circulation market for the property rights of SOEs, develop the corresponding circulation market for liabilities and further develop and perfect the securities market. It is necessary for the agency to actively organize and promote the transaction of property rights owned by enterprises and to activate bad debt assets. Property rights are a kind of commodity composed of actual rights and money claims, and occuring in physical and value forms, and of tangible assets and intangible assets. Transaction of property rights owned by enterprises is in fact a way of breaking down stock so as to bring about the optimum stock allocation, which is also a market means for dissolving faulty assets of banks. With the development of the property rights transaction market and the further deepening of the opening up to the foreign market, investors in China, especially foreign business people, will become more and more interested in the practice of buying out certain enterprises through purchasing the creditors' rights from the trusteeship agency. Promoting annexation and merger of enterprises to solve part of the bad debt problem is also an option. At present, quite a number of profit-generating enterprises in China have not yet accomplished the objective of economies of scale. Therefore, through annexation it is possible for enterprises to accomplish the target of expanding their production scale and reducing the costs of production by investing only a small amount of capital and adjusting production management. In the process of merger, a new production organization will be formed which will help to set free the productive forces and which is conducive to the activation of part of the bad debt.

Some enterprises may be allowed to go bankrupt or be auctioned off to settle some of the bad debts. It should be pointed out that, owing to historical and institutional factors, some of the bad and uncollectable debts between banks and enterprises are impossible to straighten out. Under such circumstances, enterprises should go into bankruptcy. The trusteeship agency should be totally involved in liquidation of the enterprises so as to do its utmost to rationally and legally settle all liabilities. As to small and medium-sized enterprises with no potential for growth, whose assets cannot pay off the debts and which are not important for the national economy and people's livelihood, it is necessary to turn them into civilian-run enterprises either through auctioning them off by public bidding and fair competition or through paid transfer so as to recover part of the capital.

Part of the liabilities of small-sized enterprises may be equally shared by their staff and workers. Employees may hold the shares of enterprises through buying creditors' right from the trusteeship agency, and thus correspondingly possess the property rights of the enterprises, which will be restructured into share cooperative enterprises. In this way, the trusteeship agency can activate part of the money claim, and the restructured enterprises will be able to bring about changes in the leadership and management system, which will result in the improvement of the operational mechanism and better economic benefits. By transferring part of the cost of reorganizing the liabilities to the employees, the latter may obtain the corresponding property rights of the enterprises and become income beneficiaries in the future.

5. When liabilities are entrusted the government should make a definite promise to establish a new type of marketized relations between banks and enterprises through institution-

al restructuring

During economic transition, entrustment of liabilities is a measure adopted by the government which has no alternative but this, and which is of positive significance with regard to unravelling the knots of debts between banks and enterprises and which would help to alleviate the debt burden for both parties. However, enterprises should not be misled into thinking that it is possible for them to avoid repaying their debts, as this would result in a disastrous outcome situation in the overall credit situation.

Accordingly, in entrusting liabilities the government should send out a definite message: fiduciary liabilities apply only to debts bequeathed over the years, and this shall not be taken as a precedent. As the commercialization of the state commercial banks has already begun and since banks are also enterprises, loans will be provided based on the principle of beneficial results, and both enterprises and banks should aim at maximizing profits. Taking trusteeship of liabilities as an opportunity, both the enterprises and the banks should set up a normal relationship in terms of borrowing and lending, and create a healthy cycle of "borrowing large sums of money for the development of production to generate profits and to repay all debts."

II. Bringing About the Transformation of State-owned Specialized Banks into Commercial Banks in the Establishment of a State Holding Structure or Structure of Multiple Ownership with Public Ownership Playing the Main Role

1. Accomplishing the commercialization of banks through making property rights distinct

(1) The fundamental issue in the setting up of commercial banks resides in property rights. Equivocal property rights and indistinguishable relations with regard to power and responsibilities are obstacles that inhibit the achievement of the maximization of profits for commercial banks.

Many of the existing problems such as disorder in the financial system, ineffectual incentive mechanism of state banks, ineffective restraint mechanism, inferior quality of assets, low profit awareness, lax credit, low efficiency in assets allocation and various other phenomena known as "offering leasing for money" and "seeking opportunities to barter power for money" may be traced to the deep-seated problem of equivocal property rights, as the state-owned banks have still a long way to go before they can fully play their roles in monetary interest, responsibility and power. In the market economy the property rights relations of commercial banks must be clear and distinctive. Therefore, to establish a commercial banking system oriented toward marketization, the key resides in carrying out the reform of the property rights system.

The prominent issues in the property rights system of China's specialized banks are:

The blending and intermingling of operational functions of specialized banks with the government's administration of assets, resulting in excessive intervention on the part of the government in the business activities of the banks and the property rights relations between the government and the banks becoming indistinct.

The state incorporates the ownership and right of operation into one, while the banks integrate managerial and operational functions into one. The result is blurred property interest relations between the owners of property rights and operational personnel.

(2) The realization of distinct property rights is the core of bank commercialization.

Distinctive property rights are prerequisite to the realization of corresponding power and risk responsibilities, which pave the way for the establishment of relations which contribute to a balance among shareholders, boards of directors and managers. Such relations will in turn bring about a self-restraint mechanism and corporate profits that are closely related to the personal benefits of each individual. Consequently, driven by the desire for the maximization of profits, self-development will emerge and the optimum allocation of resources will be accomplished.

One could say that the essential question with regard to the commercialization of China's state banks is whether a property rights system based on the operation of the market mechanism can be established. Only when this question is satisfactorily answered can commercial banks operate properly. The answer involves:

The establishment of an operational mechanism that fits in with the needs of the market economy and a complete corporate system of modern finance which is mainly composed of legal-person financial enterprises with full autonomous power in operation and management within the limits of law;

Strict constraint, conditioning and balancing in property rights, and the possession of requisite property rights by independent legal persons responsible for value preservation and value increment, and eventually a system of legal persons in the form of corporate businesses;

The development of operational and business activities in accordance with the needs of the market;

Operational principles based on "economic benefits, security and mobility"; and

A basic business objective of bringing about sustained and stable growth of profits while minimizing risks.

2. Maintaining a uniform banking system for state commercial banks is not only impractical but also unnecessary

(1) It is impossible to set up a genuine commercial bank while the state monopolizes banks' property rights.

The modern enterprise system is an institutional innovation resulting from the necessity to conform to modern production methods and spread risks. The shareholding corporation is a typical version of the modern enterprise system which successfully spreads the risks to the extent of each components bearing capacity while restricting the possibility of using personal capital to directly intervene in the operation of an enterprise. To this end, multiple ownership and multiple property rights are prerequisites. With sole ownership there is only one source of investment, and the sole owner must undertake all the risks. Consequently, it is impossible to reflect the objective needs of the enterprise in the operational activities of production. Only under conditions of multiple ownership and the spreading of property rights can the interests of an enterprise be separated from these of the original owner. The modern enterprise system has evolved from the corporate system through highly distributed stock rights. Owing to the highly decentralized stock rights, the capital owner can no longer directly intervene in the enterprise by simply holding a major share of stock rights; in fact, the manager has control over the operations of an enterprise and thus brings about the separation of ownership and the right of business operation.

For a long time the state was the owner of all bank assets in China, as well as the only owner of property rights. Under such a system the operation of banks was subject to the command of the state. As a result, it was normal for agents acting on behalf of governments at all levels to intervene in the banking business. "Having full authority in management" was only empty words. As the sole owner of property rights, the state was ultimately responsible for the success or failure in bank management since it was impossible to realize the principle of sole responsibility for profits, losses and risk, and impossible to achieve effective self-restriction.

(2) Multiplicity of property rights is the objective demand of bank commercialization.

The essence of property rights ownership is assets ownership, and such ownership should be based on multiplicity rather than on singularity, which is demanded by the nature of commercial banks themselves. Commercial banks are characterized by greater amounts of capital and relatively greater risks. Only by realizing the multiplicity of property rights ownership is it possible for the commercial banks to maintain and increase their assets based on their business operations and undertaking investment risks, and to spread risks through realizing multiple assets and investment in actual operations. Thanks to the involvement of corporate and personal stocks, the government's extra-market intervention in the business of banks has been greatly restricted since the law does not allow any of the shareholders to infringe on the rights and interests of other shareholders. Instead of arbitrary intervention, a government's aims can only be realized through its proportion of shares in the total and the corresponding right to vote on the board of directors. Meanwhile, internal finance is approaching integration through introducing operations based on the shareholding system; state-owned banks are beginning to operate according to international practices, which make it easier for them to gear up to international conventions and be recognised by international financial circles. Therefore, so long as the public ownership system is in the central position it is unnecessary to operate state commercial banks based on sole ownership.

3. Establishing a shareholding commercial banking system based on public ownership in the central position

(1) The stockholding system is conducive to the establishment of an administrative structure for modern corporate entities.

The socialist market economy is one characterized by a mixture of types of property ownership. The organizational form of modern commercial banks can no longer be defined in accordance with the nature of ownership; rather it is defined in accordance with the composition of assets and the legal responsibilities undertaken. Through their long experience of economic development Western commercial banks have formulated a set of complete corporate organizational systems which are worth emulating. The organizational mode of the stockholding corporation is the most ideal choice for a commercial bank.

The fundamental principle for the prosperity of the market economy resides in independent property rights and free mobility. A modern bank founded on a stockholding system has clearly defined rights and responsibilities. The defining and balancing of powers among shareholders, boards of directors and managers are all established, which is conducive to self-restriction and self-development. Therefore, it is necessary for the commercial banks of China to take the road of the shareholding system.

To transform state-owned banks into genuine commercial

banks it is necessary to carry out reform in the property rights system as in other SOEs so as to change the mode of relations between the banks and the state, and eventually allow them to become market-oriented. It is necessary to draw upon the experience gained in the development of China's stockholding commercial banks and carry out reform based on the stockholding system in state-owned banks. Changing the monolithic structure of property rights will not only expand the banks' capital and strengthen their capability for self-development, but also clearly identify the ownership of state-owned assets and the location of responsibility and power on the part of the property right owner. Founded upon the conventions of the stockholding system, shareholders' meetings and boards of directors of banks shall safeguard the status of the banks' independent legal persons and power while exercising effective supervision over the operational behavior and management approach of the executive departments in order to enforce financial self-discipline in accordance with the law of the market.

Upon the completion of reform carried out in line with the stockholding system, the structure of property rights of state banks is no longer one of single ownership, rather it is a kind of "structure of collective property rights" with each share representing a typical transferable property right, which is conducive to the realization of separation of ownership from the right of operation. The power of each shareholder must be exercised and safeguarded on a collective basis, and the behavior of the owner is governed by a framework characterized by institutionalization, legality and programization, developing into an administrative structure suitable for a modern corporate entity.

(2) The proportion of state-owned stock should be appropriately reduced to draw more and diverse investment on an extensive scale.

The state-owned principal of the state banks will be appropriately reduced when their creditors' right is entrusted to the trusteeship agency. Under such a circumstance, it is proper to encourage local governments, enterprises and individuals to hold stocks on an extensive scale so as to bring about a relatively rational stock right structure composed of state-owned stocks and stocks held by the public.

(3) Financial institutions should be encouraged to further open up when conditions are ripe, and foreign capital should be attracted.

To revamp the stock right structure of the state banks, it is necessary to have foreign capital participate as is an effective avenue for China's state-owned banking industry to develop in accordance with international practice and to participate in international competition. At the same time, foreign financial institutions should be introduced, based on the principle of equality and mutual benefit, to establish a co-funded financial setup. Commercial banks with substantial economic strength should be encouraged to develop overseas branches selectively in a planned way and to expand foreign markets, which is important for the acceleration of banking commercialization.

(4) Commercial banks should be urged to be listed for transaction.

It is necessary to actively create conditions to encourage stockholding banks to be listed for transaction, so as to increase the degree of openness in terms of operation and to intensify their competitiveness.

4. Constructing a system of commercial banks with the four major specialized banks as the principal body and bringing about a competitive financial system composed of modern commercial banks as the mainstay supplemented by other types of banking and financial institutions

With the development of the socialist market economy, the status and role of the financial services industry, particularly banking, will become more and more important in the national economy. Therefore, the reform of banking is closely associated with the institutional economic restructuring over the whole period of economic transition in China. The basic framework of China's commercial banking system in general consists of the following three aspects: one is the gradual transformation of the existing major specialized banks into commercial banks; next, the active and stable development of the existing commercial banks of various descriptions; and finally, the establishment of new urban-rural cooperative banks and other types of banks. Since banks are not only closely related to all sections of the national economy, but also to the vital interests of the public and ultimately to the economic, political and social stability of the nation, bank reform should be actively and carefully carried out. We have learned from the reform practice over the past 17 years and from the experience of the developed countries that, in establishing a system of commercial banks, it is necessary to abide by international conventions while taking the Chinese situation fully into consideration. The operation of China's existing commercial banks must conform to international standards, and rules and regulations must be perfected. It is necessary to accumulate experience in practice and to continue to explore and innovate. With unremitting efforts we should strive for the initial establishment of a modern commercial banking system that conforms to both international practice and the Chinese situation by the end of this century.

III. Creating a Market Environment of Fair Competition and Speeding Up the Marketization of the Operational Mechanism of Commercial Banks

As a corporate entity with independent operations, a commercial bank has its own independent economic benefits. It standardizes its economic activities or economic behavior in accordance with the principle of profit maximization. The ultimate goal of profit maximization of a commercial bank is realized in the process of market competition; a commercial bank can duly recover its loans, both principal and interest, under conditions of fair competition and accomplish its own goal of operation. Commercial banks must continue to expand their share of the market in the midst of intense market competition, upgrade their technology, cut costs, and increase the quality of assets and service standards. There should be a continuous inner dynamism to ensure their vitality and efficiency. The most pressing task at present is to create a market environment on the basis of fair competition with interest rates as the lever so as to promote the marketization of the operational mechanism of commercial banks.

1. It is necessary to remove control over interest rates so as to create an environment for fair financial competition

Interest rates as the prices for the use of funds are the reflection of the most general and most essential relationship between fund supply and demand. In a mature market economy the marketization of interest rates or the fair and natural need for interest rates is one of the basic conditions for economic factors to participate in fair competition and to enjoy economic freedom. At present, with regard to the reality of the economic transition in China, such a basic condition is distorted. The state banks impose official interest rates on some enterprises, mainly SOEs, but market interest rates on other enterprises, mainly non-SOEs. Such a dual interest rate system violates the principle of fair competition inherent in a market economy, which is one of the major causes of the distortion of the capital market and the chronic phenomenon of "seeking opportunities to barter power for money." Since the first half of 1993 "interest rate wars" have occurred in many places, which have seriously disturbed the normal financial market order, and despite strict rectification across the nation the war still breaks out occasionally in a more camouflaged form. Such a phenomenon explicitly shows that the existing dual interest rate system is detrimental to the transformation of the state banking system from planned economy to market economy functions. What is worse is that such a dual system has become a barrier inhibiting fair competition between banks. Accordingly, it is necessary to proceed from reality and to actively create the conditions for the establishment of a genuine operational mechanism for commercial banks on a marketization basis through removing controls over interest rates and allowing the market to dictate them.

It is necessary to remove controls over interest rates and to allow free floating of deposit rates and loan interest rates. As a transitional measure, it is proposed to let the People's Bank decide the interest rates of reloans and rediscounts and the benchmark interest rate for deposit loans. Interest rates for split-borrowing should be gradually governed by market supply and demand. At the same time, in order to avert provoking "interest rate wars," the central bank may put forward strict and unified upper and lower limits of deposit interest rates for all commercial banks as well as urban and rural credit cooperatives. It is necessary to try to work out the ceiling and floor interest rates on a scientific basis during the transition period to bring about a situation in which the control of interest rates is removed without causing confusion and the administration of interest rates is exercised without causing inflexibility.

Loan limits should be decontrolled, and either discriminatory or preferential rates of interest should be applied to any enterprises. It is necessary to create an identical and impartial financial environment of fair competition for all enterprises, and to get rid of the hotbed that breeds the bartering of power for money through decontrolling loan limits. At the same time, to prevent enterprises from opening several bank accounts each, it is necessary to provide that an enterprise is allowed in principle to open only one account at a commercial bank to handle business such as deposits, loans, remittances, etc. Such regulations apply only in principle as it is inappropriate to ascribe the practice of some enterprises' attempts to obtain bank loans from several sources as absolute "loan swindling." Under the conditions of economic transition, "when it is dark in the east, it is light in the west," and it is normal for an enterprise to try to obtain loans from several sources. It is necessary to endeavor to explore how to provide limited loans to enterprises with rational interest rates and to provide assistance in the true economic sense to enterprises to tide over difficulties.

On the premise of actively developing a commercial banking system with public ownership playing the main role and with Chinese characteristics, non-governmental commercial banks should be permitted to develop and foreign banks should be gradually allowed to participate in the competition in the banking industry in China. Only by making an effort to create a relaxed external environment of fair competition for all commercial banks will it be possible for a commercial banking system in China to possess a genuine vigorous internal operational mechanism. Likewise, only through fair market competition will it be possible to bring about the marketization of the operational mechanism of the commercial banks in China. Though it is always necessary to pay attention to stamping out unfair competition in financial activities and to formulate accordingly rules and regulations with regard to competition and cooperation within the finance business, as far as the realities of the economic transition in China are concerned, such rules and regulations should aim at promoting competition which should be healthy, standardized and well grounded. But one should not expect a print-out of rules and regulations to instantly bring about perfect competition; it is worth understanding that the process of the marketization of the operational mechanism of commercial banks is full of hardships and difficulties.

2. In accelerating the marketization process of the financial system it is necessary to overcome the barrier of monopoly and to bring about a financial market environment based on fair competition

Since the 3rd Plenary Session of the 11th CPC Central Committee in late 1978, the four major state-owned specialized banks—the Construction Bank of China, the Bank of China, the Agricultural Bank of China and the Industrial and Commercial Bank of China—have been restored or established and have been playing an important role in the national economy. With the deepening of the economic restructuring in China there has emerged an objective need for the development of an economic operational mechanism that is autonomous, liberal, assures equal status and is competitive for the allocation of social resources. A serious challenge has emerged for the state specialized banks, the essence of which is their transformation into genuine enterprises and their revamping through fair competition into ones that have the following five traits: autonomous management, sole responsibility for profits, losses and risk, self-restriction, the ability to promote liquidity and having a profit-oriented business objective. It is obvious that there are difficulties in many dimensions with regard to the conversion of state-owned banks into commercial banks, of which the monopoly factor established under the planned economy system is doubtless one that is unignorable and that must be overcome as a major obstacle to the economic restructuring of the commercial banking system. First, for a long time, under the guiding principle of "ensuring the key construction projects of the national economy," priority was given to providing loans from the central bank to state-owned specialized banks, which created risk-free monopoly benefits for the latter. Even now, when the reform measure to promote management through assets-to-liability ratio has been introduced, the state-owned specialized banks can still make requests to the central bank both for funds and for expanded scale of investment under the pretext of "shortage of funding for key projects." The unceasing intensification of monopoly benefits shows that the introduction of fair competition into the financial market is by no means something that can be accomplished overnight. Second, the immense state-owned banking system extending from the central to the grassroots levels, that has been formed through years of development, has almost monopolized over 75% of the business of borrowing and lending in China's national economy. Moreover, such a monopoly is closely associated with regional development. In addition, administrative intervention in many forms has given the whole system the color of "official commerce." In deepening the reform, the difficulties created by the integration of economic monopoly and political distortion are obvious. To realize the marketization of operational mechanism for the commercial banks of China and to create financial environment for fair competition it is necessary to fully understand the tenacious nature of monopoly within the state specialized banks themselves and to intensify the reform by overcoming the tenacity of such a monopoly.

It is necessary to positively remove all policy-related loans that have nothing to do with the profit-oriented objective of commercial banks from the domain of the existing specialized banks so as to fundamentally undermine the economic foundation of monopoly benefits. Meanwhile, based upon the summary of experience, it is essential to continue to intensify administrative work with regard to the assets-to-liability ratio of state specialized banks, to strengthen their self-restriction capability and weaken their motive for obtaining monopoly benefits, so as to promote the progress of commercialization of state specialized banks through risk management.

It is necessary to undermine the organizational foundation of monopoly and to eliminate the political factors of monopoly through changing the existing organizational pattern of state-owned specialized banks based on reorganization. The stockholding system may be an option. Also, the assets of the original specialized banks may be split up into capital, funds for special use, funds for accumulation and circulation assets. At the same time, shares may be separately owned by local governments, enterprises and individuals on a decentralized basis. Further along this train of thought, one could consider reorganizing state-owned specialized banks into bank groups through adopting the mode of shareholding by each administrative level.

IV. An Important Factor in Realizing the Commercialization of State-owned Banks is the Properly Display of the Economic Function of the Government

The economy of China is now undergoing a fundamental change which is a transition from the traditional planned economy system to a socialist market economy system. During this transitional period the role of traditional planning is gradually fading away, as it cannot effectively regulate the overall operation of the national economy except within certain narrow areas.

The operational mechanism of the market economy, which is just in the process of formation, likewise cannot be itself effectively regulate the overall operation of the national economy. However, it has already displayed its role or exerted an impact on the national economy within a certain sphere and to a certain extent, while there is still a certain sphere which neither the planned economy system nor the market economy system can effectively regulate for the time being.

Facing the reality of the economic system of China in transition, the government can no longer allocate social resources as it used to do, through formulating mandatory plans for implementation under the planned economy system. On the other hand, it must set the goals and propose feasible methods for the reform program in order to promote economic growth and to regulate economic operations so as to prepare stable social conditions for the reform program. As far as the practice of economic restructuring of the commercial banks of China is concerned, the government should, instead of exercising total intervention in finance, create a lively financial environment; on the other hand, it should persist in exercising effective financial supervision through diversified, non-programmed mandatory management to invigorate finance in an orderly manner. At the same time, it is necessary to correctly handle the relations between finance and the banking sector through deepening the reform and properly displaying its economic role.

1. It is necessary to liberalize the financial environment to realize the commercialization of state-owned banks

A major breakthrough which took place in the reform of China's financial system in 1983 was the separation of the central bank from the specialized banks. Though this means that the plan put forward by the central bank for exercising macro control over the national economy has been intensified, as reform still follows the established principle that "the government should control finance," the central bank has not yet in essence changed its attribute of being the "general counting house" of the government. This is markedly manifested in the fact that the central bank still essentially maintains administrative control of the planned monetary economy by carrying out plans for lending scale, ceilings on its own loans, determination of interest rates, etc. Such a condition is in conflict with the marketization reform of the financial system which is under way in China: First, the planning for cash input works in the reverse of the soft budgetary restraint of an enterprise, which can hardly meet the need of price fluctuation and the development of finance. Second, induced by high interest rates resulting from the disorderly state of the financial market, the control of loan limits cannot rationally and scientifically regulate the supply of money. Third, the practice of dual rates of interest has failed to accomplish its goal of alleviating the cost burden on enterprises; rather it has become the physical foundation for "bartering power for money" or "rent seeking" activities. It is evident that in persisting in the orientation of marketization with regard to the reform of the financial system it is necessary to remove the controls from finance and create a liberal financial environment.

It is correct to establish the genuine independence of the central bank and properly define the financial and economic functions of the central bank and properly define the financial and economic functions of the government so as to enable the central bank to leave certain operations to commercial banks and focus on studying the changes in the macro economy and to gradually adopt indirect means for the exercise of macro control. It is necessary to comprehensively utilize means such as re-loaning, reserve ratio against deposit, rediscount rate, open market business, exchange rates, etc., to control the money supply and scale of lending, to maintain monetary stability and to prevent inflation. It is in this sense that we hold that it is important to treasure and protect the hard-earned orientation of reform in the financial market to achieve marketization and a subsequent liberal environment for finance. It is necessary to research and cultivate the economic relationship that fits in with the laws of the market economy and that is suitable for running the central bank, commercial banks and policy banks in order to gradually develop an ideal financial environment that meets the standards required by a mature market economy system.

As far as the reform of the financial system, or rather, the reform oriented to the commercialization of China's specialized banks is concerned, the essential question is whether the central bank can attain, in a concrete economic sense, independent and autonomous power in making monetary policy which stabilizes the value of currency rather than inappropriately pursuing the overall government macro-economic objectives under the guise of monetary policy. Rather than resorting to direct intervention, the government's financial function will be transformed into a function of indirect intervention through the intermediary of the market, economic levers and economic policy with the progression of economic transition. Thus, the operation of a commercial bank in the macro-economic environment will be secured on a genuine marketization basis, which will, on the one hand, enable it to work jointly with the central bank as a restraining force in terms of overall monetary policy, and, on the other, enforce reciprocal restraint on macro-economic policy that functions as a driving force. Consequently, an ideal liberal environment for monetary and financial activities will be created to ensure the sustained, stable and concerted development of the national economy.

It is noteworthy that the efficiency of the allocation of financial resources is mainly exhibited through the commercial banking system. The stability of the financial system also depends on the soundness of the commercial banking system. Hence, as far as the overall situation of the reform of China's financial system is concerned, the creation of a liberal financial environment implies that commercial banks of diversified ownership should be boldly developed. State-owned commercial banks with public ownership as the mainstay should be developed based on standardization, while conditions for the vigorous development of other forms of commercial banks, including non-governmental commercial banks, should also be created.

2. Financial disorder is mainly responsible for the chaos in the economic setup. It is necessary to accomplish the commercialization of the banking system through establishing a financial monitoring and control system based on market economy principles

With the development in breadth and depth that is taking place in the market-oriented financial reform, a competitive mechanism has been gradually introduced, while banking business risks have become more and more obvious and the problem of the credit standing of banks has become more and more outstanding. The chaos in the financial order over a long period of time has had an inestimably negative effect on the overall development of China's national economy. Though the State Council promulgated the *Interim Regulations of the PRC on Bank Management* in 1986, this did not fundamentally improve the situation in which bank supervision remained weak and ineffective. The major reasons are that the objectives of bank supervision are not clearly defined and that the process is not scientific. In many countries where the market economy is well developed and there is a sound legal system, whether supervision is enforced by the central bank or by an independent institution, the objective of bank supervision is separated from the central bank's monetary policy, thereby ensuring the impartiality of bank supervision. China's bank supervision leaves much to be desired in terms of being scientific, giving undue emphasis to administrative means and lacking scientific standards. It is in fact highly subjective and arbitrary. There is still a long and arduous way to go with regard to introducing diversified means of supervision, setting standards of supervision based on sound scientific principles and preventing a restoration of the old planned economy order in the process of reforming the commercial banking system. It is necessary to enforce the relevant clauses in the current *Law of the People's Bank of China* and the *Bank Law of the People's Republic of China* with regard to bank supervision in order to set up a normal supervisory mechanism between the central bank and commercial banks, between commercial banks themselves, and between commercial banks and the depositors. It is necessary to make an earnest effort to construct a bank supervision mechanism that is unified, authoritative and concerted. What is most pressing at present is the question of how to genuinely establish the legal status and authority of the People's Bank as the sole organ of bank supervision so as to execute its legal rights, including the right of supervision, management right and the right of sanction on a genuinely independent and objective basis. At the same time it is necessary to strive to uphold the *Commercial Bank Law* and act in accordance with the principle of "the Law's enforcement must be strict and violators must be brought to justice" when dealing with major cases related to the protection of depositors' interests, delegating business operations, improving the quality of credit assets, etc. It is especially important to intensify supervision to make financial supervision serve the interests of financial macro control as exercised by the central bank and help monetary policy moderately tighten the money supply so as to effectively curb inflation. Therefore it is necessary to adopt effective measures to amend or revoke conflicting clauses in the two legal documents mentioned above and to make preparations for the drafting of supplementary rules and implementation regulations.

It is necessary to act in accordance with international standards as defined in the Basle Agreement and draw on international experience to execute effective and reliable bank supervision. For instance, the central bank should exercise strict supervision with regard to business risks by formulating and enforcing standards related to capital classification and ratio of capital to risk assets for all banks. It is important to establish a strict auditing system and to adopt a universally acknowledged standard for accounting. For banks and non-banking financial institutions that fall below the standards, penalties should be meted out accordingly; they should be ordered either to take steps to improve the situation within a definite period or to suspend business pending rectification. Others may have their licences revoked. Market access should be strictly controlled. Those who wish to join the world of finance should have their fund sources, social background, sponsor, managerial capability, credit worthiness and business strategy strictly examined.

It is necessary to gradually perfect the mode of supervision through the reform and create ideal external conditions for the establishment of a regular commercial banking system. In conducting business a commercial bank must see to it that the relations between its business development and the supervision of the central bank are properly handled, based on dialectical unity rather than antagonism. In terms of the significance of economic transition, the supervision system for commercial banks set up by the central bank is still far from perfect. As the present supervision system regards the central bank as a department of financial management under the government, obviously it is in conflict with the concept of genuine independence for the central bank. The policy and mode of supervision of the central bank will continue to improve as the reform deepens and the function of financial supervision becomes independent of the operations of the central bank, resulting in more impartial, objective and accurate supervision. It is also possible to set up, under the guidance of the central bank, trade associations of commercial banks at different levels which are capable of self-service, self-restraint, mutual coordination and self-discipline, and which could become good supplements to the financial supervision system.

3. **The distorted relations between overall finance and the banking sector during the economic transition period is attributed to the blurring of economic functions in the government itself. So it is necessary to straighten out these relations through deepening the reform so as to clear away the obstacles to the commercialization of banking**

Under the influence of the long-established planned economy system, the relation between finance and banking was seriously distorted and blurred. A striking manifestation of the distorted relations and sharp contradictions is in the sphere of finance-related credit capital and credit-related finance capital. Finance-related credit capital implies the conversion of credit capital into capital to be used for a long time without obligation, such as loans or overdrafts obtained from banks by the financial department of a government, subsidies for loss-incurring enterprises which are supposed to be paid by the government, with the result that the banks have to advance credit capital to finance the expenditure. Meanwhile banks, on the government's orders, provide all sort of loans such as "loans for security and unity," "front-end finance," "loans for clearing up defaults," "relief loans," etc. The revenue of the banks is converted into financial revenue and financial bonds, etc. Credit-related finance capital refers to the utilization of intermittent funds by financial departments directly involved in providing loans or making fiduciary investments on a non-gratis basis, as is the case when a financial department turns the gratuitous capital invested by enterprises into non-gratis capital for use. They also directly provide part of the extra-budgetary funds as credit loans to enterprises. Financial departments establish their own credit institutions directly involved in lending and other credit activities, issue various local government bonds to the public and enterprises and directly obtain bank loans by drawing on the circulating funds of enterprises. Such a distorted and criss-crossing relationship between the banks and the financial departments in the economic transition period is especially harmful in yet-to-be positioned marginal spheres or vacuum areas formed in the process of economic restructuring. First of all, the effectiveness of the central macro control is greatly weakened. Due to the distorted functions of the financial departments and the banks, the true picture of fiscal balance is falsified, thus intensifying the potential contradictions in the operations of the economy. Second, when a financial department overdraws from a bank, the latter is compelled to increase the money supply, which in turn aggravates inflation, hindering the stable development of the economy as a whole. Third, finance-related credit capital reduces the fluidity of credit stock, which directly affects the regulatory role of credit capital in optimizing the economic structure. Fourth, due to the abnormal lending formed by finance-related credit capital in the failure of circulation of a considerable sum of credit results and this money becomes risky assets. Finally, the large-scale development of financial credit has already resulted in the squeezing of credits and loans, which is detrimental to the standardized management of social credit. Straightening out the relations between finance and the banks, and properly defining the economic functions of the government will no doubt have a major realistic significance in revamping the state banks based on commercialization during the economic transition period.

It is necessary to draw a clear line between finance and credit, and to properly define the scope of finance and credit capital. It is necessary to make a clear distinction between financial allocation and credit allocation. Financial allocation is mainly responsible for satisfying the financial requirements of branches of non-material production, while bank credit should be based on the principle of efficiency to accomplish the goal of regulating social resources through market leverage. The scope of investment of finance capital should focus on satisfying the long-term financial requirements of enterprises and the input of money into the energy, communications and other key and basic industries. It is not advisable to make use of long-standing and stable financial resources to pursue instant benefit, and it is likewise improper to let bank credit take over the funding which should be arranged by the financial departments. It is necessary to make clear that it is forbidden to overdraw from the central bank when a deficit occurs in the central finance. Instead, capital should be raised from the market by issuing long- and short-term bonds. Therefore, it is necessary to vigorously advocate open market operations and use treasury bills and government loans as a practical choice for drawing a strict demarcation line separating finance from credit.

It is necessary to increase the transparency with regard to the utilization of finance capital. Financial departments should periodically make known the allocations of finance capital. It is proper to strengthen the differentiation of the relations between finance and credit through the market mechanism. Therefore, it is necessary to formulate long- and medium-term financial and monetary policies with feasibility and transparency, which should be interlinked with the annual financial budget and credit plan. At the same time, it is necessary to be realistic with regard to the strengthening of the management of extra-budgetary funds and finance credit so as to fundamentally change the long-established status of the "government standard" which governs the plan for financial capital allotment and the target of money supply. Instead, it should let both of them find their natural places in the operational mechanism of the market through their organic and transparent linkage with the market. Only when the relations between finance and banking are clearly defined can they genuinely catalyze the transformation of the state banks into commercial banks, provided that their functions are properly displayed in the market mechanism.

It is necessary to properly understand the relations between financial departments and the banks during the period of economic transition, which have already been converted from a hierarchical setup to one of cooperation and growth on an equal basis. Such cooperation and growth on all equal footing dictates that monetary policy should be compatible with financial policy, the banks should support the floating of treasury bonds and promote financial operations through financial supervision, and the financial departments should create a better economic environment to serve the banking sector. Beneath the surface of the finance-bank relations on a basis of equality and cooperation is a deeper implication, that is, when emphasizing the role of the bank's monetary policy in regulating the macro operation of the national economy one should not overlook the identically significant and important role of the government's financial policy. In fact, in full-fledged market economies finance and banks are employed alternatively in economic macro control. What we should strive hard for is, through economic transition, to let finance represent part of the government's economic behavior and let the banks represent the monetary behavior of the market so as to bring about a sound development of the operational mechanism of commercial banks based on marketization and further accelerate the transition toward a socialist market economy.

(Paper read at the *International Symposium on the System of Restructuring of Commercial Bank in China*, in Haikou, Nov. 15, 1995.)

Marketization of State Assets: Laying a Micro-Economic Foundation for China's Socialist Market Economy

I. Introduction

—Why do we advocate the marketization of state assets?

1. Marketization of state-owned assets (SOAs) is a total negation of the outdated economic system

Under the traditional planned economy system SOAs were characterized by: (1) plural management; (2) administration-based operations; (3) monopoly; (4) focus on concrete products; and (5) inertia.

The most evident feature of the traditional management and operation modes of SOAs is that the allocation of resources is directly carried out through administration rather than through the market. It is evident that such a practice has many drawbacks and is not a successful mode. Total negation of the traditional system is to introduce the mode of resources allocation through the market. This implies that SOAs should directly enter the market and be regulated by the market in accordance with market laws for the purpose of optimizing resources allocation and the maximization of their economic returns.

2. The key to the economic restructuring lies in the tackling of the issue of property rights, the core of which resides in the marketization of SOAs

The central link in the economic restructuring is the invigoration of enterprises. To this end, a series of "deregularizing" measures have been adopted since the introduction of the economic reform and opening policies. It is evident that the outcome has been far from being satisfactory, as invigorating enterprises is a systems engineering project which far exceeds the capability of the enterprises. Property right is the fundamental issue, and without finding a proper solution to this it is difficult to genuinely invigorate an enterprise.

Needless to say, it is important to push state enterprises into the market and to transform the operational mechanism of enterprises. However, this is far from enough, because the issue of property rights of an enterprises is not only one that calls for clarification, but also one that is related to the internal mechanism. In the conditions of a market economy, it involves a series of issues such as possession, definition, circulation and operation, etc., and in fact pertains to the effective management, allocation and operation of state-owned enterprises as a whole. The market alone cannot enable the state-owned enterprises to free themselves from the conventional management framework and from the restraint of the old administrative mechanism. The way out is to put state assets to the market; this is the most fundamental issue related to state assets and also a fundamental requirement of the socialist market economy.

The issue of property rights is not only a prerequisite for the recreation of the micro foundation of a socialist market economy, but also the foundation and basic content of macro institutional reform. Therefore, the issue of property rights has a direct bearing on the overall situation of economic restructuring, which will trigger off a succession of things. Therefore, the reform of property rights is of great significance.

3. Selection of the outlets with regard to the reform of state-owned enterprises

The reform of state-owned enterprises in China has all along been governed by the concept of "delegation of power and concession of profits." But this has already been proved to be ineffective as such a train of thought has not yet been freed from hackneyed precedents and cannot exert any substantial impact on the core of the conventional economic institution.

The idea of reform based on "delegating power and making concession of profits" was put forward at the initial stage of economic restructuring in China. This was a time of exploration in terms of the orientation of the economic restructuring, during which the objective of socialist economic restructuring had not yet been explicitly established and a break from the traditional system had not yet been achieved. Therefore, the idea of "delegating power and making concession of profits" has its own historical limitations. Now, the orientation and objective of economic restructuring in China have been established and the progress of reform accelerated to shift to a market economy as soon as possible. This being the case, the train of thought with regard to enterprise reform should be adapted to the new objective and situation. Therefore, it is necessary to achieve a major breakthrough and make bold strides.

What are the problems to be solved in terms of the reform of state-owned enterprises and what is the fundamental solution? Opinions are divided on this matter. We hold that reform of state-owned enterprises is neither an issue related only to the mechanism of these firms themselves, nor is it possible to solve their fundamental problems and all their difficulties through such a reform. Reform of state firms is the central link of all the economic restructuring, and the reform that focuses on this central link is inevitably a comprehensive one, an issue of compatibility for the system which is not just a micro one or one that belongs to a certain aspect or linkage. Reform of state-owned enterprises in a socialist market economy involves at least three major issues:

First is the problem of SOA allocation. The SOAs of an enterprises which is static and administratively monopolistic cannot enter the market for circulation to realize the maximization of returns from the assets based on the law of the market economy. The socialist market economy demands that the principal role of public ownership of SOAs should be safeguarded by enterprises, that the circulation of SOAs in the capital market and assets market be allowed, and that reorganization and optimized allocation be realized through the market mechanism so as to achieve the maximization of assets efficiency and value.

Second is the problem relating to the administration of state-owned enterprises by the state itself. Under the planned economy system the administrative power of the state, the ownership of SOAs and the right of management of state enterprises were a combination of "three in one"; enterprises were directly operated by the state and became virtually appendices of the administrative departments. At the same time, the administration exercised by the state was decentralized, stratified and placed under multiple leadership. Consequently, SOAs belonged nominally to the state, but in practice, the ownership was indefinite in terms of definition and authority. Such a system of management not only created problems like lack of autonomy for enterprises in decision making as well as lack of vigor, but also brought problems like waste of SOAs, serious losses and low efficiency and profits.

Third are the problems relating to the management of state firms themselves. They include those of the property rights of an enterprise, responsibility for assets, organizational structure and internal management system, which are directly related to developing the enterprises into genuine components of the market economy.

Therefore, the fundamental way out for the reform of state firms resides in the marketization of SOAs, that is, to push the SOAs of general enterprises onto the market and make them operate in accordance with the laws of the market economy to realize the maximization of their benefits and value. It is necessary to carry out reform in the overall management and operation system of SOAs through marketization. At the same time, reform in other aspects of economic management should be promoted to totally free the management system from the cycles and the mode of the traditional economic system and to adapt itself to the needs of the socialist market economy as soon as possible.

4. Marketization of SOAs is an issue of both practicality and urgency

The reform of the economic system has already made big progress—such as in the elimination of most of the mandatory planning and the removal of control from the prices of most commodities. Consequently, the old system has been subject to significant change, but has not yet disappeared as it should, because the key issue of property rights has not yet been tackled and still remains an impediment to carrying on the reform.

In the course of reform, further experiments have been carried out in China with regard to the marketization of SOAs, such as the establishment of stock markets, the setting up of property rights exchanges in some areas, the authorized operation of SOAs and the extensive trials carried out in the establishment of stockholding enterprises. Though the experiments have not yet developed into a system and the reform in property rights has not yet been thoroughly carried out, sufficient preparations have been made for the systematic and overall reform of the marketization of SOAs.

At present, China is in a period of transition from the old system to the new one for the establishment of a socialist market economy in the shortest possible time. It is urgently necessary to carry out a thorough reform of the property rights system and to push state enterprises onto the market so as to deepen the economic restructuring and promote the realization of the economic transition. Marketization of SOAs is a very practical and urgent issue, and the conditions for this are basically complete at this stage of the reform.

II. Theoretical Basis and Explication
—What does the marketization of SOAs involve?

1. The meaning of the marketization of SOAs

(1) Mobilization of the market. This is necessary for the full circulation of SOAs in the capital and assets markets to reorgan-

ize property rights transfer in accordance with the law of market competition so as to optimize resource allocation.

(2) Maximization of value. It is necessary to seek the maximization of money value and economic benefits in the process of market circulation of SOAs to ensure that the latter not only preserve their value but also realize value appreciation.

(3) Independence in business operation. Independent business operation will be exercised in terms of SOAs in the market. In general, the state will not get involved in the direct operation of SOAs. The operators of SOAs are enterprise legal persons.

(4) Indirect management. Unified management of SOAs will be carried out through the combination of centralized and decentralized management. Generally, it is necessary to exercise indirect management through intermediary business operations to ensure the autonomous operation of SOAs in the market free from direct intervention of the government.

2. Characteristics of SOA marketization

The marketization of SOAs represents the inherent demand of the socialist market economy, which is markedly different from the status of SOAs in the traditional economic system in the following aspects:

(1) Converting physical SOAs into SOAs of value. SOAs in the planned economy were represented in physical form, the state exercising direct control over both means of production and products. But SOAs in a socialist market economy are represented in the form of value through the measurement of assets and related economic benefits by referring to commodity value. Apart from a small number of cases in which the state still exercises monopoly, generally there is no need for the state to exercise direct control over physical property.

(2) Converting coagulation into fluidity. Under the old setup SOAs were under the direct control of the administration and were relatively solidified and unable to be mobile on their own. The socialist market economy demands that SOAs must circulate freely by themselves and fair competition should be the norm.

(3) Converting indistinct property rights into distinct ones.

In the old market economy system, state-owned enterprises were nominally owned by the state, but, owing to the multi-tiered management system and multiple investment channels used by the administrative authorities, the ownership of SOAs was ambiguous in terms of possession and definition. But in the new system the majority of SOAs are converted into shares, which behave in accordance with the corporate system. Corporate legal persons enjoy the rights of ownership, thus ensure the clarification of the property rights.

(4) Converting monotonous business operations into diversified business operations. In the traditional system the business operations concerning SOAs were under the direct monopoly of the state; under the new system, apart from few SOAs in trades and industries directly controlled by the state, most SOAs are operated through intermediary agencies based on diversified operations.

(5) Converting integration of government administration and enterprise management into separation of government administration from commercial management.

To ensure the completion of the planned economy, in the traditional system the general administrative functions of governments, the function of the proprietorship of SOAs and operational function were mixed up and performed by relevant leading government departments. But the socialist market economy requires that (1) government functions be separated from SOA management; and (2) government functions be separated from those of enterprises, that is, the functions of SOAs management should be separated from those of SOA operation.

—Will the marketization of SOAs change the basis of socialist public ownership?

1. A fresh understanding of the aims of socialist public ownership

The marketization of SOAs requires that the physically based management of SOAs be converted into value-based management. This does not imply changing the foundation of the public ownership under socialism, but it is necessary to renew our understanding with regard to the aims of socialist public ownership in the socialist market economy.

(1) In the planned economy system "public ownership" referred to publicly owned means of production, as decided by the requirements of the planned economy. As Engels said, society drew up plans to control the economy in accordance with the availability of resources and the needs of the society, and money was not all economic lever.

(2) In the socialist market economy in most cases the physical form of public ownership is unnecessary, and the measurement of assets is represented by commodity value and its external form as money; as multiple ownerships co-exist and compete against each other it is impossible for the state to control the general means of production (in fact the complete ownership of the means of production does not exist any more). The market economy requires that available resources be re-allocated in the whole society in accordance with the law of the market, so the public ownership of the means of production in physical form obviously runs counter to this. Hence, public ownership under socialism should be public ownership in the form of commodity value rather than public ownership of the means of production in the traditional sense.

(3) The conversion of property from a physical form into a value form will not change the foundation of socialist public ownership. Conversion of SOAs in physical form into value form is carried out on the basis of the principle of exchange at equal value—the state recovers the capital at equal value and takes possession of the ownership of assets in value form. Consequently, the state does not lose anything that is being exchanged. The state then invests this money in other highly profitable areas and reaps greater value of assets against the original value. Thus, the foundation of socialist public ownership will not be subject to any changes, rather it will be consolidated, developed and expanded.

2. Renewing the understanding with regard to the function of the foundation of socialist public ownership

The marketization of SOAs requires that they circulate and compete in the market to select the superior and to eliminate the inferior. But will this weaken the function of the economic foundation of public ownership? To answer this question, it is necessary to renew our understanding of the function of the economic foundation of public ownership.

(1) In the traditional economic system public ownership was the base and had a dominating position and absolute superiority in the overall national economy, just as Engels said that all capital, all agriculture, all industry and all transport, and the whole of trade and exchange would be concentrated more and more in the hands of the state. The non-state economy could at the most become a supplement to the socialist economy in a subordinate position.

(2) In the socialist market economy the function of public ownership as the economic foundation should remain. a) Those trades and industries which have a close bearing on the national economy, the people's livelihood and public utilities, and those which are unfit for competition should be controlled and managed by the state. b) General trades and industries should be jointly developed and managed by the public sector and other economic sectors based on fair competition and the principle of survival of the fittest. By continuously improving management and enhancing efficiency, the publicly owned economy will display its resilience. c) In the past the principal role of public ownership resided mainly in the pursuit of quantity to make the publicly owned enterprises hold the dominating position. In fact, the role of public ownership resides in quality, meaning efficiency and competitiveness, rather than in quantity. So long as its leading role is established in quality, the role of public ownership will be fully displayed. d) The role of the publicly owned economy is in fact determined by the leading role of the SOAs.

(3) The leading role of public ownership conforms with the theory of the primary stage of socialism. In this stage economic

101

sectors of various ownership exist side by side; they all contribute to fully developing the socialist market economy and increasing social productivity. The non-publicly owned economy is not only a supplement of the national economy but also an economic form that exists alongside the public economy. But, it does not occupy a leading position. If we overemphasize the dominating position of the public economy and concentrate everything in the hands of the state, thus restricting fair competition from other economic sectors, then the positive role of the non-state economy will be greatly cramped, which will be detrimental to the development of the socialist market economy and does not conform with the requirements of the theory and practice of the primary phase of socialism.

—Will the marketization of SOAs lead to "privatization"?

1. The marketization of SOAs does not mean "privatization"

The circulation and transfer of SOAs and their property rights in the market does not mean that the state gives up ownership of its assets. In the socialist market economy the conversion of the physical form of ownership into the value form does not involve any changes in its nature.

2. Several principles for the marketization of SOAs

(1) The state should directly manage a small number of trades and industries as monopolies which are not to be put to the market.

(2) State-owned joint stock enterprises should in general be run by the state. In traditional theory the state's holdings should comprise 51% of the total stocks, but when the stock rights are widely disseminated the percentage of holdings may be smaller.

(3) It is necessary to consider the leading role of public ownership in transferring SOAs and their property rights so as to prevent the non-public economy from totally controlling some

major economic areas.

(4) It is necessary to prevent the drain of SOAs, strengthen the supervisory mechanism and exercise strict assessment.

III. Operational Scheme (1)
—Establishing a market system for SOAs

1. Structural framework of the market system for SOAs

SOA markets may be classified into four types: market for stocks, market for the transfer of stock rights, market for the transaction of property rights, and market for the transfer of operation rights.

(1) Market for stocks. This is directed for state-owned joint stock enterprises that issue stocks to the public. The stocks can be listed in the primary and secondary markets for the liquidity of SOAs.

(2) Market for the transfer of stock rights. This is suitable for joint-stock limited companies and limited liability companies in capital raising. Such companies are joint stock enterprises whose stocks are not listed. However, with the approval of a shareholders' meeting or the board of directors, the stock rights may be sold or transferred and circulated in the market for stock rights. Methods of transfer include mutual equity participation, stock owning, stock holding, pooling, etc.

(3) Market for the transaction of property rights. This is suitable for the transaction and transfer of assets or property rights owned by non-joint-stock enterprises. Methods of transaction include transfer in whole or in part, auctioning, take-over through purchase, assets swapping, pooling, etc. It is also suitable for joint-stock enterprises in transacting or transferring assets other than stock rights, such as auctioning bankrupt stock and swapping residual assets.

(4) Market for the transfer of operation rights. This is suitable for companies which are directly controlled by the state and are not directly involved in business operations or do not need to adopt the form of joint-stock organization for capital

raising. For these enterprises there is neither the need for the transfer of stock ownership nor the need for the state to get involved in direct business operations. Rather, the rights of business operation are publicly sold in one of the following forms: trust business operation, business operation under contract or business operation based on leasing. The rights of business operation bought may be re-transferred in the relevant market when all parties concerned agree. The sale or transfer of the rights of business operation should be conducted through public bidding based on competition or through bilateral or multi-lateral negotiations arranged by intermediary market agencies and a contract signed. It is a principle those that possess the rights of business operation should be economic entities with the capability of business operation rather than individuals.

2. Essentials of the operation of the SOA market

(1) The SOA market should be composed of relevant departments such as the Ministry of Finance, banking and auditing departments at state level, State Economic and Trade Commission (SETC), State Planning Commission and State Commission for Restructuring the Economic System (SCRES), under the supervision of the State Commission for SOA Administration.

(2) Specialized agencies for market transaction and administration should be established for the four markets respectively, securities exchanges, exchange centers for the transfer of equity rights, property rights exchanges and exchange centers for the transfer of business operation rights.

(3) National-level and local-level operations should be established for all four markets, that is, a system composed of a unified national market and local markets to be established in accordance with the necessary circumstances to enliven the market and promote circulation and competition.

(4) All markets to be established should be standardized in accordance with legal provisions to ensure fair, just and reason-

able competition.

IV. Operational Scheme (2)
—Establishing a three-tier system of SOA administration and ensuring the marketization of SOAs

1. The framework for the three-tier system of SOA administration

(1) SOA administration center

The State Council exercises administrative control over SOAs on behalf of the state. The administration operates on two-levels: The first level exercises unified coordination and supervision; the second level exercises separated administration based on a combination of decentralized and centralized administration modes.

A commission for SOA administration composed of responsible members from relevant departments will be established under the State Council. The commission will be responsible for the formulation and coordination of all the principles, policies, plans and laws with regard to the administration and operation of SOAs, and will supervise their implementation. The State Administration of State Property is to be abolished.

SOAs will be classified into: a) Trades and industries under the control and monopoly of the state, such as posts and telecommunications, railways, banks, weaponry, key mineral resources and public utilities. These are to be put under the administration of relevant leading departments at the central level which are subject to the policy-based coordination of the State Commission for SOA Administration; and b) General competitive trades and industries which should be put under the unified administration of the SOE Administration Department under the State Commission for SOA Administration rather than having each department act on its own. The existing relevant departments at the central level will be responsible solely for formulating policies for their respective trades rather than exercise direct control over state-owned enterprises, and will be replaced gradually by semi-official trade and industry associations.

(2) SOA investment center

Apart from a small number of state-monopolized sectors which should be directly managed and operated by the relevant departments in charge under the State Council, other SOAs should be operated by specialized intermediary investment agencies. The departments in charge of SOAs should not get directly involved in the operation of SOAs. Instead, their representatives will serve on the boards of directors or management committees of the intermediary investment agencies to participate in making policies concerning the business operations and to exercise supervision.

The SOA intermediary investment agencies, which enjoy the status of legal persons of corporate business, are responsible only for capital (assets) investment and yield and are not directly involved in specific business operations.

The SOA intermediary investment agencies can take such forms as investment corporations, holding corporations, enterprise groups, insurance companies, commercial banks and foundations of various types.

Intermediary investment agencies are not entitled to serve as the sole agencies for trades, because this will result in economic monopoly and hamper competition. And it is inappropriate for an intermediary investment agency to become an overly massive institution, which will lead to low efficiency in decision making.

(3) SOA business operations center

The specific business operations involving SOAs will be handled by specialized state firms which will be responsible for concrete production and operation activities, cost effectiveness, enhancement of economic benefits and increase of profits. The SOA business operations center will also be the principal assets market. Most of the existing SOAs belong to similar specialized bodies.

V. Operational Scheme (3)

—Revamping the existing state firms trade by trade to thoroughly transforming their operational mechanism

1. Basic conception with regard to the categorized revamp of existing state enterprises

(1) State-owned self-run enterprises

Enterprises that should be directly operated by state departments or enterprises that should be operated by agencies directly affiliated to relevant state departments at the central level. This applies only in a small number of trades and industries in which it is inappropriate to carry out free competition and that must be monopolized by the state.

State-owned self-run enterprises will not be pushed to the market and their property rights will not be transferred. However, some foreign countries have transformed such enterprises into joint-stock ones.

(2) Other types of state-owned third-party-operated enterprises

Enterprises of this kind are categorized as follows: a) infrastructural and key firms, and a small number of loss-incurring enterprises that are covered by state mandatory plans and cannot be allowed to go bankrupt. These enterprises do not need the state to get directly involved in management, but to improve their management they may be contracted or leased to economic entities with the operational capability of managing them; b) enterprises for which the joint stock system is unsuitable may adopt the mode of state-owned third-party-operated companies. Such enterprises include small retailers, small industrial enterprises, and firms involved in tertiary trades. These enterprises, which employ relatively few people and need little capital, are suitable for decentralized operations and may adopt the operational modes of the contractual or leasing systems.

Generally, state-owned third-party-operated enterprises

should transfer their rights of operation through the market for the transfer of business operation rights. The forms of operation include trust operations, contracted operations and leasing operations.

If necessary, state-owned third-party-operated enterprises may also be converted into joint-stock enterprises or privately run enterprises.

(3) State-owned joint-stock enterprises

Apart from the conditions set above for state-owned self-run or third-party-run enterprises, other large and medium-sized state-owned industrial enterprises may also be reorganized on the basis of the joint-stock system, i.e. to be transformed in accordance with the modern corporation system. The legal forms of joint-stock enterprises are as follows: joint-stock limited company, limited liability company or solely funded limited liability company.

State-owned joint-stock companies enjoy the ownership status of legal persons and have the right to handle corporate property, such as selling off fixed assets, disposing of idle assets, re-allocating assets, mutual-holding of equity rights, reciprocal transfer of equity rights, selling or buying stocks and even auctioning or taking over enterprises. Ownership by legal persons of a corporate business does not conflict with state ownership, since the state remains the largest shareholder and, as a member of a corporate legal entity, determines the execution of ownership by a corporate legal person. Ownership by the state incorporates that of a corporate legal person, and ownership by a corporate legal person is in essence ownership by all the members of the corporate entity, which include the state.

(4) Privately run enterprises

Privatization of an enterprise means turning a state-owned enterprise into a non-state-owned one. This mainly refers to small and medium-sized firms that are of little importance to the national economy and loss-making ones that need not be shored up. Turning them into private enterprises is conducive to promoting their economic development and to enhancing their productivity.

Privatization should generally be accomplished through the

property rights exchange market so that the transfer, annexation and auctioning of property rights are dealt with properly.

2. Revamping state firms based on the corporate system

A great number of large and medium-sized state-owned industrial enterprises will have to be reorganized into stockholding enterprises, that is joint-stock enterprises based on a corporate system. The modern market economy is composed of all forms of corporations, but the transformation of state firms should be based on the three forms as follows:

(1) The joint-stock limited company is a form suitable for firms that need to raise funds extensively from the public and those that need to spread risks. Their stocks may be listed for transaction. Limited liability companies based on capital raising may transfer their equity in the relevant market.

(2) The limited liability company is a form suitable for joint-venture enterprises, joint-management enterprises, enterprise groups and other enterprises based on mutual stockholding and equity participation. Enterprises of this kind do not issue stocks to the public and their equity may be transferred in the equity transfer market upon the approval of a shareholders' meeting or the board of directors.

(3) The solely-funded enterprise is a special form of stockholding system with only one shareholder, with limited liability. Such a form is suitable for wholly state-funded enterprises. Apart from the applicability of the forms of joint-stock limited companies and limited liability companies as mentioned above, the transformation of other large and medium-sized state-owned industrial enterprises into joint-stock enterprises may adopt the form of the solely-funded limited company with a board of directors as the top leadership. Solely-funded limited companies may transfer all their stock rights on the equity market. If only part of the stock rights are to be transferred, the corporation should be converted into a limited liability company.

(Read at the *International Symposium on the Theoretical and Practical Issues of the Market Economy in China*, in Haikou, July 1, 1993.)

Development of the State-Owned Economy in an Environment of Market Competition

The First Working Conference on the UN Asia-Pacific Network Cooperation Project (UNAP Network Project) was held from February 24 to 25, 1994. As the CHIRD is the executive organ of the UNAP Network Project, over the past year or so it has invited scholars from the member countries on three occasions to participate in international symposiums to address issues of common interest on economic reform.

In the Asia-Pacific region some countries have already been practicing market economies and progressively dovetailing their economies with the global market, while other nations have been shifting from traditional planned economies to market economies. In such circumstances many countries in the region are confronted with major issues like how to speed up the reform of state-owned enterprises, how to fit in with the macro environment of market competition, how to improve management and how to promote the growth of the state sector of the economy. In 1994 the CHIRD and the UNDP jointly sponsored an international symposium on the reform of state firms in China, and both domestic and overseas participants, especially those from member nations of the network project, contributed valuable proposals and comments.

We hold that in the conditions of the market economy the reform of state firms should focus on the overall competitiveness and overall soundness of the state-owned sector and that the guiding role of the state-owned sector in the development of the national economy should be fully displayed. The management of state firms calls for the establishment of stable interest relations among the managers, laborers and the enterprise, as such stable interest relations will contribute to the laying of a lasting dynamic foundation.

I. Maximizing the Efficiency of State-owned Assets and Fully Displaying the Guiding Role of the State-owned Sector

To meet the needs of the market economy, to bring about the organic integration of state-owned assets (SOAs) with the market economy and to reap the maximum benefits from SOAs are problems of the greatest importance and practical significance during the transition from the planned economy to the market economy. Solutions to these problems can spur the reform of state firms and the reform of the management of SOAs, and consequently give full play to the guiding role of the state sector of the market economy.

In a market economy the proportion of the state-owned sector should be reduced in the areas of general competition, and SOAs should be focused on basic industries, key areas and public utilities.

The common characteristic of market economies is the maximization of profits and economic advantages in the course of market competition. This tends to give rise to temporary and limited decision making, with attention focused on those areas that promise speedy returns at the expense of economic projects that require long-term planning, and promise tardy and comparatively low benefits. The market economy is also characterized by the contradiction between local and overall interests, between short-term and long-term interests, and between individual and social interests. Therefore, it is necessary for the state to formulate economic and industrial policies utilizing powerful physical means to play a dominating role in key areas of business and for the control and regulation of economic operations so as to guide the development of the market economy in a sound direction.

Proceeding from the overall social efficiency, macro-economic efficiency and long-term development efficiency of SOAs, the optimum efficiency of SOAs should be reflected in terms of basic efficiency, guiding efficiency and the efficiency of public service.

Basic efficiency dictates that the bulk of SOAs should focus on investment in infrastructural facilities and basic industries to lay a solid foundation for the development of the entire national economy.

Guiding efficiency means that, abiding by the principle of fair competition, SOAs should also command a principal position and play a leading role in key industries and areas such as finance, insurance, posts and telecommunications, aerospace and aviation.

Efficiency of public service entails the duty of SOAs to play important roles in the realms of public services and educational and cultural undertakings, and to increase investment in these spheres progressively.

The guiding role of the state-owned sector should mainly be manifested in competitiveness and efficiency, ensuring that it commands an unrivaled position in the total social assets and has a controlling power over the national economy. To truly display the efficiency and competitiveness of the state-owned sector it is necessary to shift the SOAs from general competitive industries and concentrate them in basic industries, key areas and special trades.

But, instead of withdrawing from competition, SOAs should actively participate in competition in trades and industries that have a predominant bearing on the national economy and people's livelihood and that require the dominance of the state sector.

Second, the operation of SOAs should be carried out through competition in basic industries and in the area of public utilities, which will help to enhance the efficiency and benefits of SOAs. SOAs may engage in competition not only with the non-state sector but also among themselves.

Third, the competition between SOAs in basic industries and

public utilities should be carried out moderately. Efforts should be made to avoid the dislocation of resources resulting from the malpractice of dividing up government functional agencies, developing multilateral ownerships, proposing questionable projects, duplicating construction projects, etc.

The roles and functions of the state-owned sector do not lie in the absolute quantitative superiority of state firms, as it is unwise to bring all the economic areas together under state control. The state-owned sector should exercise control and conduct operations in areas that have a vital bearing on the national economy and people's livelihood. As to general types of trades and industries, the state-owned sector may also play a leading role in terms of quality, efficiency and competitiveness on the basis of mutual development and fair competition with the non-state sector.

In accordance with the market mechanism of letting the successful survive and having the unsuccessful eliminated, it is essential to boldly adjust the structure of state firms to let those that cannot survive die and those that can survive live.

To deepen the reform of state firms, it is imperative to develop market competition to let enterprises with comparative advantages grow and expand through shifting and infusing capital and resources into such highly efficient enterprises, which in turn will invigorate the whole national economy. Developing the guiding role of the state-owned sector does not mean invigorating every state firm, which in fact is both unnecessary and impossible.

Therefore, enterprises that suffer long-term losses and are unable to turn themselves around should be declared bankrupt in accordance with the pertinent law. Their residual assets should be put up for auction or absorbed or bought by other legal persons. Some small enterprises may be leased out or sold. Those enterprises that have developed advantages in the market economy should be encouraged in terms of policies and investment to develop into backbone and pillar enterprises of the state-owned sector. Special prominence should be given to large-sized enterprises and conglomerates that have an important bearing on the national economy and people's livelihood to sharpen the competitive edge of the entire national economy in the domestic and international arenas so as to accelerate the progress of industrialization.

II. To Turn State-owned Assets into State-owned Capital, It Is Necessary to Invigorate the National Economy in a Comprehensive Manner

The modern market economy centers on invigorating capital in the pursuit of maximum profits, maximum value and maximum benefits. The key lies in the successful transformation of SOAs into state-owned capital, that is, shifting from the pursuit of quantity of SOEs to the realization of the overall benefits of state-owned capital. This is what the reform of state firms should strive to tackle in the transition from a traditional planned economy to a market economy.

The transformation of SOAs into state-owned capital does not mean discarding some of the major social responsibilities shouldered by state firms. Some of those responsibilities can be regulated by economic means. It is essential to eliminate policy-based monopolies to allow non-state firms to participate, to a certain extent, in economic operations and competition within certain limits, such as in the construction of basic facilities. It is also necessary to formulate policies for open economic compensation for all participating enterprises, including state firms. The same may apply to a few state firms in carrying out policy-based tasks or voluntary social services. In such cases, a special account may be kept to calculate the cost involved and to make compensation accordingly. An indicator of the "public pay-out ratio" may be designed, which, together with the indicator of the rate of profit, may serve as a basis for meting out rewards and punishments as well as for performance assessment. During the process of transition from the planned economy to the market economy state firms are still obliged to be run as self-contained work units which should be disintegrated into different functions for the eventual progressive transfer to society. In the conditions of a market economy the social responsibilities should be shared so as to maximize the profits of state firms and to bring about their advance to the market together with non-state firms, based on mutual competition. Only by so doing can the national economy be invigorated in an overall manner.

To bring about the transformation of SOAs into state capital, efforts should be made to tackle the deep-seated contradictions in the traditional managerial system of SOAs. The deep-rooted institutional factors that lead to the drain and waste of state-owned assets are due to the traditional planned economy, characterized by the lack of separation between government administration and investment on the one hand and enterprise management on the other, as well as by the practice of multilateral ownerships. These man-made restraints inhibited the circulation and optimal composition of state capital. Therefore, in shifting towards the market economy, the key lies in the re-establishment of managerial and operational systems which include: (1) The establishment of a unified system of management over SOAs is necessary. The state should set up a commission for SOA management and all operational SOAs should be placed under the proper authorities in the government. (2) The Commission for SOA Administration should be set up, composed of two managerial tiers characterized by both integration and division. The first tier should be administrated and coordinated by the Commission, and the second tier should exercise divided management, in which the trades and industries under state monopoly and control will be subject to specific management. Other industries and trades will be subject to unified administration under the Administration of State Property, which will replace the traditional practice of having the latter in charge of various trades. (3) A structure of separate ownership and management of SOAs should be established, and corresponding local commissions to oversee SOAs should also be set up. (4) An independent operational system for SOAs should be established. The control of state-owned capital will be the exclusive responsibility of an intermediary agency, while it is necessary to realize the separation of capital control of

SOAs from business management.

To bring about the conversion of SOAs into state-owned capital it is imperative to invigorate SOAs in an overall manner. The invigoration of the national economy and the pursuit of the optimization of the benefits from SOAs does not lie simply in invigorating every state firm. The latter should conform to the requirements of the market economy in terms of survival for the fittest. It is imperative to push, in the realm of competition, the assets of state firms and their property rights into the market for reimbursable assignment and reorganization, for the reallocation of resources and factors of production and optimal composition so as to ensure the maximization of asset values and the optimization of economic returns. Especially noteworthy is the intensity of competition in both the domestic and international markets. In such a context there arises an urgent need for the selection and organization of a national contingent of leading enterprises through reform and new establishment of state-owned holding companies which can fully play the role of the main force in market competition. Proceeding from the invigoration of state firms to that of SOAs and eventually to that of state capital entails a qualitative leap in the reform of state enterprises.

III. Establishing State-owned Holding Companies as Intermediary Agencies Is an Effective Way to Separate Government Administration from Enterprise Management

International experience has shown that the low economic benefits of state firms and the serious losses they incur are attributable mainly to the lack of separation of government administration from enterprise management. The arbitrary intervention in enterprises by the government and the lack of independent decision-making power on the part of the enterprises make it impossible for enterprises to fully bear the responsibility for the outcome of business operations. Consequently, there arises a conflict between the business system of state firms and the law that governs the market economy. This is especially true in those countries that are shifting from planned to market economies, and where the contradiction that arises out of the lack of separation between government administration and enterprise management has become even more striking. Major topics such as how to tackle the above contradiction by finding an effective way for the separation of government administration and enterprise management are subjects that are under exploration during the reform of state firms in many countries.

In exploring the separation of government administration from enterprise management one of the major means is to rely upon the intermediary agency that lies between the governmental department in charge and the state firm, serving as a barricade preventing direct ties between government administration and enterprise management. This is vital for overcoming governmental inertia in the process of shifting from the planned economy to a market economy. The state holding company is a major form of the intermediary organ in this respect.

State-owned holding companies are intermediary investment agencies that specialize in the management of SOAs. They are vested with the status of independent corporate legal persons. In the practice of many countries, there are both successful and unsuccessful examples with regard to the establishment of state-owned holding companies. The reason for the lack of success lies in the failure on the part of the holding companies to check government intervention, or, worst still, the degeneration of the holding companies into vehicles for governmental intervention. Therefore, to accomplish the goal of separation of government administration from enterprise management it is essential to prevent the holding companies degenerating into administrative bodies, that is to say, being only a company in name, and in fact being an administrative agency of a government, or functioning as a company while vested with the administrative functions of a government department. Such a holding company is in fact controlled by the government while it intervenes in the management of its subordinate enterprises through administrative means.

Therefore it is actually a reproduction of the old economic setup. In establishing a state-owned holding company it is essential to prevent it from turning into an administrative company; it is necessary to avoid the establishment of an administrative company in disguised form on the basis of the original government agency in charge. A real holding company must be established based upon assets as linkage through the methods of integration, merging, shares purchasing, etc.

To establish a state-owned holding company it is imperative to reform the traditional state firms on the basis of the corporate system. The state-owned holding company will mainly exercise control through holding a sufficient percentage of shares. Thus, it is necessary to, first of all, turn a large number of state firms into liability limited companies. This calls for both reforming the managerial mechanisms of state firms in the process of transition from a planned economy to a market economy and exercising control over the many business-type enterprises.

The establishment of state-owned holding companies requires protecting the independence of the property rights of enterprises. Two aspects of the problem require particular attention: One is the relationship of authorization and entrustment of property rights between the SOA administrative departments and the state-owned holding companies, which hold the ownership over SOAs in accordance with the law and are vested with independent property rights. Under no circumstances should the SOA administrative departments or other government agencies arbitrarily and illegally interfere in the business activities of the holding companies. The other is the operational relationship between the holding companies and their subsidiaries, which is an economic relationship arising from investment and shareholding. Both of them enjoy independent legal person status and independent property rights based on autonomous operation. It is necessary to guard against monopolizing any line of business through the establishment of a holding company.

IV. Intensifying the Interest Incentive Mechanism for Enterprises Based on the Establishment of the Property Rights of Labor and Fundamentally Tackling the Ever-increasing Contradictions in Enterprise Management

Practice shows that the problems relating to low efficiency are also directly related to inefficient management. A survey found that in over 2,000 loss-making enterprises, mismanagement was the cause of losses for 81.7% of them. During the process of economic institutional conversion, problems related to management have become more and more prominent. Many factors contribute to this phenomenon, such as the transitional factors during the process of the economic institutional conversion, but more important and prevalent are the factors related to the quality of the workforce and management of enterprises. The problems in management arising from the adjustment of interest relations are the most pressing ones. In the macro-economic environment of the market economy the scientific management of an enterprise will have a sound foundation provided that the interest relations among the enterprise, managerial personnel and employees are correctly handled. Only then can there be a stable infusion of dynamics and vitality for the further growth of the enterprise.

With the deepening of reform the original interest pattern can no longer meet the needs arising from the transition to the market economy. Consequently the internal contradictions within enterprises tend to surface. The question of prime importance in the management of enterprises now is how to coordinate the conflicting interests.

Fundamentally speaking, reform implies the rational adjustment of interest relations and the optimization of the interests of all aspects. In the reform towards marketization the original interest pattern of the whole society has been broken down, and a pattern characterized by the multiplicity of interested parties, the complexity of the interest structure and the surfacing of

119

conflicts of interests has emerged. In the economic institutional conversion conflicts of interest fueled by the indepth adjustment of interest relationships in state firms have become increasingly striking, such as:

The clash of interests between labor and enterprises.

With the abolition of the traditional egalitarian system of distribution and with the marketization of labor resources, the labor force tends to flow spontaneously towards posts with most benefits. Under constraints from several aspects, the labor force flow is characterized by spontaneity and blindness. However, the higher the skill of the labor force, the greater the mobility. People with high-tech backgrounds tend to seek posts in general management and in labor-intensive enterprises. Such a trend is bound to exert a greater influence on enterprises as time goes on.

The contradiction between short-term interest and long-term interest.

Economic practice indicates that the myopic behavior of enterprises is directly related to the excessive pursuit of short-term self-interest. In the conditions of the market economy the pursuit of short-term interest by managerial personnel and workers is inevitable. This will in turn bring about short-sightedness in the managerial behavior of an enterprise, which will do harm, to a certain extent, to the long-term interests of both the enterprise and its employees.

The contradiction between the interests of monetary capital input and labor capital input.

In a market economy people tend to, on the one hand, over-emphasize the input of capital in the form of money, and, on the other, overlook the role of capital in the form of labor. There is a fairly big difference in the return on investment between monetary capital and labor capital. Such being the case, enterprises tend to utilize all opportunities and means to gain income derived from short-term monetary investment while ignoring investment in labor capital.

Through the establishment of the property rights of labor it is necessary to correctly coordinate the interest relations among enterprise, managerial personnel and workers, and make a solid foundation for scientific enterprise management.

The so-called property rights of labor implies that, apart from income in the form of wages, the labor force is entitled to earnings derived from property rights to a certain extent, that is to say, part of the earnings from the enterprise should be converted into shares owned by the employees in accordance with the value of labor. The shares should be decided in accordance with the length of service, position, contribution, etc. Shares obtained through the property rights of labor should be non-negotiable, non-tradable and non-inheritable.

The establishment of the property rights of labor and the conversion of part of the profits from enterprises to the labor property rights will greatly boost the economic efficiency of enterprises. The essence of the property rights of labor is not simply that a quantity of public property is measured for distribution to the individual workers, nor is it equivalent to individual ownership. It is property rights of a special type.

Property rights of the labor force in the form of shares held by employees ensure that such shares will grow along with public accumulation, and this will provide a good way to tackle the contradiction between individual earnings and public accumulation. Due to the fact that extra dividends based on shares are closely tied to the profits and losses of an enterprise, such an elastic income replaces the original fixed income, and this pattern of distribution incorporates the interests of staff and workers with that of the enterprise. Consequently more and more concern will be shown by the staff and workers for the performance of the enterprise, and the awareness of participation in management and in decision making will be intensified. As the staff and workers share the weal and woe with the enterprise, such a union provides a good solution for tackling the conflict between the long-term and short-term interests, thus unravelling the contradiction between the worker and management.

The realization of property rights of labor is conducive to recruiting a team of managerial personnel and staff and workers of higher caliber. With the development of the socialization of production, the labor capital will play a greater and greater role in the economic growth. Over a score of years, Western countries practising market economies have adopted the modes of expanding partnership, extensive shareholding, staff shareholding, etc. All these aim at regulating the relationship between labor and capital, at intensifying the management of the interest of enterprises and promoting economic growth. In implementing the market economy it is imperative to provide a better solution for handling the relationship of interest distribution in an enterprise, so as to provide a better interest basis for its management. The establishment of property rights of labor is a revolution in the system of distribution. The effective incentive mechanism will ensure the optimum combination of human capital and physical capital for optimum efficiency, which in turn will lay a dynamic foundation for the long-term development of enterprises. At the same time, as the shares given to the workers depend on factors like tenure of service, position, contribution, etc., such a practice will motivate the staff and workers to improve their own contributions and intensify the competitiveness of labor capital, thus giving fuller play to the role of human capital.

The close combination of enterprise and staff and workers on the basis of interest relations is an important goal to accomplish in the conditions of the market economy. The promotion of the property rights of labor, which is both an important part of the reform of enterprises, and a fundamental measure for improving the management of state firms. The management of interest that gives rise to management of efficiency is an effective avenue for the scientific management of enterprises in the conditions of the market economy. This deserves further discussion and analysis.

(Read at the *International Symposium on Comparison of Reform and Management of State-owned Enterprises in the Asia-Pacific Region*, in Haikou, April 25, 1995.)

Reform of China's State-owned Enterprises During the Economic Transition Period

The reform of state-owned enterprises has always been the central link in the economic restructuring of China. This reform has basically undergone the following three stages: First, beginning in 1978, the basic train of thought with regard to the reform was to transform the highly centralized planned economic system, that is, to expand enterprise autonomy through delegation of power and concession of profits by giving more financial resources to enterprises so as to enhance their vitality and by adopting the profit retention system and a two-stage substitution of tax payments for profits. Second, since the Third Plenary Session of the 12th CPC Central Committee, the reform of state firms has gradually unfolded. The basic concept of the reform is to further separate ownership from the power of management and to turn enterprises into both relatively independent producers and dealers of commodities. The major measures taken include the implementation of the Enterprise Law and the introduction of the management responsibility system. Most state firms carried out the responsibility system of management on a contractual basis, while a small number of SOEs adopted the leasing or shareholding systems, etc. Third, beginning in 1992, when Deng Xiaoping made his important remarks during his inspection tour of south China and the convention of the 14th CPC National Congress was held, a series of policy documents have been promulgated one after another—Regulations for Changing the Management Mechanism of Industrial Enterprises Owned by the Whole People, Company Law, and Regulations for the Supervision and Management of Assets of State-Owned Enterprises, and these created conditions for changing the enterprise management mechanism. The Decision on Some Issues Concerning the Establishment of a Socialist Market Economic Structure made at the 14th National Congress of the CPC clearly set out the establishment of a modern enterprise system as the goal for the reform of state firms. In the process of this reform, the Chinese government has seized the opportunities to try out several experimental reforms, and accumulated rich experience through explorations for the institutional renovation of state firms. For instance, the trial reform aimed at the establishment of a stockholding system initiated in 1984 and the experimental reform which started around 1987 with regard to property rights in terms of merger, auction, bankruptcy and transfer, have made considerable progress. Besides, the incorporating of group enterprises, the reform based on the corporate system, the introduction of foreign capital aimed at "grafting" enterprises and the entrusted management of state-owned assets on a contractual basis, etc., have all been boldly carried out. Efforts have also been made by the Chinese government to improve the external environment of the reform of state firms. Especially in 1994, the introduction of a series of macro-economic reform measures in fiscal matters and taxation, foreign exchange and foreign trade have created conditions for the acceleration of the reform of state firms.

Through 17 years of exploration and practice China has accumulated rich experience as the theory of reform has become increasingly mature, the legislative environment for the reform of state firms has been continuously improved and state firms have undergone drastic changes, and a batch of enterprises which are characterized by good mechanism, great vitality and high efficiency, and with excellent reputations in both domestic and international markets have emerged. However, judging by the actual results, a breakthrough has yet to be made in the process of reform. Problems confronting state firms have become more and more serious, such as serious losses, low efficiency in input and output, declining production growth rates, irrational allocation of state-owned assets, serious waste of state-owned assets and heavy social and economic burdens. In addition, the problem with regard to the separation of administration from management has not been fundamentally solved, which seriously hampers the development of state firms. Since 1992, when China has set it the objective of reform to establish the socialist market economy system, the economic restructuring of China has entered a new stage, and the pace of reform has accelerated. Since 1994 the introduction of the reform measures for the macro economy have exerted a major impact on promoting the overall situation of reform. Compared with reform in other areas, the reform of state firms has obviously lagged behind, and this, to a great extent, has affected the results of reform measures in other areas. Especially, the failure to separate administration from management and the series of problems arising therefrom has fundamentally inhibited further reform of state firms. Therefore, how to tackle the problem of separating administration from management and how to bring about the change in government functions and promote the reform of state firms have become pressing tasks that have aroused widespread attention. There is no doubt that the issue of separation between administration and management is a long-standing one which is characterized by great difficulty and the solution to which calls for a long process. In 1995 the Chinese government decided to place the emphasis of economic restructuring on the reform of state firms, to lose no time in firmly pushing ahead with the establishment of a modern enterprise system and to take the separation of administration from management as the major content of the reform of state firms so as to make a breakthrough in the reform in order to accumulate experience for its overall implementation. The reform of state firms in China is at a critical stage, as the last five years of this century are the most important period for China. It is necessary to explore continuously and find a way to invigorate the state-owned economy so as to establish a basic framework for the socialist market economy.

I. Promoting the Marketization of State-owned Assets and Invigorating the State-owned Economy on an Overall Basis

1. Invigorating the state-owned economy as a totality rather than invigorating every single state firm is a major shift in the guideline with regard to the reform of state firms and is also a fundamental issue in the separation of administration from management

In economic transformation in China the basic issue of separation of administration from management is related to how the government should invigorate the state-owned economy and how to display the guiding role of the state sector. In the planned economy system the government directly involved itself in the management of enterprises, while enterprises were directly subordinate to government departments. Every enterprise was guided by a "mother-in-law," and as a result the enterprises were deprived of any autonomy and independence. The establishment of a socialist market economy system requires that enterprises become independent bodies in line with the principle of letting the superior survive and the inferior eliminated. Therefore, both the mode and means of government administration should undergo a fundamental change. The government should no longer administer every single enterprise. Instead, enterprises should be given a free hand to enter the market. It is necessary to bring about a shift from the direct administration based on the micro economy to indirect administration based on the macro economy, and both legal and economic means should be applied to strengthen macro control and focus on invigorating the overall state-owned sector.

In China the state-owned sector has always and will always be the most important pillar of the national economy. It is more than a decade since the reform program was introduced and the state-owned sector has made rapid development. However, of the aggregate GNP, the state-owned sector still accounts for a proportion of around 40%; of the total industrial output, the proportion of the state-owned sector accounts for about 55%. The economic lifelines of the state, such as infrastructure, energy and communications, public utilities and backbone enterprises are all state-run. The fiscal revenue contributed by state firms still accounts for more than 60%. The practice of reform and opening up has proved that different types of ownership have their own advantages in their respective fields. In light of the specific situation of China, public ownership is the basis and the state sector is the guiding force. The state-owned sector is not only the representative of the development level of the productive forces but also a basic force supporting the reform and opening up, promoting economic growth, maintaining social stability and being involved in international market competition. It is also an important means for the Chinese people to accomplish common prosperity.

In the market economy the leading role of the state-owned sector is vastly different from what it was in the past. On the whole, the status of public ownership and its leading position in the national economy are mainly reflected in its advantage in assets owned by the state and the collective, which in turn demonstrates the control of the lifeline of the national economy by the state-owned sector and its guiding role in the national economic development. Henceforth, the proportion of the state-owned sector in some industries may change slightly. However, so long as the state-owned sector keeps its leading position in important industries, it will continue to play its guiding role.

China's experience of reform over the past decade has increasingly proved that for state firms to play an effective role the key lies in the rational and optimal allocation of state-owned assets in accordance with the basic principles and laws of the market economy. In the planned economy system in the past emphasis was given to the idea of "larger in size and having a higher degree of public ownership," which resulted in an overall pursuit of the superiority of state firms only in quantity and scale and the setting up of state firms which could not be disbanded. Consequently some enterprises that lacked competitiveness and should have been eliminated could not be screened out, while social and economic resources could not be rationally allocated or effectively utilized. The practice of reform for more than a decade has proved that a minority of state firms that should have been disbanded could not be disbanded, while the majority that should have been invigorated could not be stimulated, and the effort to invigorate every state firm will only result in the deterioration of the majority that should have been invigorated because of a minority that should have been disbanded. Consequently, the burden on the state finance and state banks has become increasingly heavy. According to statistics, by 1993 the total value of state-owned assets in China stood at 3,495 billion yuan, of which assets of an operational nature accounted for 74.5%. With liabilities deducted, the actual amount was only 898.215 billion yuan, and the net assets of state firms generally accounted for only around 20% of the total. Based on this liability ratio, state firms owed the banks as much as 2,596.785 billion yuan, which was almost equivalent to the total household savings deposits during the same period (By 1994 the balance of savings deposits of urban and rural residents in China was 2,151.88 billion yuan). That is to say, 82.87% of the bank loans to state firms was derived from the public's savings deposits. In 1994 the annual interest rate on such savings deposits was 10.98%, which was much lower than the 22% inflation rate, while the annual profits of state-owned industrial and commercial entities were only 7.4%, much lower than the interest rate on bank deposits. This means that the larger the scale of state firms which were developed under the traditional system the more the public and the state lose. In reality, the state is already incapable of maintaining all the existing state firms.

The guiding thinking of the state firm reform, whether proceeding from the actual conditions of the reform of the present state firms or from the demand arising from the market economy, is that the focus should be shifted from invigorating every enterprise to invigorating the overall state-owned sector through the liquidity of assets and imposing strategic reorganization on state firms so as to strengthen the function of the whole state-owned sector, enhance its overall strength and give better play to its guiding role.

2. "Grasping the bigger while giving up the smaller" so as to adequately reduce the operational scope of the state sector

The financial resources and stamina of the state are limited. The excessive scope of the state-owned economy has landed the government in a predicament in which it is at loss as how to eradicate factors that will eventually dampen the vitality and efficiency of the state firms. Therefore, it is necessary to "grasp the major ones while leaving aside the minor ones" and to make a rational adjustment of the distributional setup by category of state-owned assets and to adequately shorten the operational front line of the state-owned economy.

The method of shortening the front line is to adequately reduce the proportion of state investment in minor yet relatively highly competitive fields and transform those enterprises which the state needs not manage and is incapable of controlling (the majority of which are small enterprises) into non-state-owned or non-publicly owned firms, so as to concentrate the limited financial resources and energy in key areas. The economic development of a country, the achievement of industrialization and the enhancement of economic capability mainly depend upon large-sized enterprises and groups. Through grasping well the key state-owned large-sized enterprises which play the role of mainstays in the national economy and creating a batch of large-sized enterprise groups with economies of scale and international competitiveness, it is possible to spur a large number of other state firms to develop, promote the adjustment of the industrial structure and optimize the allocation of resources. For the small-sized state firms, it is necessary to further open up, and invigorate and strengthen the reform. As for the state firms which are small in scale, and backward in efficiency and management, it is possible to resort to various ways to deregulate their operations, such as contracting, leasing, merging, reorganizing into stock-holding cooperative entities or auctioning.

Reducing the sphere of state operations and creating favorable conditions for the transformation of government functions. On the premise that most assets belong to the state, it is difficult to realize the separation of administration and management. This is because the managerial functions produced through the assets relationship are rigid. The state could sell off some unimportant assets or enterprises could effectively cut their assets ties with the government, consequently removing the basis for direct intervention by the government in a considerable number of enterprises. Hence, reducing the operational sphere of state-owned assets will not only enable the government to get rid of unwanted burdens, but will also help the government to concentrate its efforts on handling major issues. At the same time it will help the government to transform its functions and shift the priority of its work to macro control, services and supervision, while limiting direct intervention to the most needed areas.

Of the existing several million enterprises in China, there are over 70,000 industrial ones, of which large and medium industrial enterprises amount to only 14,700. Though small in number, they occupy an important position in the national economy. Of the 500-biggest industrial enterprises in the nation, their assets account for 37% of the total assets of state-owned industrial enterprises, their volume of sales accounts for 46%, and their profits, 63%. It is necessary to concentrate efforts and adopt effective policy measures to develop these into superior and strong enterprises with good prospects for development and market competition capability. They will then be the main force for China's economy to advance to the international market. With the strong radiative power of these enterprises, it will be possible to spur a large number of other enterprises in the domestic market while creating a vast arena in which these core enterprises can undergo reorganization, merger or bankruptcy. Therefore, it is highly necessary to make a study for the implementation of the strategy of big groups and big corporations. Concentrating on the decisive minority of firms in the nation or region will not only ensure their guiding role in the national economy but also create important conditions for the separation of administration from management.

3. To optimize the efficiency of state-owned assets and to

accelerate the adjustment and reorganization of their structure, it is necessary for state-owned assets to shift toward key areas and basic industries

At present, state firms on the whole are low in economic returns. According to statistics issued in 1994, 40% of them are in the red. Apart from actual losses, about two-thirds of state firms are subject to "latent" losses as well, with more and more enterprises suspending or slowing production. The input and output efficiency of state firms is very low and the earning capacity of investment funds dropped from 13.2% in 1985 to 2.7% in 1992. In recent years the state has devoted over 70% of its fixed assets investment and current fund loans to state firms. However, the proportion of growth of state firms in the total economic growth accounts for only around 20%. According to estimates, in the 17 years since the reform and opening up started, based on the calculation of net output value of growth, the growth of state firms derived from the improvement of efficiency has accounted for only 12.2%, although input has grown by 87.8%. That is to say, the limited growth of state firms depends basically on the increase of input. These enterprises maintain their operations while bearing as high as 70% liabilities. The result is poorer and poorer efficiency and lower and lower profits with larger and larger deficits, which results in the increasing irrationality of allocation structure (repeated undertaking of industrial construction projects complicated by bottleneck constraints) and heavier and heavier debts for the state.

The guiding role of the state-owned sector lies neither in maintaining the large scale of the state firms formed under the old system, nor in expanding their number, nor in the state controlling all the economic fields. The guiding role of the state-owned sector is mainly manifested in its efficiency and competitiveness, so as to occupy a dominant position in the total social assets and thus exert control and influence on the national economy. The national economy should proceed from the overall social benefits, macro economic benefits and long-term development benefits to bring about the optimization of the efficiency of the existing state-owned assets to give full play to their guiding role.

To be specific, the optimization of the efficiency of state-owned assets is mainly reflected in the aspects of basic efficiency, guidance efficiency, and social and public service efficiency.

—Basic efficiency. From the point of view of overall and long-term benefits, it is necessary to concentrate investment in state assets in infrastructure facilities and basic industries, such as posts and telecommunications, communications, harbors, water and electricity supplies, resources exploitation, coal, petroleum, steel, chemicals, non-ferrous metals, large-sized irrigation projects, etc. Thus, we can lay a solid foundation for the development of the overall national economy.

—Guidance efficiency. In compliance with the premise of fair competition, it is necessary for the state assets to play a principal and guiding role in some critical industries and domains, such as finance and insurance, aerospace and aviation, high technology and the defense industry.

—Social and public service efficiency. It is necessary for state-owned assets to play a significant role with a strong sense of duty in social and public service domains, in environmental protection, and scientific, educational and cultural undertakings. More investment should be made progressively in this respect.

It is necessary to genuinely display the economic benefits and competitive capability of the national economy, and the state-owned assets should gradually shift away from general competitive industries to concentrate on basic, key and special industries. The state should exercise control and management mainly in the fields that have a vital bearing on the national economy and the people's livelihood. As for general industries and trades, the state-owned sector should display its guiding role through competing with the non-state economy on the basis of mutual development and fair competition in terms of quality and efficiency. Therefore, the allocation structure of state-owned assets should undergo major adjustments, not only in their incremental quantity but also based on the principle of optimization of their efficiency.

4. Pushing state-owned assets onto the market and bringing about a fundamental transformation of state-owned assets into state-owned capital to assure their maximum value

In the planned economy system state-owned assets were used only for the purpose of fulfilling mandatory planning quotas rather than to pursue the maximization of their revaluation. State-owned assets were not regarded as capital. As a result, nobody was concerned about protecting or increasing their value. The state firms risked their equipment and funds in disregard of whether the products met the market demand or were piled up in stock. Consequently the state-owned assets were often wasted. Since the reform and opening up started this situation has not been fundamentally changed. In 1994 loans to state firms increased to almost 100 billion yuan all over the nation, but state firms' stock lying idle increased by several thousand million yuan, and the waste thus incurred was immense.

The modern market economy concentrates on invigorating state-owned capital, the essence of which is to pursue the maximization of profit and magnitude of value, and to pursue the greatest economic returns of the capital. Though people differ in opinion as to whether it is proper to pursue the greatest economic returns and the magnitude of value of currency for state assets in a market economy, we hold that state-owned assets should be treated as capital and operated in accordance with the law of capital operation in a market economy. There is not only an urgent need for China to improve the current status of state-owned assets to maintain and increase their value, but also a basic need to comply with the common law of the market economy. To bring about the change of state-owned assets into state-owned capital to try to maximize the capital value is a fundamental issue.

Bringing about the transformation of state-owned assets into state-owned capital will not prevent state firms continuing to shoulder social functions. Some social functions that must mainly be assumed by state firms may be regulated through economic means, such as adopting an open and comprehensive policy of economic compensation and formulating targets for public pay-out ratio.

As a large number of state firms still perform community services it is necessary to disintegrate such functions through deepening reform and gradually turn them to the whole society to shoulder.

Should state-owned assets be allocated through the administrative mechanism or through the market? In the traditional system, state-owned assets were allocated through the administrative mechanism. The state had a monopoly of them, and so they could not enter the market for circulation, and thus the maximization of assets efficiency was impossible. The administrative allocation of state-owned assets has resulted in a large amount of state-owned assets either lying idle or being operated at a low efficiency rate. According to estimates, now about 30% of the state-owned assets are either lying idle or have a low rate of utilization, and so a huge amount of funds is tied up in thousands of small and medium-sized enterprises. Meanwhile, social funds, and particularly money in the hands of the public, are looking for investment channels. If only 5% of the stock of state-owned enterprises entered the market for circulation, that would be equivalent to an increase of 170 billion yuan of working capital, which means over 100 billion yuan-worth of productive forces brought into play. The circulation of the stock of state-owned assets cannot bring about optimal allocation through the traditional administrative mechanism. The effective way for state-owned assets to realize rational structural adjustment, optimal allocation of resources and effective utilization of resources is for them to enter the market as objects of transaction. To invigorate the state-owned sector on the whole is to transform state-owned assets into state-owned capital and, to achieve this aim, it is necessary to push state-owned assets onto the market.

To do this it is necessary to solve the contradiction between management of state-owned assets in kind and management on the basis of value. State-owned assets in the planned economy system are manifested in material form, with the state directly controlling the means of production and products in their physical forms, whereas in the market economy it is required that the resources of the state-owned sector be reallocated based on the law of the market in the whole society. Consequently it calls for changing the state-owned assets in physical form into state-owned assets in the form of value. Such a process of transformation is based on the principle of exchange at equal value in a market economy—the state recovers monetary capital of equivalent value and holds the capital ownership in the form of value. The state does not lose this portion of the assets, rather it invigorates the state-owned economy through such a transformation and enhances its strength. The state utilizes the recovered monetary capital to invest in other domains of higher efficiency and reaps greater assets value. This being the case, the foundation of the socialist public ownership does not weaken, rather it is consolidated and developed, and becomes stronger.

II. The Organization of State-owned Holding Companies as the Key to Exploring Effective Ways for the Separation of Administration from Management in Large-sized Enterprises

1. Taking the establishment of state holding companies as a turning point to gradually develop a national "leading team"

A holding company is an organizational form for stock rights operation often adopted by countries practicing market economies. Unlike an ordinary enterprise that directly deals with the production of commodities, a holding company mainly deals with the management and operation of stock rights through the form of investment holding, or spurs the commodity operation of controlled enterprises through such means as equity participation and investment holding. Holding companies have in fact developed into group enterprises with assets as ties.

In 1995 China designated 100 enterprises as pilot units for the establishment of a modern enterprise system, and at the same time carried out experiments in establishing state-owned holding companies in the aviation, petrochemicals and nonferrous metals industries. State-owned holding company is taken as one of the major forms for the transformation of state firms based on corporatization. It is an especially effective way to transform the state-owned large backbone enterprises and enterprise groups based on the modern enterprise system. Large-sized backbone enterprises are always the core of China's state economy and its pace-setters. They also play an important role in international economic relations.

At present, in the large-sized state-owned enterprises in China, apart from their inherent institutional drawbacks the outstanding problem is low efficiency and lack of competitive capability. Of the 500 strongest industrial enterprises in the world, none was listed from China prior to 1994, and in 1995 three were listed, whereas Japan had 128 listed in 1992, accounting for more than one fourth of the total. The degree of concentration of most of China's industries is generally lower than in Europe and North America, especially the metallurgical, chemicals, petrochemicals, building materials, electric power, heavy machinery, automobile and household electrical appliance industries. The total assets of the several big groups in the aviation industry put together cannot match that of one US aircraft corporation, and the assets of all China's steel companies put together fall short of those of one Japanese steel company. China has several hundred automobile factories, but their total output is only 1.3 million vehicles a year, which cannot match the output of one subsidiary of the US Ford Company. China's further opening to the international market, particularly the linking of the domestic market with the international market, will exert a huge impact on quite a number of trades and their relevant products; the most seriously hit will be the heavy and chemical industries and high-tech industries, which account for about one third of the total industrial output of China and which are mainly state firms. China has a large number of industrial enterprises which are small in scale, high in resources consumption and cost, and low in output and efficiency.

In front of the serious challenges coming from both national and international markets, China urgently needs to adjust its enterprise structure, elevate the efficiency of its economies of scale, and improve its present division of labor on the basis of specialization and a higher level of cooperation. At present, the development of enterprise groups has been seriously restrained by the traditional setup, and the course of development has been full of obstacles. The main problems are: First, the establishment of group enterprises is mainly confined to their own sectors or regions, and the ownership, affiliation and fiscal systems remain unchanged. Second, owing to the lack of a foundation for the corporate shareholding system, enterprise groups are linked together more through ties of production technology and supply and sales and less through the linkage of assets. Third, the internal management system of group enterprises is imperfect, and it has not yet been standardized based on corporatization, resulting in some enterprise groups possessing highly concentrated power, infringing on the autonomy of the subsidiary enterprises, while some group enterprises are found to lack cohesive power. Therefore, it is necessary to take the establishment of holding companies as a breakthrough for restructuring the intermediary operational system of state-owned assets and to remove the restraints of the traditional system. We must greatly spur on the adjustment of enterprise structure and the transformation of group enterprises, and introduce a new type of group companies.

2. The key to the establishment of state-owned holding companies lies in sectors that the state needs to monopolize and control

Proceeding from the actual needs of China, especially from the need for more effective management of state-owned assets, to bring about the efficiency of economies of scale and to sharpen the competitive edge through cooperation the country should organize holding companies in the following areas:

—Industries that the state needs to monopolize and control, such as public utilities, posts and telecommunications, aviation, railways, banking, energy, important raw materials industries, etc. Such industries should be put under the direct control of the state. It is possible to adopt the organizational form of the holding company which the state controls on a full holding or partial holding basis, or through entering into an control agreement.

—Industries that need to enhance their efficiency through economies of scale, to strengthen the division of labor based on specialization and cooperation, and that need to be further developed, especially those industries that need to intensify their international competition, such as steel, automobiles, machinery, etc. The auto industry is one of the pillar industries of China, but at present, the country's auto enterprises are scattered, small in scale and weak in terms of competitiveness in the international market. It is essential to enhance their size, efficiency and international competitiveness by organizing several state holding companies to meet the ever intensifying international competition, especially the need for international competition after the China market opens up.

—Science and technology industries that receive priority from the state, such as the electronics, fine chemicals and biological engineering industries. High-tech industry often calls for the joint efforts of enterprises to tackle key scientific and technological problems, to input large amounts of funds for scientific research and to organize competent research personnel to conduct research. The holding company mode will help enterprises in the same sector to join hands and cooperate, which will be beneficial for giving key support to certain high-tech industries.

—Industries that urgently need to adjust their enterprise structure and product mix, strengthen technological transformation, spur the upgrading and enhance the professional and technological levels, such as the textile industry, building industry, etc. At present, the textile and building industries in China are large in number but small in scale. Their equipment is outdated and their product quality is poor. It is highly necessary to adjust their industrial structure and establish group enterprises, intensify technological revamp, and improve the labor productivity and management levels.

3. Scientifically defining the nature of state-owned holding companies and rationally standardizing the stock rights-based administrative functions of government departments over state enterprises

A state holding company specializes in dealing with the operation of state-owned assets; it is authorized by the state to exercise the ownership of state-owned assets and is responsible for investment in and operation of those assets. Generally, the state holding company does not engage in specific business operations; instead the professional enterprises under its control engage in specific business operations. The holding company is the intermediary investment organ of state assets, and helps to sever all direct ties between the government and the professional enterprises. This is conducive to the complete separation of administration from management and ensures the independent business operation of the enterprises.

The state holding company is not an administrative organ, rather it is an independent economic entity in the form of a corporate. A holding company is a type of company which is subject to the Company Law. The relationship between state-owned assets management departments and holding companies is one between the assets authorizer and authorized. The state-owned holding company exercises, in accordance with the law, the ownership of state-owned assets, and possesses independent enterprise property rights. The business activities involved are free from all wilful and unlawful intervention by the state assets administrative departments and other government departments. A state-owned holding company is different in nature from China's current administrative corporations based on trade. The state-owned holding companies do not perform administrative function. Therefore special attention should be paid in this respect when establishing state-owned holding companies.

A holding company is also known as a parent company, while a company under its control is known as a subsidiary. A state-owned holding company exercises control over other companies through holding sufficient stock rights or through entering into a contract of eminent domain. That is to say, there are two kinds of relationship between the parent company and its subsidiary: One is for the former to hold a majority vote at the shareholders' meetings of the subsidiary by controlling a certain amount of stock rights; the other is for the former to exercise actual control over the latter through entering into a contract to enable it to exert a decisive influence on the other company, thus becoming its major creditor.

Both the state-owned holding company and the company being controlled by it are independent corporate legal persons. Although the controlled company is subject to control, it has its own name and articles of association, and assumes independent civil responsibility over assets and external business contacts. It also possesses autonomy in production and operation. Therefore, in establishing state-owned holding companies it is essential to abide by the regulations of the Company Law and to ensure that the specific enterprises enjoy the status of independent legal persons and autonomy in business operations.

The key to the relationship between the government and the holding companies is in the managerial functions, with a standardized assets relationship as its base. Through establishing state-owned holding companies, the government's administrative behavior is "purified" into a pure assets relationship which ensures that the intervention in the enterprise by the investors (backed by the government) is confined within the limits allowed for any member of the board of directors and within the lawful and standardized procedures.

4. Diversified forms may be adopted in establishing and developing state-owned holding companies

The basic requirement for the establishment of a state-owned holding company is that the stockholding system must be adopted by state-owned enterprises. State-owned holding companies mainly adopt the method of controlling stock rights through holding sufficient ownership rights of the subsidiaries to control them. The basis of percentage of ownership right to be held is to be decided by the actual control of voting in the shareholders' meetings of the subsidiary by the parent company. Normally, 50% of the stock rights of the constituent company are held, but if the shareholders are considerably decentralized the percentage may be less than 50%. Through this control method it is necessary to transform the many existing specialized enterprises into limited joint-stock companies. There are several specific modes with regard to the relations of ownership right: One is to acquire in great quantity the stocks of specialized companies so as to realize ownership right holding; second, one or more constituent companies can be established; third, the existing group enterprise may be reorganized into a holding company; fourth, assets can be reinvested in a state-owned holding company and controlled company; fifth, specialized state firms can surrender or transfer profits to a holding company so that the latter will gain a relationship of ownership.

It is also possible to enter into an agreement to reorganize enterprises that are either specialized state-owned sole-funded companies or limited liability companies. This method is applicable especially to the trades and industries over which the state has to exercise monopolized control.

Therefore, it can be said that only by adopting diversified types of company forms in the light of different circumstances can we bring about an organic integration that fits with the internal laws of the market economy, that fulfills the state macro control plan and macro market control and that brings about the optimal allocation of state capital and social capital.

5. The government should define the profit targets and social targets for the state-owned holding companies

On the one hand, the government claims that state firms should be regarded as commodity producers, and that it should exercise indirect control over them and carry out examination and assessment based on the identical operational index as that for private enterprises. On the other hand, the government requires state firms to abide by and safeguard the interests of the state, to carry out the government mandate and to act as instruments for the implementation of the government's economic policies. As a result, as a foreign economist has pointed out, two common problems crop up: First, it is very difficult to establish an objective function for state firms as their many objectives are often in conflict. Second, no matter what its political hue, a government cannot help interfering in state firms. Since the state-owned holding companies are large ones engaged in the operation of equity they are often at the top of the huge national economic system. Therefore, the contradiction between the operational objectives is often more acute than in ordinary state firms.

How can we evaluate the role of state-owned holding companies in implementing the government's economic policies? On this, theorists and business managers have different views. In establishing and developing state-owned holding companies the government should pay great attention to tackling the contradiction in the dual operational objectives: striving to reduce the social objectives of state-owned holding companies and strictly differentiating between the two types of operational activities of state-owned holding companies and providing necessary compensation. In addition, it is necessary to make public the social objectives and standardize the aims of the state-owned holding companies to prevent government departments from interfering in the business activities of the companies.

III. Accelerating the Reform of the Property Rights System and Straightening Out the Relationship Between the Functions of Government and Those of Enterprises

1. The main thrust of China's reform of its property rights system

Since the mid-1980s China has actively explored the reform of its enterprise property rights system and has achieved remarkable success. The country began its merger of enterprises at quite an early stage, and the progress has been smooth. Since the beginning of the 1990s the merger of enterprises has been even more successful. By early 1993 over 10,000 enterprises had been merged, which helped reduce the number of loss-incurring enterprises and freed a large amount of frozen assets. As early as 1986 China formulated its *Bankruptcy Law*, which went into effect in 1988. In recent years experiments with the shareholding system have progressed rapidly, and by 1993 there were over 13,000 shareholding enterprises across the country, of which the number of newly established shareholding enterprises totaled 9,440, a 1.55-fold increase, compared with the previous year. Securities markets have also developed robustly. At present there are two securities exchanges in China—one in Shanghai and the other in Shenzhen—as well as two exchanges for shares held by legal persons in Beijing. Chinese enterprises have also been listed on exchanges in Hong Kong and the USA. A transaction market for property rights has also been established. By the end of 1993 a dozen provinces and over 20 cities and regions in China had established property rights transaction markets, and the transactions have become increasingly hectic. In addition, in recent years experiments in the reform of the state-owned assets management system have been developing rapidly. In 1993 the state began to carry out reform toward the authorized transaction of state-owned assets on a trial basis. In the past two years basic work related to the reform of property rights and to the establishment of fund sources through physical inventory has unfolded on a nationwide scale, while assessment authorities for state-owned assets and other intermediary organs for property rights have also been established.

In the reform of state firms in China it took quite some time to arrive at a correct understanding of the property rights relationship, starting from the understanding of "delegating greater power and benefits to lower levels" to the understanding of implementing "separating two powers," followed by establishing "the property rights of corporate legal persons." However, the biggest problem in the practice of state firms' reform is the ambiguity in property rights. Unclear property rights of enterprises will inevitably create difficulties, and it will also be difficult to separate government functions from those of enterprises. No one takes responsibility for the property rights. The problem is how to ensure that the state-owned property belongs to the state while giving management autonomy in operation to the enterprises.

2. The reform of the property rights system is the key to solving the deep-seated problem of state-owned enterprises

The more than a decade of China's enterprise reform has shown that the reform based on mere "delegation of power and concession of profits" cannot solve fundamentally the various problems confronted by the state-owned economy. Owing to the fact that the property rights of enterprises are not clearly defined, resulting in unclear responsibilities and duties, the outcome of "delegation of power and concession of profits" is either that the enterprise does not really enjoy autonomy or abuses its autonomy, resulting in a great amount of revenue from profits being turned into personal gain. Therefore, even though the productivity of a state firm is raised, without solving the problem of erosion in the link of distribution through wages and various other types of abnormal consumption that eats away the profits, the efficiency of an enterprise will remain low and the problem of serious losses cannot be fundamentally solved. Due to the lack of clearly defined property rights and a constraining mechanism over property handling, simply delegating more power of operation to a state firm will not make it genuinely responsible for all its profits and losses.

In the realm of macro management with regard to state firms the problem of vaguely defined property rights and responsibilities also exists. Government departments that directly take over the management of state firms have not solved the problem of careless use of state-owned capital, a phenomenon characterized by eager efforts for personal gain when profits are being made but a total lack of responsibility for losses. It is exactly because of the lag in the reform of property rights of state firms that the reform of the financial and investment systems and other reforms related to the macro economy can hardly get off the ground, or worse, some already accomplished reform has been forced to backtrack, hampering the leverage role of macro economy.

Since 1992, as the reform of state firms has entered a new stage, the reform of property rights has become more and more urgent. In the market economy state firms should be on an equal footing with other entities of the market economy, assuming civil responsibility and owning independent property rights and equity. The basic requirements for every market economy entity are clearly defined property rights, full authority for distribution and sole responsibility for their profits and losses. Otherwise, it is impossible for market economy activities to be carried out on a normal and orderly basis. In reforming state firms, no matter whether it is the relation between the state and the enterprise, or that between enterprises, or that between the enterprise and the society or the internal relations of an enterprise, all the relations involve the relation of property rights without exception. Especially in the relations between the state and the enterprise, it is necessary to solve the problem of separating the functions of government from those of the enterprise, and the key is to straighten out the relations between the state and the state firm over property rights. In the market economy, the ties between the state and state firms are different from those in the past, which used to be made up of both property rights and administrative relations, which was in fact simply a relationship between the investor and the legally entitled persons of a corporate business. However, any change of such a nature must be realized through the reform of the property rights system. Therefore, the Decision of the CPC Central Committee on Some Issues Concerning the Establishment of a Socialist Market Economic Structure, adopted at the Third Plenary Session of the 14th CPC Central Committee, for the first time stated the reform of the property rights relations in the state-owned economy in a programmatic document. The reform objective for the establishment of a modern enterprise system put forward at the Third Plenary Session of the 14th CPC Central Committee determined that one of the major features of a modern enterprise system is "clearly defined property rights, powers and responsibilities." The reform of the property rights system is a stage in deepening the reform of state firms which cannot be bypassed. The key content of the reform of state firms in future will include the reform of property rights together with the reform of the management of state-owned assets and the reform of the government administrative system, which are all closely related.

3. **Proceeding from the actual conditions of China to actively explore the establishment of a new enterprise property rights system**

—Accelerating the reform of enterprises by setting up a corporate system and realizing the multiplicity of property rights of state firms. In the planned economy system, unitary property rights were the theoretical basis for government intervention in enterprises. The realization of the multiplicity of property rights will ensure the independence of property rights of state firms and prevent the departments in charge of them intervening at will. It is also conducive to the reorganization and rational allocation of state-owned assets and their efficiency optimization. In practice, the multiplicity of property rights of state firms should focus on two points: (1) It is necessary to accelerate the reform process on the basis of a corporate system and give special attention to the reform toward the stockholding system, so as to disintegrate the structure of property into stock rights which are easy to circulate and transfer. The internal legal entity rectification of state firms established on the basis of the corporate system can help to lay down an institutional foundation for the effective operation and management of property rights. (2) The multiplicity of state firms' property rights may appear in diversified ways, such as stock mutually owned by legal persons of a corporate business, equity rights transfer, enterprise reorganization and issuing to the public stocks, and listing for transaction. Multiplicity of property rights can not only be carried out inside the state-owned units, it can also be carried out between non-state-owned units such as collective enterprises, privately owned enterprises, foreign-funded enterprises, etc. The state may take specific circumstances into consideration to exercise investment holding over state firms or give up holdings to transform them into non-state firms. Thus the umbilical cord enabling direct intervention by government departments in enterprises will be severed.

—Establishment of a corporate stock rights structure with stocks owned by legal persons of a corporate business. In reforming state firms based on corporatization, one crucial problem confronting the reform of their property rights is who should act on behalf of the state to own the stock rights of a company. One effective way is to establish an intermediary as a representative organ of the state-owned stock rights and of state-owned assets operation between state-owned assets management departments and the enterprises. These intermediaries may be state holding companies or investment companies, or some kind of investment foundation, but all must be independent legal persons. In practice, it is possible to work in conjunction with the reform of state firms based on corporatization and turn the state-owned property rights of the existing state firms into the stock rights of state holding companies, at the same time, vigorously encouraging financial institutions or legal persons of corporate businesses outside the state organs to own stocks, thus developing a corporate property rights pattern with the legal persons holding the stocks mainly.

—Reorganizing enterprises and promoting the renewal and change of property rights structure. The reorganization of enterprises, that is the adjustment of the organizational and assets structures, is an important means to spur the optimal allocation of state-owned assets. The reorganization of enterprises and the assets liquidity mix leads to a kind of self-regulatory mechanism inherent in the market economy. In the operation of the socialist market economy, imbalance among property rights, and the trade and industrial structures will inevitably occur, in addition to the maladjustment of enterprise organizational structure and undesirable capital structure that gives rise to low efficiency and stagnation in the utilization of assets. To accomplish the recombination of asset liquidity among enterprises it is necessary to accelerate the construction of a new economic structure while paying special attention to property rights, establish a market for property rights transactions and promote the reorganization of enterprises on the basis of property rights reform.

Reorganization of enterprises may take the following forms: (1) joint reorganization; (2) reorganization based on annexation, merger and acquisition; (3) discrete reorganization; (4) reorganization through bankruptcy.

At present the reorganization of enterprises may start with reorganizing their liabilities. Creditor's right can be turned into stock right which, rather than being held by a bank, should be transferred to various financial intermediaries, enterprise groups, foreign enterprises or the public through the property rights market. Retirement pensions and unemployment funds may also be appropriated from the property rights. The disseminated stock rights and the multiplicity of stock rights thus formed may also be effective in straightening out the relations between enterprises and the government.

—Distributing assets rights among the central and local authorities and exercising supervision from the central to the local levels. At present, China implements the principle of "unified ownership by the state, level-by-level supervision by the government and autonomous operation by the enterprises" in dealing with state-owned assets. However, in practice, how to fully display the initiative of the local government in regulating the publicly owned assets and how to improve the efficiency of management and operation of state-owned assets are issues worth study.

Over the past few years state-owned assets have in fact been divided into "assets under central management" and "assets under local management," and in terms of income apportionment of state-owned assets, into "central income" and "local income." Under such circumstances, it is necessary to follow the general trend to rationally establish the property rights for publicly owned assets by the localities. China has a vast territory, and the level of development of the productive forces across the nation is very uneven and complicated. For the central authorities to control all state-owned assets in fact proves very difficult. The highly centralized and unified possession of the state-owned assets is detrimental not only to the effective utilization and allocation of publicly owned assets, but also especially to the effective formation of a capital market, the transaction of property rights, and the optimal allocation of state-owned assets. Consequently, it is necessary to empower the local authorities to possess and operate some of the state-owned assets. Whether the central authorities or the local authorities deal with property rights, the ultimate owner is the state. The central government obtains revenue through taxation and exercises macro control through financial levers.

Sharing out publicly owned property rights among local authorities is helpful for stiffening the budgetary restraints on state firms in the localities. At the same time, the division of local publicly owned property rights will also enhance the initiative of the local governments in regulating publicly owned assets. It is necessary to promote the reform on a corporatization basis and spread the risks involved in property reform among the local authorities, strengthen the management of state-owned assets and enhance the efficiency of and benefits from their operation.

Part of the property rights may be appropriately given to the local authorities to regulate. Two approaches are available: One is to allocate the existing local state firms to the local authorities for regulation; the other is to delegate part of the property rights to the locality, that is, for the central government to give up part of the property rights.

—It is necessary to actively explore and establish a property rights system for the labor force so as to strengthen and coordinate the internal interest relations of the enterprises. Practice indicates that problems like low efficiency are mainly the direct consequence of mismanagement. According to an investigation, among 2,000 loss-incurring enterprises, as high as 81.7% of the losses were caused by mismanagement. During the economic transition period the problems of management of enterprises have become increasingly striking. The reasons include: transitional factors during the institutional conversion, factors related to the sub-standard quality of management and staff and workers. However, the adjustment of interest relations is a deep-rooted factor that affects the management of enterprises.

During the reform toward marketization, the former interest

pattern of the whole society has been replaced by the situation of multiple bodies of interest, complex interest structure and conspicuous interest contradictions. During the course of economic transition, these contradictions arising from the deep-seated adjustment of interest relations of enterprises, especially of state-owned enterprises, have become more and more striking, resulting in contradictions between the interests of the worker and those of the enterprises, between short-term and long-term interests, and between the interests of monetary capital input and those of labor capital input.

With the deepening of the reform, the original interest pattern of the enterprises can no longer meet the needs of the economic transition toward a market economy. Consequently, coordinating the interest contradictions has become the primary issue in the management of enterprises. Through establishing the property rights of the labor and correctly coordinating the interest relations among enterprises, managerial personnel, staff and workers, and on this basis intensifying the interest-incentive mechanism, it is possible to fundamentally solve the contradictions embedded in the management of enterprises.

The so-called labor property rights implies that workers should not only receive wage incomes but also to a certain extent are entitled to earnings from property rights. In other words, to turn part of the incoming profits of the enterprise into shares of that enterprise to be held by staff and workers of the same enterprise. The share to be obtained by the employee is to be determined by factors like length of service, position, contribution, etc. The property rights obtained by the workers and staff are non-negotiable, non-transactable and non-inheritable. To establish the property rights of labor and to turn part of the incoming profits of an enterprise into the earnings from property rights for the labor force of the enterprise means establishing an effective direct linkage between the interests of staff and workers and those of the enterprise, resulting in a community of interests and destiny. Such a practice can intensify the interest-incentive mechanism of the enterprise and correctly coordinate the interest relations among the enterprise, managerial personnel and staff, which in turn enhances the economic returns of the enterprises. The essence of property rights of the labor force does not mean changing publicly owned assets into privately owned ones. It is not equivalent to personal ownership, rather it is in fact a special kind of property rights.

4. The government should fully exercise its responsibility as regards the property rights market in the capacity of social regulator, so as to progressively develop a unified property rights market

In establishing a property rights market, the government should accelerate the pace of transformation of its functions and bring about the separation of governmental functions from enterprise functions. It is necessary to overcome the drawback of unclear property rights relations and ambiguous property rights caused by the dual functions and dislocation of roles on the part of the government, which serves both as the owner of state-owned assets and as the regulator of social administration. It is necessary to let enterprises freely enter the market. The transaction of enterprise property rights should have its base in the market, but the market should be placed under the supervision of the state, which should provide guidance and standardized regulation in accordance with law. It is essential to eliminate all uncalled-for intervention by the government in enterprises during the course of transferring property rights and speeding up the development of the property rights market. It is necessary to gradually establish a new mechanism based on the property rights market for the overall flow of the factors of production and the partial transfer of property rights. Therefore, as the owner of state-owned assets, the state has the ultimate decision-making power with regard to the transfer of the state firms' property rights. The establishment of a specialized organ to take charge of the defining, assessing, transferring and supervising of state property rights will help protect the rights and interests of the owner of the state-owned assets.

It is necessary to strengthen legislation and enact a set of laws, decrees and regulations with regard to the property rights market. In a socialist market economy the state is both the owner of state-owned assets and the administrative regulator of the whole of society. Therefore, the government should not only exercise control over the transaction of state-owned assets, but also carry out supervision and control as regards the operation of the property rights market. In formulating the law on securities transactions and other related laws, it is necessary to speed up the legislative procedure to enable both parties to property rights to dispose of their property while the state regulates the property rights market in accordance with law. On the strength of the legal means, it is essential to check and remedy all property rights transactions that violate the law and all behavior that harms the ownership of property rights and the rights and interests of the state.

It is necessary to empower a specialized organ to carry out effective control over the operation of the property rights market. To establish both a central- and a provincial-level macro control system may be a proper solution. The specialized organ should, under the guidance of the state's industrial policy, bring into play the role of the market mechanism and be responsible for the overall planning of the national property rights, enforce all laws and policies promulgated by the state, collect and release at regular intervals information related to domestic and international property rights transactions, establish a report system with regard to the statistics of surplus and deficiency of assets, and make analyses of the distribution of assets and their increase and decrease. It is necessary to organize and coordinate the transaction of property rights, to examine and supervise the operation of the national property rights market and seek to halt all illegal transaction activities.

All necessary auxiliary reform measures that go in tandem with the development and efficient operation of the property rights market should be worked out. The key to the normal operation of the property rights market lies in transforming the operational mechanism of enterprises and in making it clear that property rights of assets are to be owned by enterprises. It is necessary to establish and improve all laws and decrees that are complementary with the implementation of the Enterprise Bankruptcy Law, which include the social security system and unemployment insurance system, and which constitute the external environment to ensure the entry of property rights into the market for transaction. By so doing we will be able to promote the rational flow of all production factors, especially by promoting the scope of business operations, the rationalization of organizational structure and the acceleration of optimal allocation of state-owned assets for the eventual enhancement of their operational efficiency.

IV. Promoting the Commercialization of Banks and Creating an Ideal External Environment for the Separation of the Functions of the Government from Those of Enterprises

The promulgation and implementation of the Commercial Bank Law of the People's Republic of China indicate that the reform of China's banking system has entered a new stage. Over the past few years the state-owned banks have undergone a process of perfecting their internal economic mechanism and tightening management. As a result, they are playing an important role in supporting the development of state firms and stabilizing the market economy. However, with the steady development of the market economy, problems such as excessive burdens borne by the state-owned banks and decreasing efficiency have become more and more striking. Therefore, how to accelerate the commercialization of banks and create conditions for the separation of government functions from managerial ones have become urgent tasks for carrying out the deep-going reform.

1. The ratio of assets liabilities of state firms, as high as 79%, is the most outstanding problem in their reform

(1) In the reform of state firms the huge amount of debt (owed mainly to the state specialized banks) has become the most

outstanding problem. Owing to this problem of liabilities, other measures of state firms' reform, such as the transformation of the assets structure, the reorganization of the basis of shareholding, the adjustment of assets stock, and the annexation, merger and reorganization of enterprises have all come across obstacles.

Since the early 1980s the state has turned the investment made in state firms into bank loans. For more than a decade the ratio of assets liabilities of state firms has been on continuous rise. In 1980 the assets liabilities of state-owned industrial enterprises was only 18.7%. However, by 1993 it had risen to 67.5%, of which the liability ratio of current assets reached 95.6%, which means that almost all the working capital of the enterprises derived from debt. At the end of 1994 the State Property Administration conducted an investigation known as "appraisal of fixed assets and circulating funds," the result of which indicated that the assets liability ratio of state firms stood at 79%, of which the equity-debt ratio was 70%, much higher than the international standard, which is 50%. Two figures stand out most prominently: One is the assets pay-out ratio by state firms, which is 6-7%, and the other is the average interest rate of loans, which is 12%. Judging by these two figures, it is obvious that, when the assets pay-out ratio is only 6-7% while the liability ratio is as high as 70%, it is very difficult for an enterprise to pay the interest. In 1995 the ratio of liability of assets of state firms was on the increase. At the same time, the liabilities of enterprises cover not only a large amount of debt that the state has invested in basic construction and technological upgrading, but also short-term debts employed to supplement the working capital. These liabilities are composed of both debts in arrears and also default loans from non-banking financial institutions and counterpart cooperative units. The heavy burden of debt incurred by state firms has become a very pressing problem confronting the normal operation of China's economy.

(2) Heavy debts have already put the state firms at considerable operational risk and have become a big obstacle in deepening the reform of state firms and carrying out institutional innovation.

The international established equity-debt ratio is generally 50%. By exceeding this limit, enterprises will be confronted with big operational risk. At present, liabilities incurred by the large and medium state firms are generally higher than this limit, and quite a few of them cannot make repayment upon the maturity of their debts and often they obtain new loans to clear off the old, with liabilities becoming heavier and heavier until they have little hope of reversing their loss-making position. Overly high debt ratio and heavy burden of liabilities bring about the situation in which the increase of profit cannot catch up with the growth of loan interest. State firms are in the predicament that they cannot operate normally.

From the point of view of specialized banks, enterprises have shifted their losses to the banks by repudiating their debts, resulting in overdue debts and bad or dead accounts, with bad assets accounting for about 25% of total assets, large amount of debts whose principal and interest cannot be recalled upon maturity, and the yield of banks falling drastically. This seriously impairs the banks' credit standing and the utilization of the loan mechanism. Without eliminating the large amount of bad assets and the mechanism that generates bad loans, it will be difficult for specialized banks to become modern commercial banks.

(3) The liabilities of state firms are mainly due to the policy factors employed to adjust the difference in the transitional period between the traditional planned economy system and the new system.

Under the traditional planned economy system decisions on investment were completely made by the government. Less efficient investment and losses arising from erroneous decisions made by the government were borne by the state firms, which have been operating for a long time inefficiently or unproductively, therefore losing the capability for debt redemption. In replacing the fund appropriation system with loans, a batch of state firms have been established that almost totally depend on bank loans. Most of them have all along been operating in debt and cannot rid themselves of the heavy debts incurred. At the same time, not only were depreciation rates very low, but also most of the little depreciation funds have been turned over to the state as profits or used to develop new projects. Consequently most of the enterprises can only be upgraded under heavy liabilities.

With the deepening of the reform of the price, distribution and social security systems there has been a persistent increase in the expenses of non-operating subsidies. At the same time, the rapid changes of policies related to interest rates, taxation and exchange rates have far surpassed the actual capacity of state firms to bear them, thus resulting in policy-based losses.

The traditional system of having state firms running community services and corporate social insurance have led to part of their assets being encroached upon by non-operating undertakings. The reduction of operating assets has greatly reduced the efficiency of overall assets in operation. State firms are having a hard time to maintain their normal operations, resulting in borrowing to tide over difficulties.

2. On the basis of combination of debts in trust with various measures, it is necessary to strive to solve the overall debt problem to speed up the pace of bank commercialization

Proceeding from the actual conditions of the creditor's rights and liabilities between the specialized banks of China and state firms, it is urgent for the government to establish authoritative and transitional trusteeship organ both at the central and local levels which should be responsible for the overall handling the current bad assets of the state commercial banks, and further promote the reorganization of enterprises. The said organ may be established on the basis of the current State Property Administration.

The major tasks of the debt trusteeship organ are as follows:

First, to take over the bad debts of enterprises from state banks and to leave the banks to conduct normal business operations so as to embark on the road of commercialization. Henceforth, commercial banks will no longer undertake any mandatory policy loans and will operate totally in accordance with the principle of commercialization with regard to the placement of debt.

Second, through holding the creditors' rights of relevant enterprises, the trusteeship organ will take part in the reorganization of enterprises and further push forward their overall marketization reform. Through reorganizing the enterprise creditors' rights and adjusting the structure of enterprises, it is necessary to accelerate the flow of property rights of state firms, especially of small and medium ones. It is also essential to intensify the management of state firms to enhance their overall economic benefits while paying attention to solving the historical debt problems. Measures should be taken against the development of new bad debts between the enterprises and the banks.

Debts of China's state firms have their own special characteristics. The operation of the debt trusteeship organ should take into full consideration the coordination of the interests of the state, enterprises, banks, etc. In China there is in fact only one creditor, which is the state-owned bank. Owing to the fact that the creditors' rights (state bank) and debtor (state firms) are owned ultimately by the same "person" (the state), in principle the problem can be instantly solved by writing off the debts. However, under one nominal ownership (the state), the three departments with major interests in the debts of state firms have different expectations: The firms expect to write off debts and be exempted from more debts; the state banks oppose doing so unless the banks can obtain sufficient compensation; and the treasury department is reluctant to use more financial revenue to renew the financial input into state firms. This results in the tightening of the state treasury funds and the expansion of deficits. Therefore, the key to smooth implementation of the scheme of debt trusteeship lies in all parties concerned making sacrifices to seek an equilibrium of interests for all parties.

In the meantime, an important operational issue that merits earnest study is how to scientifically and rationally define the bad credit assets of a given time and place, which should then be separated totally from bank loans and handed over to the debt trusteeship organ. Schemes under consideration include: In making appraisal of the fixed assets and the circulating funds, the grassroots branch of a commercial bank should register case by case all the bad debts prior to the promulgation of the Commercial Bank Law of the People's Republic of China; upon the joint confirmation of the local People's Bank branch,treasury, auditing authorities and department in charge of enterprises, the registration should be submitted to the respective department at a higher level and handed over to the trusteeship organ after going through a certain segregation procedure.

Upon the trusteeship organ taking over bad creditors' rights, the banks, government, enterprises and the trusteeship organ should all work together to solve the debt problem.

—Banks, as creditors, should make effort to solve the problem of bad assets once and for all. In the process, it is necessary to offer attractive discounts for the trusteeship organ to take over creditors' rights and strive to settle about 20% of bad debts through this approach.

—Such a discount should be deducted from the doubtful account reserve and from a certain amount of capital in cash. In stripping the debts, it is worthwhile for creditors to make some necessary contribution, even though the bank will have to reduce its capital in cash by a substantial amount and reduce its scale. However, this will be conducive to invigorating the bank's state-owned assets on the whole and instrumental in helping banks shake off these historical burdens and genuinely take up commercialized operations, as well as strengthening control of debts.

—The debt trusteeship organ needs a proper fund input from the government. It is necessary for both the central and local treasuries to jointly input a certain amount of funds to help the trusteeship organ to take over bad debts from the banks. It is assumed that this input would account for about 10% of the bad debts.

By doing so, it will not only be possible to alleviate the debt burden of the banks, but also to improve the quality of the banks' assets, and thus satisfy the need for bank asset liquidity and effectively adjust the credit structure. It is planned that during the Ninth Five-Year Plan the government will invest in large and medium-sized state firms which occupy important positions in the national economy but are ridden with heavy historical and social burdens. It is proposed that the funds should be directly put into the trusteeship organ to solve the debt problem of large and medium-sized state firms on an overall and planned basis, and it is expected that there would be some ideal output.

—The government should support the trusteeship organ in its efforts to raise funds through diversified ways to buy creditors' rights. It is necessary to strive to raise about 25% of the total fund to buy bad assets.

The debt trusteeship organ may resort to means such as issuing bonds, establishing debt reorganizing funds, etc., to raise domestic and foreign funds to buy from the specialized banks the bad credit assets of relevant enterprises so as to own the creditors' rights of the enterprises concerned which are in debt to the banks.

The trusteeship organ may convert part of the property rights of state firms into bonds. It may also take over bad creditors' rights from the banks, which should be followed by a bond-oriented conversion process. Then the converted bonds may be transferred in the circulation market for state firms' debts, or be transferred to other investment banks, non-bank financial institutes or other enterprises. By means of such a strategy it is possible to alleviate the debt burden of some state firms and recall part of the funds to make up for the bank losses. Needless to say, this calls for the development of a circulation market for state firms property rights and a counterpart debts circulation market, both of which depend upon the further development and improvement of China's securities market.

—The compensation obtained for part of the creditors' rights in reorganizing enterprises means that efforts should be made to obtain about 20% compensation for bad creditors' rights.

In accordance with the common international practice, when an enterprise is landed in a predicament in which it is heaped with excessive debts and finds that it is impossible to redeem debts falling due, generally two approaches are adopted to handle this problem: One is to sell the assets of the enterprise or to declare it bankrupt for liquidation to recoup debts; the other is to reorganize the enterprise and adjust the assets liability structure through various means to provide the enterprise with a new foundation for survival and seek a new opportunity for development.

Upon the trusteeship organ taking over bad debts it is necessary to accelerate the reorganization of the enterprise and adopt corresponding measures based on discrimination to activate stock funds. It is also necessary to resolve bad creditors' rights through converting debts into shares, leasing, transferring or auctioning.

—About 25% of the bad creditors' rights should be converted into good ones.

In the process of entrusting creditors' rights, it is necessary to identify bad debts and handle them accordingly. For some bad debts, even though they are heavy, if the products are marketable and have good prospects it is proper to adopt measures such as interest exemption, stopping interest payment, postponing servicing, etc., to help the enterprise to develop. A new debt redemption agreement may be signed between the trusteeship organ and the enterprise so as to convert part of the bad creditors' rights into good ones.

(1) Acting in accordance with the principle of the market economy, it is necessary to establish a market economy relationship between banks and enterprises based on each party's own choice and on equality and fair cooperation.

The linkage that brings enterprises and banks together is the fund movement which is manifested as a behavior of credit and is a temporary transition of funds based on the terms of repayment of principal plus interest. Due to the restraints of the planned economy in the past, both banks and enterprises depended upon the government, all their business activities were regulated through plans, and the credit relationship between them was distorted because of administrative intervention, which resulted in alienation devoid of compensation, harming the basic characteristic of credit and giving rise to an abnormal credit relationship between the banks and enterprises.

The commercialization of specialized banks calls for the establishment of an autonomous cooperative borrowing and lending partnership based on credit. Banks do not have the obligation to provide funds to enterprises, and enterprises in turn do not have the right, by means of a third party, to force banks to provide loans. In this way, it will be possible both to develop an overall environment of fair competition and to urge the two parties to honor credit and stress efficiency, consciously overcoming short-term behavior.

(2) It is necessary to have both creditors' rights and debts protected by law.

Traditionally, the business activities of specialized banks were under the administrative intervention of the government. Loans provided by the banks used to be characterized by recklessness, which resulted in a large amount of bad creditors' rights between state firms and specialized banks, with no effective legal protection.

With the transition of state firms into modern enterprises and the deepening of the commercialization of specialized banks, the debtor and creditor relationship between banks and enterprises must obtain the confirmation and protection of the law. Banks have the right to utilize the legal means of filing lawsuits or auctioning to recall all sorts of loans, so as to reduce the loss of credit assets as far as possible.

(3) Restraints by banks upon enterprises should be by economic means.

Both enterprises and banks are part of the market economy, which is based on a relationship of mutual benefit and equality. Both parties exercise rights and obligations in accordance with the credit and contract. Enterprises need support from banks, and banks needs cooperation from enterprises. By using complete economic means to impose restraint upon enterprises by banks, enterprises regain the right to regulate working capital under autonomous management and thus become the genuine subject of investment and interest.

(4) The government should play an important role in regulating the relations between banks and enterprises.

With the conversion of the planned economy into the market economy, in handling the relationship between banks and enterprises, the government should convert its former administrative intervention into organizational coordination. In fact, the government was both the match-maker and the witness of the relationship established between banks and enterprises under the traditional system. During the transition period of the economic system, when new disputes and contradictions arise between banks and enterprises it is reasonable for the government to fully display its role as a coordinator. The key lies in the local government, which should take the interests of the whole into account, proceed from the overall situation and handle the various contradictions between the banks and the enterprises impartially, attend to the needs of both parties concerned and safeguard their legal rights and interests.

V. Speeding Up the Conversion of Government Functions and Spurring the Fundamental Transformation of the Economic System

1. The biggest issue for the reform of government institutions raised in the reform of state firms is to accelerate the separation of government functions from those of enterprises

The reform of state firms in the past 17 years has shown that the root of failure to invigorate them and the difficulty in promoting the reform lies in one critical problem: The lack of separation between government functions and those of enterprises. Under the traditional system, the relationship between enterprises and government departments used to be one of administrative subordination. The government was entitled to directly administer enterprises and intervene in their operations. Even government departments and regional offices could directly enforce control over enterprises. But since the introduction of the reform program the series of reform measures aiming at enterprise reform, such as "delegation of power and concession of profits" and the contractual responsibility system, have all failed to solve the problem at the core, i.e., separating government functions from enterprise functions. The corporate enterprise system, which includes the shareholding system and is a typical form of modern enterprise systems, has failed to deter unnecessary government intervention in shareholding companies set up in line with the corporate system. The reason is the failure to totally separate the government functions from those of enterprises, which is also an important reason why the reform of state firms is hard to accomplish. Separation of administration from enterprise management calls for streamlining government departments and changing government functions. Since the reform and opening up were introduced, conversion of government functions has been repeatedly stressed and government organs have also undergone reform. Yet the outcome has been just the reverse; instead of reducing the numbers of organs and departments in the government, the number of employees working in the state organs and institutions has gone up while the government organs are still under the administrative system of the planned economy, and the government's functions have failed to be totally changed. It is precisely because of such a failure that the problem of separating administration from enterprise management cannot be fundamentally solved, thus becoming a big obstacle to deepening the reform of state firms.

The difficulty in changing government functions lies not only in the transformation of mentality, but also in, and more importantly, the fact that the transformation is directly related to the readjustment of the power structure already formed under the former system, which involves government departments at all levels and administrators who hold both power and interest, and it also pertains to the relocation of large numbers of government employees. Therefore, it is a reform of great difficulty, and considerable efforts are needed to carry it out.

2. To accomplish the separation of policy-based management from true business management and to transform government functions, at present priority should be given to finding a solution to the system for controlling state-owned assets and accelerating the pace in establishing the social security system

The Chinese government has already taken the separation of government functions from those of enterprises as an important part of the current reform of state firms. To tackle the problem of separating the two functions, it is necessary to proceed from the actual conditions of state firms and act in accordance with the principle of separating the government's socio-economic administrative functions from its ownership function regarding state-owned assets and actively find a rational form and avenue for the administration and operation of state-owned assets, so as to standardize and systemize the behavior of government and enterprises. The key problems pending are:

It is necessary to fundamentally alter the mode of administration of state-owned assets and to carry out the separation of administration from assets ownership. "Lack of separation of administration from assets ownership" is the root of the lack of separation of administration from management. The government department in charge of an enterprise is both the "boss" that exercises ownership and the "mother-in-law" that exercises administrative power, merging two functions and integrating two powers, tightly putting the enterprise under control. The separation of administration from assets ownership means strictly differentiating the government's socio-economic administrative functions and the function as owner of state assets, consequently separating the function of management of state assets from that of state administration in terms of the setup of organs and personnel placement, introducing two different systems based on the division of responsibilities and duties. One feasible scheme is to set up a state-owned assets management committee in the State Council to unify the management of state assets and act as the sole representative of the ownership of state assets. Thus, other government departments will no longer be involved in the direct administration of state assets.

(Read at *MDP Workshop on Comparative Studies of the Role of Government in the Productive Sectors in Countries in Transition*, in Haikou, March 11, 1996.)

Development of China's Non-Public Economy in the Period of Its Economic Transition

The fundamental task of China's economic system reform is to successfully realize the transition from the traditional planned economy to a socialist market one, to preliminarily establish a socialist market economic system by the end of this century and to have in place a relatively well-established socialist market economic system before the year 2010. One of the most important aspects of China's progressive reform is permitting and encouraging the development of non-public sectors including the private, individual and foreign-funded economies on the precondition of taking public ownership as the main form of ownership. In the past 18 years the proportion of the non-public sectors in the overall national economy has been expanding step by step, which is one of the most important reasons not only for the continuous rise of the marketization level of China's national economy but also for the market mechanism to play an increasingly important role. To build a socialist market economy China needs further development of the non-public sectors, because this is conducive to continuous improvement of the economic performance and market competitiveness of state-owned enterprises. It also enhances the opening up of China's economy and contributes to the maintenance of rapid and sustained economic growth. Therefore, China shall continue to encourage the development of the non-public sectors in the future.

I. Adhering to the Principle of Having Public Ownership as the Main Form of Ownership, and Permitting and Encouraging the Development of the Non-Public Economy

Since the policy of reform and opening up to the outside world was adopted in 1978, the non-public sectors have regained vitality and has seen rapid expansion. Particularly since 1992, when China began its all-round economic reform, the non-public sectors have been developing very fast through market competition. In 1993 and 1994 the number of private enterprises grew by 70.39% and 81.68%, respectively, as against the previous year. And the proportion of state revenue from the non-public sectors in the total increased from 0.7% in 1980 to 16.3% in 1994. This clearly shows that the non-public sectors have become a new growth point of China's national economy.

1. The economic strength of the non-public sectors have been getting ever stronger and its added value has been growing very fast

By the end of 1995 the number of private enterprises reached 600,000, a 6.1-fold increase over the figure in 1990. By the end of June 1994 the number of privately owned small industrial and commercial undertakings amounted to 22,386,000 and their number of employees to 39,580,000, up 68.5% and 89.1%, respectively, as compared with the figures at the end of the Seventh Five-Year Plan period. In the just ended Eighth Five-Year Plan, the individual and private sector created a total output value of 660 billion yuan, their business turnover amounted to 1,471.9 billion yuan and their tax payments to the state were as much as 11.7 billion yuan.

At the same time, the value of assets of non-public enterprises which have relatively larger profitability has been expanding at a very fast pace. Some enterprises of this type have gone through the stage of primitive accumulation and entered the stage of rapid development. Moreover, some of them have large enough assets values to be regarded as large and medium-sized enterprises. By 1993 the number of non-public enterprises whose assets value surpassed 1 million yuan each had topped 4,000. In some areas there have emerged non-public enterprises whose assets value is 10 million yuan or even over 100 million yuan each.

2. Changes have taken place in the organizational pattern of non-public enterprises, and the number of limited liability companies has been growing relatively fast

By now, China's non-public economy has attained some new characteristics. For instance, the private sector has infiltrated the public sector and vice versa through many means, such as trans-regional, trans-industrial and trans-ownership participation, leasing and merger. All this has helped maximize favorable factors, minimize unfavorable ones and bring the "advantage of hybridization" into full play. With the flow and reorganization of property rights the ownership structure of some private enterprises is no longer unitary. And a new type of property rights structure is gradually taking shape. In 1993 the number of private limited liability companies reached 41,549. Their size is usually quite large. Though their number only accounts for 23% of the total number of private enterprises, their registered capital accounts for 59% of the total registered capital of all private enterprises.

3. The industrial structure of the private sector is getting increasingly rational and the quality of its investors as well as its management has been continuously improving

At present, 44% of China's private enterprises are in the tertiary trades (62.5% in urban areas). However, some private enterprises have begun to enter high-tech industries, turning out brand-name products for the international market.

Apart from this change, the composition of investors has also changed, and their quality has improved. In the past, most investors in the private sector were young people waiting for employment, retirees and other people without jobs. Nowadays, professionals, government functionaries and factory workers constitute the majority. In private businesses which have newly started up the proportion of people with academic and technical qualifications is increasing.

The practice of China's economic reform has proved that the development of the non-public sectors has a very important role to play in maintaining the rapid economic growth and in accelerating economic marketization. Since 1992 China has further relaxed policy restrictions, consistently permitting and encouraging the non-public sectors to develop rapidly. Nevertheless, in the whole process of the economic reform it is still necessary not only to combat the adverse influence of some traditional ideas but also to create a healthy market environment for fair competition as well as to provide all-round legal protection for the private sector. This is extremely important for a smooth and healthy development of the non-public sectors.

II. Further Promoting the Development of the Non-public Sectors Through the Transformation of the Property Rights System

1. Transformation of non-public enterprises into shareholding ones should be encouraged

China's non-public economy is still in the initial stage of development. Its intrinsic limitations in development are very obvious. Generally speaking, non-public enterprises are usually small in scale, unitary in form of operation and lack effective means to raise funds from society as a whole. All this makes it difficult for them to achieve minimum economies of scale. Moreover, there exist in almost all non-public enterprises many economic problems stemming from unclear definition of property rights. Therefore, to encourage and support the adoption of the shareholding system by qualified non-public enterprises, their property rights must be clearly defined in the first place. On the other hand, they should be helped to achieve minimum economies of scale.

At present, some non-public enterprises are spontaneously seeking to adopt the shareholding system or to step onto the road of amalgamation. This can be seen quite clearly from the following statistics:

First, the proportion of non-public enterprises which have adopted the form of limited liability company in the total number of enterprises in the non-public sector has been continuously on the increase. Between 1989 and 1993 this proportion rose from 4.2% to 23%, and in the past two years it has continued to increase.

Second, the number of non-public enterprises which have adopted the shareholding system has increased by a large margin, and quite a few of them have become listed.

Third, there has appeared a trend for non-public enterprises to become shareholding cooperatives. This is particularly noticeable in rural areas. For example, from 1987 to 1992 the number of shareholding cooperative enterprises in Wenzhou, Zhejiang Province, grew to 24,000, and their tax payment made up 45.4% of the local revenue in 1992. In terms of the distribution system, they combine distribution according to work with distribution according to capital contribution. And the proportion of distribution according to work to distribution according to capital contribution approximately ranges from 7:3 to 6:4.

Fourth, not a few non-public enterprises have begun to be transformed into mixed economy ones through joint management in different degrees and forms. According to a sample survey in 1993, among the randomly selected 143 private enterprises all over the country whose assets value was each over 1 million yuan, 3% had joint operations with enterprises of public ownership, and 23.14% were preparing for this type of operation.

Under China's present conditions, the non-public economy must proceed from the needs of its own existence and development to carry out institutional innovations. First of all, the government should encourage the transformation of qualified non-public enterprises into shareholding companies. To this end, research must be done on how to promulgate or readjust relevant policies and regulations. For instance, the government should: (a) encourage more non-public enterprises which can meet the requirements of the Company Law to establish limited-liability companies; (b) encourage and support through policies the development of the shareholding cooperative economy, and legally recognize this economic form which has been created out of practice; and (c) permit and encourage non-public enterprises to hold shares of enterprises of other types of ownership in order to enhance amalgamations and mergers through the shareholding system. In particular, it should permit non-public enterprises to buy stocks of general state firms.

2. Creating a larger and more favorable arena for the development of the non-public sectors in the process of strategic adjustment of the structure of the national economy

In the period of economic transition the reform of state firms in China is of crucial importance. The principle adopted is to "grasp large ones and give up the small ones." The state-owned economy is the lifeline of the national economy. It covers infrastructure, basic industries and pillar industries as well as macro regulatory means such as public finance. Such firms should remain in the hands of the state and be the focal point of attention in enterprise reform. However, small firms could be revitalized through auctions, mergers, declaration of bankruptcy or leasing. Some of them could be reorganized into shareholding companies, and others could be sold to collectives or individuals. In this way, the strategic adjustment of the national economy would accelerate the reform of the property rights system. This would be conducive not only to bringing the leading role of the state-owned economy into full play but also to the further development of the non-state economy.

Some of the state firms should be sold in order to transfer state-owned assets into compensation. Selling state-owned assets is an effective method for the state to exercise economic administration in the form of value. The practice in some areas can be described as follows: First, enterprises whose assets value is not large are sold to their employees after evaluating their assets and then are operated and managed as shareholding cooperative enterprises; second, for those which are large in size and could be better managed in a decentralized manner, their assets are divided and then sold bit by bit; third, for those which cannot be operated and managed well as a whole, some of their assets are sold to their employees; and fourth, for those which are legally declared bankrupt, their employees have precedence over others in buying the liquidated assets for the purpose of organizing new enterprises.

Next, some state firms could be leased out, that is, they could be publicly owned but privately operated. Employees of leased enterprises should raise working funds on their own, have the autonomy of independent operation and management, assume sole responsibility for their profits and losses, and pay taxes in accordance with laws and regulations.

Finally, some state firms could be grafted onto enterprises with other types of ownership in order to have their assets jointly operated. In the process of attracting investment and introducing capital, some places have actively guided state firms to set up joint ventures with foreign firms. Their purpose is to graft the property rights of the state firms onto foreign-funded enterprises in order to optimize their industrial structure and to improve the operational efficiency of their assets. For example, Hainan Airlines transferred 25% of its total capital stock to Air America, and thus became the first Sino-foreign joint airline in China.

3. Enhancing the development of diversified economic elements through promoting the flow of property rights

Transaction of property rights is an important means in optimizing the allocation of resources in modern market economic conditions. According to statistics, over 6,900 enterprises were merged throughout the 1980s through the flow and reorganization of property rights, with more than 8 billion yuan worth of assets in stock transferred, the number of loss-making enterprises reduced by 4,095 and the amount of losses reduced by 522 million yuan. According to incomplete statistics, nearly 3,000 enterprises and over 6 billion yuan of assets were transferred through property rights transaction agencies in Shanghai, Nanjing, Shenzhen, Guangzhou, Wuhan and other places. With the development of China's market economy, property rights transaction activities are getting more and more brisk and have shown some new features.

First, property rights transaction has become an important means to readjust the industrial and ownership structures. Property rights transaction restarted in China in 1984. At first, it was done mainly through the taking over of loss-making enterprises by profitable ones. Through the practice of over a decade, it has developed from the spontaneous growth stage to the stage of being consciously cultivated.

Second, property rights transaction has become diversified in form. For example, one form is the transfer of property rights through securities. In other words, some enterprises have been acquired or merged through the securities market. Another form is the internal transfer of property rights, which means that assets in the form of stock of small and medium-sized state firms are divided into shares which are sold to their employees. In this way, this type of enterprise is transformed into a "shareholding cooperative" one.

The third characteristic is the entry of foreign capital into China's property rights transfer market, which refers to the fact that foreign capital as well as capital from Hong Kong, Macao and Taiwan has begun to enter the mainland of China by way of purchasing all or part of the stock rights of enterprises.

However, due to some drawbacks in China's property rights system, transaction of property rights is far from standardized. And in the process of property rights transfer there has been a serious drain of state-owned assets. Therefore, there exists an urgent need to establish a unified and standardized property rights transaction market and to comprehensively enact laws and regulations governing property rights transactions in the period of economic transition.

III. Enhancing the Competitive Development of Diversified Economic Elements by Strengthening Market Economy Legislation

1. Legal status of private businesses

The General Principles of the Civil Law of the People's Republic of China, promulgated in 1987, legally recognize and affirm some concrete forms of non-public economy, including privately owned industrial and commercial undertakings, rural contract households and individual cooperatives, which are all regarded as special types of civil subjects and natural persons. However, these stipulations only apply to the individual economic sector.

The 1988 Amendment to the *Constitution* states that "the state permits the private economy to exist and develop within legally stipulated areas" and that "the private economy is a supplement to the socialist public economy."

In accordance with these stipulations, the State Council in the same year promulgated the Provisional Regulations of the People's Republic of China for Private Enterprises, which completely standardizes all aspects of private businesses. It ought to be said that the legal status of the private economy has been established by the above-quoted stipulations.

2. The *Company Law* has provided the legal basis for the private economy to adopt standardized organizational forms

The Company Law of the People's Republic of China was promulgated and put into force on July 1, 1994. This law is of great significance for the establishment of a modern enterprise system with public ownership as the main body and with Chinese characteristics. In order to seek a healthy development, the non-public sectors must conform to the modern enterprise legal system. For this reason, the implementation of the Company Law is extremely important in the period of economic transition for the standardization of corporate organizational behavior, for the protection of the legal rights and interests of corporations, shareholders and creditors, for the maintenance of social and economic order, for the promotion of the development of diversified economic elements, and for the establishment of a market economy system.

3. A series of laws for standardizing the market and for maintaining market order

In the process of its economic restructuring, China has promulgated one after another important laws, such as the General Principles of the Civil Law, the Law on Industrial Enterprises Owned by the Whole People, the Law on Foreign-Capital Enterprises, the Law on Sino-Foreign Joint Ventures, the Law on Chinese-Foreign Cooperative Enterprises, the Company Law and the Commercial Bank Law. Apart from these, there are quite a number of laws specially formulated on major bodies of market.

Take Hainan Province for example. In a short period of eight years since the whole Hainan Province was made a special economic zone, over 100 laws and regulations on the market economy have been promulgated. For instance, it led the whole country to promulgate and implement such laws and regulations as the Regulations on Shareholding Companies in the Hainan Special Economic Zone, Regulations on Limited Liability Companies in the Hainan Special Economic Zone, Regulations for the Registration and Administration of Corporations as Legal Persons in the Hainan Special Economic Zone and Regulations on Foreign Investment in the Hainan Special Economic Zone. In the past three years another 23 local laws and 35 administrative rules and regulations have been issued. All these have greatly promoted the establishment of the market economy system in the locality.

4. Providing effective legal protection for overseas investors

Since July 1979, when the first Law on Sino-Foreign Joint Ventures was promulgated, China has enacted and issued more than 200 laws and regulations concerning foreign investment. These laws and regulations fundamentally constitute a relatively complete investment legal system which is capable of providing truly effective protection for investors.

In view of the requirement of establishing a sound legal system in conformity with international practices, China still needs to, in the period of its economic transition, (a) further strengthen legislation for investment; (b) revise inappropriate ones in a timely fashion; (c) allow an interim period for determining the time of enforcement of laws and regulations; (d) gradually give national treatment to foreign-invested enterprises; (e) gradually reduce and abolish internal stipulations and improve the "transparency" of policies; and (f) heighten the conscientiousness and strictness of law enforcement.

In recent years, with the development toward a socialist market economy, China has paid close attention to economic legislation and has transformed many important norms and standards for economic relations and economic activities into laws and regulations. With the establishment and development of a socialist market economy system as well as with the standardization and legalization of a large number of economic relationships and economic activities, a relatively complete legal system which will meet the needs of the socialist market economy is sure to be established.

(Read at *MDP Workshop on Comparative Studies of the Role of Government in the Productive Sectors in Countries in Transition*, in Haikou, March 11, 1996.)

On Establishing Labor Property Rights in the Period of Economic Transition

In the period of economic transition the main thrust of China's reform is to break down the old system and build a new one, namely, a socialist market economy system. At present, the reform of state-owned enterprises is the key link in the overall economic reform. In the process of the reform of state-owned enterprises and the establishment of a modern enterprise system a large number of state-owned enterprises have been transformed or are being transformed into cooperative companies of various types. According to statistics, the number of enterprises whose employees are part of their shareholders accounts for 865 of the total number of shareholding enterprises that have grown up from state-owned enterprises. The shares held by the employees amount to 6.1% of their total capital stock (*Economic Research References*, Issue No. 13, 1996). It is thus clear that employee ownership and the shareholding cooperative system have become major issues in the overall situation of China's enterprise reform. Regarding how to bring the initiative of employees into full play in the conditions of a socialist market economy and how to correctly handle the relationship between employees and enterprises, many regions and enterprises have done some useful exploration and experiments. However, further in-depth study is needed from both the theoretical and practical perspectives.

I. Analyzing the Concept of Labor Property Rights in Pushing Forward the Reform of State-owned Enterprises

Urgent issues at the moment are how to accelerate the reform of the property rights system of state-owned enterprises, establish an effective property rights system, enable state-owned enterprises to acquire a rational interests mechanism from the market environment characterized by increasingly intense competition and optimize the allocation of resources for the purpose of maximizing profits. In one sense, the reform of the property rights system is a revolution in the operating mechanisms and distribution system of state-owned enterprises as they march toward a market economy. Therefore, the establishment of labor property rights, in order to have an incentive mechanism for mobilizing the enthusiasm of the labor force, is becoming more and more important to the reform of state-owned enterprises.

1. **Establishing labor property rights simply means that employees not only should be paid wages for their work but should also enjoy a certain part of the income generated by property rights**

This means part of the profits of an enterprise should be changed into shares and given to its own employees, with the number of shares allocated to an individual employee being determined by his or her length of service, position and contribution to the enterprise. There should be stipulations that such shares can be neither transferred, traded nor inherited. So far as the overall situation of the development of the socialist market economy is concerned, the establishment of labor property rights is becoming more and more important.

2. **Establishing labor property rights means to forming a mechanism for state-owned enterprises' long-term, steady development through the coordination of interest relations between enterprises and their employees**

Basically, enterprise reform means adjusting the interest relations between enterprises and their work force to realize the maximization of their respective interests. With continuous deepening of the reform, the original interests pattern is no longer compatible with the requirements of the economic transition, and internal contradictions within enterprises are becoming sharper. In the period of economic transition the following contradictions between enterprises and their employees are sure to become even more prominent:

The contradiction among the interests of the work force, the interests of enterprises and the interests of the state. With the distribution system of "everyone eating from the same big public pot" having broken down and with the marketization of the allocation of human resources, labor flows spontaneously to jobs at which it can maximize its own interests. Due to various types of constraints, the present flow of the labor force is characterized by too much spontaneity and disorder. The better trained an employee is, the more likely he or she is to change jobs. Furthermore, there has even appeared the phenomenon that top scientists and technological workers are moving to ordinary work posts and labor-intensive industries, which is an obvious manifestation of the conflict of the interests of the labor force with the interests of enterprises and the state. Therefore, raising the question of labor property rights is aimed at solving the problem of how to rationally and reasonably integrate the long-term interests of employees with those of enterprises and the state, and to gradually form a community of the interests of the labor force, enterprises and the state.

The contradiction between long-term interests and short-term interests. As is shown by actual economic life, short-term actions of enterprises are directly linked to the labor force, particularly management's excessive pursuit of short-term interests. The establishment of labor property rights will enable the long-term interests of the labor force to grow in step with public property accumulation in the form of shares for the employees. This will better resolve the conflict between personal interests and accumulation by enterprises. The additional income of employees in the form of dividends, the amount of which is closely linked with the performance of enterprises, will change the rigid structure of employees' income, which is only composed of wages. As the practice of paying dividends to employees according to their shares links their interests closely with the interests of enterprises, the concern of the employees about their enterprises will be aroused and their sense of involvement in management and decision-making will be bolstered. In this way, enterprises and their employees will become a community sharing a common future and destiny, and the conflict between short-term interests and long-term interests will be better resolved.

3. Strengthening the status and role of labor capital through the establishment of labor property rights is the key to improving the competitiveness of state-owned enterprises

For a long time there has been a lopsided view that the growth of economic benefits of enterprises depends solely on the input of money capital. Consequently, the important role of labor capital has been neglected at large. With the development of modern large-scale socialized production the role of labor capital is becoming increasingly important. Though the role of capital in the conventional sense still keeps its importance, it has shown a tendency to gradually decrease. The capital in the hands of today's shareholders is money capital or capital in kind. However, information, knowledge and technological know-how are playing increasingly important roles in the process of wealth creation, so are employees who have acquired and are utilizing, processing and creating information, knowledge and technological know-how. The more important a role information plays in an enterprise and the more trained its employees are, the smaller a role the input of shareholders plays. In other words, the success of an enterprise, or the amount of wealth it creates and the speed of its wealth creation, relies more on the joint efforts of its employees. Therefore, in future enterprises will be more and more like communities of interests.

At present, the quality of the enterprise management and managers' sense of responsibility have become important factors affecting management efficiency. With the gradual establishment of a new property rights system their roles will become increasingly important. Therefore in attaching importance to the role of the labor force it is particularly important to pay attention to and bring into full play the special role of management in the development of enterprises. It is of vital importance to the reform and development of enterprises to establish labor property rights and integrate labor property rights with enterprise management.

II. Establishing Labor Property Rights by Proceeding from China's Reality and Learning from Employee Ownership Schemes of the West

With the development of large-scale socialized production, labor capital is playing an increasingly important role in economic development. In the past 20 years or so most of the countries with market economies in the West have tried to coordinate the labor-capital relationship as a way to accelerate economic growth through such schemes as partnership expansion, universal shareholding and employee ownership systems. In the process of the reform of state-owned enterprises it is very important to make it clear how to scientifically establish labor property rights by proceeding from China's reality and by drawing on employee ownership schemes.

1. Labor property right should have a wide coverage

The major goal of enterprise reform is to mobilize the initiative of employees. And the establishment of labor property rights aims at strengthening the sense of identification, involvement and responsibility of all employees in an enterprise. Therefore, wide coverage should be the first priority. The employee ownership program in the United States has the requirement of "extensive participation" which is worth learning from.

In the United States there are rigid stipulations about the requirement of "extensive participation" in employee ownership schemes, particularly the participation of employees with low incomes. An employee whose yearly pay is above 50,000 US dollars or who holds 5% of the shares of a company is regarded as belonging to the high-salary class. And the number of the shares he can own is rigidly restricted. It further stipulates that, for all enterprises which adopt employee ownership schemes, 70%

of the employees with low pay should participate and their average income from employee ownership should be no less than 70% of the average income of high-pay employees from the same source.

The establishment of employee shareholding societies within enterprises in China aims at mobilizing the initiative of the broad masses of employees. Thereupon, it requires more extensive participation. Action must be taken to prevent shares of enterprises with better efficiency from being monopolized by a minority of employees. For this purpose, it is necessary to lay down some legal stipulations on the number of shares employees with high pay can hold.

2. Increasing the proportion of labor property rights in small and medium-sized enterprises so as to facilitate and protect their development

From the experience of developed countries in the West we know that the practice of employee ownership is conducive to the protection of small and medium-sized enterprises. Specially, it enables such enterprises to get a firm foothold and grow in strength in the process of intense competition. In the face of increasingly intense market competition small and medium-sized enterprises tend to be at a disadvantageous position, more often than not, they are in danger of being bought out. According to statistics the majority of enterprises bought out are those whose number of employees is smaller than 500. However, once the share capital of a small or medium-sized enterprise is in the hands of its employees, the collectively owned position of the corporate assets will serve as a strong protection mechanism in the market competition. This is the main reason why the number of small and medium-sized enterprises in the West has been continuously growing and that the majority of them have been bought by their own employees. As is shown by statistics, among the over six million enterprises in the United States 98% are small or medium-sized ones whose number of employees is less than 100 each. Of all these enterprises, those whose employees number less than 20 account for 87%. And their output accounts for 40% of the total

GNP of the United States. Moreover, they are still showing great vitality and their number is still rapidly growing.

In our country large state-owned enterprises are characterized with huge value of assets, large numbers of employees and multitude of historical burdens. The reform of their ownership will inevitably lead to great social impacts and affect social stability. Therefore, it is better and more realistic to carry out experiments with employee ownership within small and medium-sized enterprises first. In reforming the ownership of small and medium-sized enterprises the proportion of the labor property rights to their total property rights should be as large as possible and dividends from the shares should be closely linked to their immediate performance. When it comes to experimenting with employee ownership within large state-owned enterprises, employees' dividend income should be largely retained as retirement pay. That is to say, the purpose of practicing this type of ownership should be to increase the employees' long-term interests and the long-term development of their enterprises. This is because large state-owned enterprises do not have to rely on employee ownership for their survival in view of their solid strength, diverse investment sources and strong capacity to bear risks.

3. The forms of realizing labor property rights should be flexible and diversified

When state-owned enterprises are transformed into shareholding enterprises as a way to establish a modern enterprise system, their assets transferred from employees' welfare and award funds as well as part of the assets transferred from public accumulation can be allocated as employee shares, which can be either rationed or sold at low prices to their employees as a way to realize labor property rights. To turn such corporate assets into employee shares should not be considered a drain on state-owned assets. It should be regarded as a way to return to employees the part of the property which, as a matter of fact belongs to them. Nevertheless, when determining the proportion of the assets to be turned into employee shares, careful calculation must be done to guarantee a fair and rational result. In determining the amount of shares the individual employees should have, the method used by employee shareholding societies in the West can be drawn on. And employees' length of service, posts, positions and contributions should form the basis. However, since the property rights of enterprises in our country have remained ambiguous for a long period of time and a lot of problems have accumulated, including that of retirees, how to decide the part of the assets to be turned into employee shares and how to calculate the number of shares individual employees are entitled to should be carefully studied.

III. Estimating the Role of Establishing Labor Property Rights in Accelerating the Development of Enterprises

1. Realizing labor property rights through employee ownership is helpful for the development of publicly owned enterprises

The major goal of realizing labor property rights through employee ownership in our country is to strengthen the cohesive strength of enterprises and to cultivate an incentive mechanism indispensable for the long-term development of enterprises. It is in essence conducive to the development of enterprises. Employees' income from capital is an extension and expansion of reward for labor. However, there should be clear stipulations on the use of employees' income from labor property rights. For instance, it can be stipulated that this kind of income can only be used for reinvestment and employees' welfare. Since the shares in the hands of the employee shareholding society of an enterprise as the new investor will never flow from the enterprise, the nature of the public ownership of the enterprise will not change. Furthermore, the ultimate goal of both practicing the labor property rights system and establishing employee shareholding societies is to mobilize the employees' initiative, improve the economic returns of enterprises, promote their development and strengthen the economic basis of public ownership.

2. Realizing the transformation of the property rights of small

and medium-sized enterprises by selling, or transferring them or transforming them into cooperative shareholding enterprises can not only reflect labor property rights but can also be helpful for the long-term development of enterprises

The reform of the property rights system, with selling and transfer of small state-owned enterprises as the major approach, particularly the transfer of all or part of their property rights, can promote the rational flow of state-owned assets, guide them to areas of high efficiency and create favorable conditions for the maintenance and increase of their value. In order to realize labor property rights through employee ownership, the most important thing is to bear in mind the overall situation of the state-owned economy, which poses the question of whether it is good for enterprises to remain inefficient, feed on state-owned assets and make themselves empty shells or to revitalize the factors of production of enterprises to contribute to the increase of the wealth of the whole society. To realize the reallocation of state-owned assets in accordance with the principle of "grasping the large ones and giving up the small ones" is conducive to both effective utilization of state-owned assets and mobilization of employees' initiative.

3. Bold exploration in the cooperative shareholding system which is now in the ascendant should be encouraged and the system itself should be gradually standardized

Cooperative shareholding, which is an output of a certain stage of China's economic restructuring, reflects labor property rights relatively fully. Transforming enterprises into cooperative shareholding ones means regarding labor property rights as part of the overall property rights and employees or members of an economic organization as beneficiaries of part of the ownership interest. It directly relates the income of employees to the performance of their enterprises and the shares they hold, resulting in a perpetual incentive for maintaining and increasing the value of state-owned assets. The equal rights every member of a cooperative shareholding economic organization enjoys, and his participation in and familiarity with the management activities of his enterprise, make supervision by the masses a normal, concrete, conscientious and voluntary action. At first, the cooperative shareholding system may not be perfect or even mature. Naturally, it takes some time to solve this problem. Labor property rights should be combined with the practice of the cooperative shareholding system, which will play an important role in establishing labor property rights in the period of China's economic transition.

To integrate enterprises and their employees into communities of interest is a universally pursued goal in modern market economy conditions. Since we are establishing a socialist market economy, we should set up a better interest relationship between enterprises and their employees to inject a chronic motive force into our socialist market economy and to finally enable all the members to prosper together. The establishment of labor property rights is of very important practical significance for the acceleration of the reform of state-owned enterprises and the establishment of a socialist market economy.

(Read at the *International Symposium on Shareholding by Employees and Shareholding Cooperatives*, in Haikou, April 15, 1996.)

Issues Facing China's Rural Economic Reform During the Conversion Period

I. What Role Do the Reform and Development in the Rural Areas Play in Keeping Overall Stability?

To build a socialist market economy a stable social environment is needed. In China 80 percent of the population lives in the rural areas. Therefore, the stability of the social environment depends largely on the stability of agricultural production and the rural areas. Years of practice have proved that only when agricultural production and the rural areas remain stable will the whole country be stable. And only when the whole country is stable will a smooth economic structural conversion be possible. And only when the overall situation remains stable will a continuous, fast and healthy development of the national economy be possible. But experience also shows that, when making policies concerning China's macro economy, it is extremely difficult to give top priority always to rural economic development. In some situations the interests of the rural areas have to be sacrificed and the speed of the rural reform has to be slowed down for a temporary macro-economic balance. Between the rural economy and macro-economic stability there has been agreement over a long period of time as well as some transient conflicts which have been the sources of a series of dilemmas during China's economic structural reforms.

Basically, the difficult balance between the rural economy and the overall situation originates in the old planned economy system. In the past period of socialist economic construction priority was given to industrial development. To this end, a high rate of accumulation had to be maintained on the basis of low income. To maintain the high rate of accumulation, salaries and other industrial costs had to be kept low. One of the most important means to achieve this was to bring down the prices of foodstuffs and of most light industry raw materials, including agricultural products. In this sense, the state monopoly for the purchase and marketing of agricultural products at low prices was the cornerstone of the system of the planned economy. When the rural reforms went beyond the stage of producing enough to feed and clothe the peasants and moved towards a market economy, the basis of the old system, as well as the macro-economic balancing mechanism, were shaken. But the economic reform in the urban areas, where the state economy still plays the leading role, lags behind the economic reform in the rural areas, where the non-state economy plays the leading role. Industry and commerce, with their low-level adoption of the market principle, cannot deal smoothly with agricultural products which have adopted the market principle to a much greater extent. The perplexity of this imbalance between the rural and the urban reforms has been with us since the mid-1980s. The dilemma is that if we speed up the adoption of the market principle with agricultural products the urban areas will be shaken; on the other hand, if we slow down the rural reform the peasants' incomes and their enthusiasm for production will be dampened.

What is more difficult is the fact that the whole set of former policy instruments have been changed in the reform and their effectiveness has been lost, while the new market-dominated macro-economic regulation mechanism has not yet been established. During the conversion period, when the conflict between the rural interests and the urban interests becomes tense, we can neither go back to the former state-monopolized purchase and marketing system and the isolation of the rural area from the urban area, nor can we progress to reach a fully flexible market-based regulation system. When we find ourselves caught "between the devil and the deep sea" how can we maintain macro-economic stability during the conversion period? How can we effectively put macro-economic regulatory policies into effect to meet the needs of further agricultural development during the conversion period?

So the central problem to be discussed at this symposium is not whether or not we should keep macro-economic stability, nor whether or not we should carry forward the rural reform toward the market economy system, nor whether or not we should continue with the urban reform toward the market economy system. The problem we are facing is much more complex than that: It is how can we, under the limitation of the rural and urban reforms being out of step, keep the macro-economic stability and find solutions for a series of dilemmas?

II. Carrying Forward the Reform in the Purchase and Marketing System of Agricultural Products Under the Pressure of Inflation

The purchase and marketing system of agricultural products has intermittently been undergoing several reforms. The latest one started at the beginning of 1993. The cancellation of the state contractual purchasing of grain was put into effect in most parts of China, and the supply of grain at state-set prices in most cities and towns was also canceled, so that the price controls on grain were completely lifted. In the same year the method of "fixed purchase quotas at deregulated prices" (i.e., the quotas for purchasing remain the same, while the prices change according to the market demand) was suggested and put into practice. But in 1993 the prices of grain went up so substantially that the state had to resume the former method that the state purchases in definite quantity at fixed prices and opening the market only after the purchasing is completed. In the summer and fall of 1994 the prices of common agricultural products like grain and cotton again went up by a big margin, which sharply spurred inflation. In these circumstances the state had no choice but to impose ceiling prices for major agricultural and sideline products and to close the agricultural produce market. And grain rationing was resumed in some cities and towns. So, instead of going forward, the reform of the purchase and marketing system for agricultural products retrogressed.

The reform of the purchase and marketing system fluctuated with changes in demand and supply of agricultural products. This raises a series of questions that are worth discussing.

First, how should we estimate the long- and mid-term prospects for the balance between demand and supply of basic agricultural products, such as grain and cotton, in China? For different estimates will lead to different goals for structural reforms. Experience shows that a pessimistic estimate will gain the upper hand when there is a shortage of supply of agricultural products and the prices go up, which will result in a tendency not to believe that demand and supply can be regulated by the market mechanism. This will produce an adverse impact on policy making. On the other hand, when there is an over-supply of agricultural products and the prices are steady an optimistic estimate will be widely accepted. Considering the inner link between the estimate of demand and supply, and its effect on policy making, a scientific estimate of the prospects of the long- and mid-term balance between the demand and supply of agricultural products has to be considered when discussing the reform of the purchase and marketing system. Special attention has to be given to such questions as how to analyse the relationship between a speedy realization of agricultural industrialization and modernization, and the management of individual farmers, as well as how to analyse the possibilities of China entering the international agricultural produce market. These are very difficult academic problems, and different views have to be heard in order to reach a sound judgement.

Second, how should we analyse the relationship between inflation and the reform of the purchasing and marketing system of agricultural produce during the conversion period? In the past the increase in food prices in large and medium-sized cities played the leading role in the increase in the consumer price index, the contribution of which was about 60%. This phenomenon brought forth two opposite judgments. One says the latest round of inflation has been caused by the increase in the prices of agricultural products. To prevent overall galloping inflation the prices of agricultural products must be kept under control, and to increase the supply of agricultural products through appropriate scale of operation it may even be necessary to restructure the management of individual farmers, so as to maintain overall stability. The other judgment claims that the present inflation was largely structural, which, due to some problems in the system, is caused by the excessive issuing of money. The structural inflation overshadows every aspect of our country's economic life, and it is only due to the relatively small elasticity of the demand and supply of agricultural products that the quicker price increase showed itself. Therefore, real control of inflation can only be realized by speeding up the reforms in the government departments. Controlling the prices of agricultural products through administrative means can only upset the balance between demand and supply, which will harm the balance of the macro economy.

Finally, we have to discuss whether it is possible to carry forward the reforms in the purchasing and marketing system of agricultural produce in conditions of inflation. The State Council has made the decision that the purchasing and marketing of grain, cotton, and fertilizer will be the responsibility of the governor or mayor of every province or city, which is a big advance from the previous state purchase at unified prices. Now each province or city can achieve a balance between the demand and supply of foodstuffs and industrial raw materials through its own provincial market, inter-provincial market or even international market. In other words, the central government requires every provincial government to achieve a balance between demand and supply of agricultural products, but no unified means to achieve that goal is stipulated. This means that in some provinces the market mechanism will be more fully used to achieve the balance. On the other hand, another possibility also exists: i.e., that administrative decrees will be used instead of the market mechanism, and the purchasing will be carried out through different levels of government, and

and inter-regional trade will be shut down. So, how to ensure the former possibility and prevent the latter possibility has become an urgent problem in the study of the present government policies.

III. Dealing With the Shift of the Surplus Rural Labor Force from Agricultural Production to Non-Agricultural Enterprises and to the Urban Areas

During the conversion period another acute problem facing the rural economic reform is the shift of the surplus rural labor force. A large population with relatively little land and a low level of employment is a basic fact of life in China. According to rough estimates, the present surplus labor force all over China has reached 100 million to 120 million, and there will be a net growth of six million to seven million every year. With the readjustment of the agricultural structure and the development of a modern agriculture, the shift of the surplus rural labor force to non-agricultural enterprises has happened in most industrialized countries. And this shift has helped increase the peasants' income, especially in the less-developed rural areas, so that the difference between income in rural and urban areas has been narrowed.

However, the increase in peasants' income will directly affect the effective purchasing power in the domestic market. But we should not forget that the under-capacity industrial operation in some places has become very serious. And we still remember the economic slump we experienced a few years ago. It is true that the inefficiency of the state economy is one reason for the under-capacity industrial operation and the economic slump, but the low rate of increase in the peasants' incomes and the weak expansion of the domestic market are surely others. If we only take one reason into consideration and disregard the others we may have to face not only the problem of inflation, but market stagnation as well. With this in mind, quite a few experts and scholars believe that the shift of the rural labor force and a continuous increase in peasants' incomes deserve serious attention, for they give rise to problems that will affect the national economy on a long-term basis.

But the shift of the huge rural labor force presents some tough challenges for society as a whole. Among all the problems, two are outstanding. One is whether the sharp increase in the employment of the surplus rural labor force will lead to a rapid increase in the opportunity cost, which will in turn cause an increase in the cost price. The second is what changes in the structure of the national economy, especially in the industrial structure and the urban structure, ought to be made in order to accommodate all the rural surplus labor. Besides, we cannot ignore the fact that the shift of the peasants' employment goes together with the developmental imbalance between different areas. The mainstream of the shift is not only from the rural to the urban areas, but also from the less-developed areas to the more-developed ones. What effect that will have on the balance of income between different areas is still not clear. As to the problems caused by the shift in the social administration, such as public security, urban sanitation, birth control, education, etc., China needs to learn from international experience.

IV. Forming a Social Organizational Base at the Village Level for Stable Economic Transition

The social organization at the village level is the weakest link in Chinese society during the economic transition period. In the days of the people's communes the mechanism of the administrative mobilization of rural resources reached right down to the village level. But since the reform started villages are recognized in line with the Constitution as autonomous administrative units run by villagers themselves. However, proper ways of implementing this autonomy have not yet been established. The recent problems that have emerged in the rural areas, such as the excessive financial burdens forced on the peasants, the tense relationship between village cadres and villagers, and the decline in the level of village public affairs are all due to weak social organization at the village level. The construction of the village social organization is one important aspect of the construction of the rural market economy system. First, the present land ownership mode in China is collective ownership, and land is contracted to the peasants on a long-term basis. In practice, villages are the owners of the collective land. The function of stabilizing and regulating the land contract system formed by the village, not by any other social organization. The 15-year land contracts, most of them signed in the 1980s, will soon have to be renewed. This is a tremendous job, and one which has to be done at the village level. If the social organization at the village level falls apart the land contract system will not be able to continue. Without the land contract system there would not have been the development of the rural areas in the past ten-odd years, nor would there now be rural stability or the possibility of further agricultural development.

Second, the villages, as the grass-roots social organizations in rural areas, are the vital link between the central government and the hundreds of millions of Chinese peasants. Only with their help can the government's policies be carried out by the peasants. The social organizations at the village level, as autonomous organizations of villagers, not only work for the interests of the state and the collective but also serve as spokesmen for the peasants and work for their interests as well. Therefore, how to construct the village social organizations is an urgent research subject to be researched in deepening the rural economic reform. At present, the existing village social organizations are undergoing a conversion from the old system to a new one, and because of that they are caught up in the conflicts caused by the reforms as well as in the contradictions between the government and the peasants. The absence of an institutionalized financial foundation at the village level poses a hidden threat to the long-term development and stability of the village communities. If the problem of constructing an autonomous financial foundation at the village level is solved, along with the reforms of the finance and taxation systems, it may have an important effect on China's economic and political stability. In addition, the construction of socialist democracy at the village level will also have a positive effect on the efforts to curb corruption in the villages and to motivate the peasants to take part in the management of social and political life in their own villages.

(Read at the *International Symposium on Reform of China's Rural Economy*, in Haikou, March 21, 1995.)

China's Rural Economic Restructuring and Its Development During the Period of Economic Transition

I. History and Achievements of Rural Economic Restructuring in China

China's rural economic restructuring started in 1978. Prior to that, the people's communes, a centralized system of rural economy characterized by unified distribution and management and a work-point system, was established for the execution of the strategy of giving priority to the development of heavy industry while developing the mode of primary accumulation of capital through the exchange of unequal value. Such a system produced an adverse effect on the rural economy, resulting in egalitarianism, known as "everybody eating from the same big public pot." This seriously inhibited the enthusiasm of the broad farming population. The mandatory plans and administrative decrees for agricultural production under such a system led to serious waste and disproportions in the utilization of rural economic resources and the allocation of rural labor force. Furthermore, the rather underdeveloped rural productive forces and the low quality of farm products made the income of the farming population stagnate for a long time. The result was a very vulnerable foundation for the rural economy. Prior to the implementation of the reform program, agriculture was the most stagnant sector in the national economy of China.

The agricultural responsibility system featuring fixed farm output quotas on a household basis was introduced in 1978 by farmers in Fengyang County, Anhui Province. They scored remarkable success and became the forerunners of rural economic restructuring in China. Since then, thanks to the support of the state in terms of policies, the household responsibility system has spread across the nation, ushering in a new era in the development of the rural areas of China.

The rural reform that started in 1978 was progressively carried forward, primarily in the following three aspects:

(1) The transformation of the rural managerial system based on the re-establishment of the rural economic units and the reform of the organizational system.

(2) The reform of the circulation system characterized by progressively removing price controls and getting rid of the state monopoly in the circulation of farm products.

(3) The institutional barriers preventing farmers from participating in non-agricultural production have been progressively eliminated with a view to encouraging the development of rural industry characterized by the growth of village and township enterprises (VTEs).

1. The Transformation of the Rural Managerial System

In the course of the rural reform that started in the late 1970s, nothing is comparable to the far-reaching significance of the household responsibility system.

The household responsibility system, starting in some localities and extending to all provinces across the nation, was originally regarded as an expedient measure designed to basically solve food and clothing problems. But it was acknowledged by the state in only a few years as the basic operating system that should be adhered to on a long-term basis in the rural areas of China. By December 1984, 90% of the rural economic organizations all over the country had carried out this contractual system, and consequently accomplished the fundamental transformation of the micro rural economy. In 1985 farming households across the country totalled 191 million, which increased to 228 million households in 1992.

With the popularization of the responsibility system based on the contractual system, the former system of people's communes was deprived of its foundation. After the promulgation of the new

Constitution in 1982 government functions were separated from the administrative functions of the people's communes, and the people's government was established on a village (township) basis; the former production brigades were turned into villagers' committees. By the end of 1984 the work of separating government administration from commune management was basically accomplished. By 1985 the former 54,353 people's communes had been reorganized into 83,182 village people's governments and 7,956 township people's governments. The former 710,000 production brigades had been transformed into 940,000 villagers' committees. By 1992 there were 34,115 village governments, 14,135 township governments and 806,000 villagers' committees.

The universal implementation of the household responsibility system has overcome various deep-rooted drawbacks such as the integration of government administration with commune management, administration by government decrees, and egalitarianism known as "everybody eating from the same big public pot," and fundamentally revamped the organizational structure of the rural micro economy. As the basic units participating in commodity production, the farming households have intensified the budgetary constraints and incentive mechanism which have greatly strengthened the inner dynamism of agricultural production, and have consequently spurred the high-speed growth of agriculture.

2. The Transformation of the Circulation System

The transformation of the price system of farm products and their circulation system has undergone three stages.

The first stage (late 1978-1984): During this stage, the primary effort made was to increase the mandatory purchasing price of major farm products. Next, efforts were made to open up rural produce fairs and to gradually increase the varieties of farm products that were allowed to be sold by the peasants. By 1983, apart from cotton, all varieties of farm produce were on sale in the rural fairs while farmers, on an individual or partnership basis, were permitted to transport farming and sideline products other than cotton for sale over long distances. Thus the state monopoly of the circulation of farm products was shattered.

The second stage (1985-1988): The system of unified and fixed state purchasing of farm products was abolished and replaced by a mechanism incorporating both contractual purchase and purchase through the market.

The third stage (April 1988 to date): The reform in this stage aims at promoting the overall establishment of the market system while eliminating contractual purchasing on the one hand and increasing the price of farm products on the other, with a view to eventually accomplish the objective of comprehensive market regulation of prices. During this stage the establishment of the market for farm products has made remarkable progress, symbolized by the establishment and operation of the Zhengzhou Central Grain Wholesale Market, followed by the establishment and operation of a large number of modernized central wholesale markets all over the country, thus ushering in a new era of progressive replacement of the traditional small-scale markets with modern means of circulation. Since 1993 the system of grain markets which is part of a three-level system with national wholesale markets occupying the foremost position, regional wholesale markets as the mainstay and rural primary markets as the foundation, has gradually come into being. There are over 80,000 rural grain and edible oil markets and primary product markets in the rural areas of China.

3. The Development of Rural Industrialization

The progress of rural industrialization, symbolized by the emergence of VTEs, had been noticed even before 1977. However, VTEs were subject to severe restrictions both in policy and scope. In 1984 the state formally renamed the former enterprises run by communes and production brigades VTEs and decided that the state would give the same treatment and support to them as enjoyed by state-owned enterprises. This decision marked both the end of the state monopoly of non-agricultural production and the beginning of the entry of the rural population into non-agricultural fields. Since then, VTEs have been making great progress. In 1992 the VTEs across the country totalled as many as 207,900, with a payroll numbering more than 100 million. Their total output value has reached 1,797.5 billion yuan.

The rural economic restructuring has made gigantic achievements which have become the focus of world attention. The results of the rural reform have surpassed the accomplishments of the preceding 30 years. What is more, the speed of development has been fast even in the light of international comparative studies. According to statistics, the average annual growth rate of the total output value of agriculture in China between 1952 and 1978 was 2.7%, and the average annual growth rate of total output value reached 5.91% between 1978 and 1992. The gross national product increased from 279.2 billion yuan in 1980 to 2,538.6 billion yuan in 1992. Allowing for the factor of price increase, this is a growth of 9.1 times in 12 years.

The rapid growth of agriculture has made a tremendous contribution to the development of the national economy. Between 1952 and 1978 the national income in China increased steadily by 5.98% a year, in which the contribution of growth in agriculture accounted for 37%. Between 1978 and 1988 the national income increased by 9.22%, to which agricultural growth contributed more than 69%.

The rapid development of the rural economy brought about an overall improvement and rapid growth in the supply of farm products which fundamentally changed the situation of shortage of food that had existed for a long time. The great improvement in the supply of food has led city and township residents, one third of whom used to be underfed, to a stage of affluence that ensures them sufficient food and clothing, followed by a marked improvement and increase in the quality and composition of their diet. In 1983 the caloric intake per person per day for urban and rural residents had increased by 566 large calories based upon 2,311 large calories in 1978, and protein and fat had increased by 12 g. and 17 g. respectively. In the early 1990s the level of nutrition of Chinese people had far surpassed that of the low-income countries and was getting close to that of medium-income countries.

Thanks to the overall development of the rural economy due

to the rural reform, the income of the farming population has eventually overcome the situation characterized by stagnation or even decline which lasted for as long as 25 years, and has started to enter a new stage of growth. In 1978 the net income per capita for peasants in the whole country was only 133.57 yuan, but by 1992 it had reached 783.99 yuan, an increase of nearly five times as compared with that of 1978. Leaving out the price increase factor, the average increase stands at 7.1% annually. In consequence, the living standards of the farming population have increased markedly.

With the increase of productivity of rural labor and the development of the division of labor and industries, the rural economy has switched from relying on agriculture alone to comprehensive development of various sectors. As compared with 1978, the proportion of crop and plant cultivation decreased by 21.2 percentage points while those of forestry, animal husbandry, sideline occupations and fisheries increased respectively by 1.3, 12.0, 2.8 and 5.2 percentage points in the composition of total agricultural output value in 1992. As for the total social product in rural areas, the proportion of agriculture decreased in 1992 by 33.1 percentage points, while the proportion of industry increased by 31.6 percentage points as against the figures for 1980. During this period, the coefficient of alteration in the structure of agriculture and the rural economy reached 0.425 and 0.667 respectively. The swiftness of alteration in structure was higher than in the previous 30 years.

II. Problems Confronting Rural Reform in China at the Time of Economic Transition

In the late 1980s, the long-existing and deep-seated contradictions and problems inherent in the economic development in rural China began to surface. The convergence of these contradictions and problems was manifested in the sluggish increase of income for the farming population. Since 1992, when the national economy underwent a new round of high-speed growth and the market economy became exceptionally brisk, the peasants' incomes did not show any obvious sign of improvement, or worse, compounded by various new problems and unexpected situations such as the insufficiency in the investment made in agriculture, outflow of agricultural funds, encroachment on arable land in the development zones and the increase of the already heavy financial burden on peasants, etc., rural China once again became the concern of both national and international society. At the same time, with the price controls over farm products lifted and the market economy introduced, the focus of policy research became whether agriculture should be protected, and if so, how. Also pondered was how to carry out effective macro control. All the issues and problems cropping up in the transitional process of shifting toward a market economy implied that agriculture and rural economy had once again entered a critical period.

1. Proceeding from the Overall Development of the Rural Areas, the Main Contradictions and the Prominent Problems Reside in the Reform of the Land-Use System

China's rural economic restructuring in the 1990s is vastly different from that in the 1980s. First, reform has more than ever touched upon the deep-seated contradictions between interests. Unless the problem of property rights relations totally solved and a credible property rights system established, it will be very difficult to fully stimulate the enthusiasm of the broad farming population in the new situation.

In the 1980s, the major reform that had the most far-reaching influence in rural China was the managerial responsibility system mainly based on the household contract system. Through such a responsibility system the separation of the ownership of land and the right of management were realized, with the power of management in the hands of farm workers themselves, which has greatly aroused the initiative for production on the part of the broad farming population, and greatly enhanced the level of output. In recent years, based on the new situation of rural reform, the contract periods have been extended and the legal transfer of land use right permitted. These measures have played a positive role in practice. However, they do not fundamentally solve the problems related to the property rights relations of land. Hence, the contradiction arising from land has become acute in the past few years.

(1) The problems of the expansion of non-farming use of arable land and of letting farmland remain idle have become aggravated, the area of grain growing land has decreased and the gap between grain supply and demand has widened. Owing to the craze for the establishment of development zones and the booming real estate business, the "land enclosure movement" has developed on a larger scale, resulting in decreasing farmland acreage. In the past few years the area of farmland in China has been decreasing by 4 to 5 million *mu* (one *mu* equals one-fifteenth of a hectare.—*Tr.*) per year. Farmland per person in one third of rural China is less than one *mu*. To maintain China's grain production at a rational level, the area sown to crops must be at least 16,500 million *mu*. However, the area of farming land had shrunk to 16,400 million *mu* in 1994.

(2) The frequency and arbitrariness of land readjustment have become more and more serious. The land policy at present still acknowledges that land is collectively owned. As the current fixed-output-quota farmland is evenly distributed according to the sizes of village populations, to solve the problem of land distribution based on the increase or decrease of land there is an objective need to redistribute it in accordance with the actual size of the rural population to date. Recently, in many places, due to the transfer of population and the encroachment on farmland for non-farming use, land has been repeatedly readjusted, with the intervals becoming shorter and shorter. The repeated small-scale oscillation of land is sufficient to undermine the stability of the responsibility system and damage the farmers' enthusiasm for investment.

(3) Input (including labor, capital, technology, etc.) in agriculture has been on the decline, especially the input by farming households in land has been conspicuously reduced. The problem of short-term activity has become striking. In the past few years the investment in agriculture by the state has been continuously on the decline: In the investment structure of 1994 investment in

agriculture was reduced from 2.8% in the previous year to 2.2%. That was only one side of the picture. What was even more serious was that the input by the farming households has also been declining. The negative effects of the unclear property rights of land have become increasingly obvious and, compounded by the comparatively low efficiency in grain production, farming households have become less enthusiastic about investing in agriculture. Driven by short-term interests, funds that should have been injected into agriculture have been drained through various channels in great amounts toward non-agricultural sectors and the cities. To make matters worse, a great number of skilled farm workers and agro-technicians have been drained from the agricultural sector.

2. The Problem of Macro-control Conforming with the Marketization of Farm Products Has Become Very Salient in Accelerating the Process of Marketization

Removal of all price controls from farm products, including grain and cotton, and the acceleration of the marketization of farm product prices is the key to the rural economic restructuring. It should be pointed out that the guiding ideology on this issue has been correct. In 1985 the state announced the abrogation of its system of planned purchase and marketing. With the coming of the 1990s the state has successively adopted quite a few measures in price reform, such as removing control over the purchasing prices of grain and edible oil, designating protective prices and directive prices for the purchase of wheat and rice, increasing the prices for the mandatory purchase of cotton, setting a ceiling price for major agricultural means of production, in addition to increasing the purchasing prices of grain and cotton under contract, etc. All these efforts have played a great role in stabilizing agricultural production, in increasing the income from agriculture and in safeguarding the initiative of the farming population.

However, the issue is by no means an isolated one, rather it is a domino situation; it is especially so as it exerts a direct impact on the interests of urban residents. Consequently, the conflict of interest between the urban and the rural areas fuelled by the purchasing and marketing of grain and cotton has become more and more striking. A farmer who has become gradually market-conscious with production and marketing oriented toward the market aims at the maximization of economic benefits. Nevertheless, the excessively rapid increase of costs in agriculture in contrast to the excessively low mandatory purchasing prices for farm products will give rise to the universal phenomena of farmers after harvest being "reluctant to sell" and "waiting for the highest bid." On the one hand, the state guides the farmers to organize production based on the needs of the market for the purpose of increasing income. On the other hand, the state has to take supplementary administrative measures to protect the mandatory production, purchasing and marketing of grain and cotton, which have comparatively low benefits but are important to the national economy and people's livelihood. When it is impossible to guarantee both at the same time the state is more concerned about how much farm produce farmers can supply to the market in order to ensure the stability of supplies to the cities. Furthermore, any act of deviation on the part of a local government intensifies the contradiction between the state and the farmers. When there is an insufficiency in the production of grain and cotton the government forces the farmers to produce more grain; when there is bumper harvest, the state generally forces down the purchasing price or even takes no further interest in it. This being the case, the farmers must take some self-protection measures, such as reducing the input into agriculture or giving up farming for business to pursue higher comparative returns.

A problem that is closely associated with the overall situation of rural economic development and also a pressing question for discussion in the deepening of rural reform is how to coordinate the interests of the urban and the rural dwellers, of the state and the farmers, with a view to making the policies of macro control more practical and the means more applicable, so as to gradually reduce or even to abandon the old methods of administrative intervention practised by the planned economy and to adopt new measures that conform to the laws of the market economy.

3. A Rather Thorny Problem is How to Face the Shift of Farm Labor Toward Non-Agricultural Occupations and Townships

Another characteristic of the restructuring of the rural economy is that the reform in the 1990s has begun to surmount the barricade that separates agriculture from industry, the rural from the urban. It is evident that rural reform has increasingly been associated with the urban reform, which has become a salient contradiction in the process of economic conversion. Examples are millions of farm laborers entering the cities to seek jobs, millions of farmers participating actively in the urban market for farm products, and farmers entering the cities to manage enterprises on a contract basis and building small townships in rural areas.

The transfer of surplus farm laborers has become a very striking issue that confronts the economy of China during the economic transition period. The basic situation of China is a large population with little land to cultivate, which results in a problem of underemployment. According to estimates, there are over 100 million surplus farm laborers now in China, and it is estimated that there will be a net increase of 6 to 7 million each year. With the adjustment of the agricultural structure and the development of agricultural modernization, the surplus farm laborers will shift toward non-farming occupations and the townships, which is a universal phenomenon in the process of industrialization experienced by many countries around the world. The transfer of surplus farm laborers to non-farming sectors is beneficial for the increase of income for farmers, especially for solving the problem of low income of farmers in underdeveloped regions, and further for narrowing the income gap between the urban and rural residents.

However, the migration of millions of rural laborers will definitely pose challenges to society. One is whether the fast increase of employment of farm labor in non-farming sectors will lead to the excessive increase of opportunity cost of agricultural production, which will push the cost of prices for farm products upwards. The other is what kind of changes in the structure of the national economy, especially in the industrial structure and the structure of towns and smaller cities, would be necessary for them to absorb such an enormous number of people. Moreover, the shift of surplus rural laborers is associated with the uneven development between different regions of China. The flow of rural laborers from agriculture to non-agricultural sectors, from rural areas to towns and small cities and from underdeveloped areas to developed areas merits in-depth studies with regard to what kind of impact such a migration will have on the equilibrium of income between different regions in China. In terms of social administration of laborer migration, the problems related to several levels of society are ones of residential permits, security, urban environment and sanitation, child-bearing, education, etc., which call for serious attention after summing up the domestic experience as well as referring to international experience.

4. A Vital Issue That Has a Bearing on the Overall Situation of Reform Is What Status Rural Reform and Development Should Have in Macro Stability

The establishment of an overall economic system calls for a stable social environment. Eighty percent of the population in China live in rural areas. Therefore, the social stability in China depends first of all upon the stability of agriculture and the rural areas. The practice of many years has proved that only by consolidating agriculture and by stabilizing rural areas can the whole nation be stabilized and the economic transformation be carried out smoothly, which in turn will ensure the sustained, rapid and sound development of the national economy. However, experience has also shown that it is very difficult to list rural development as top priority at all times in making decisions related to the macro economy of China. Under some specific circumstances a short-term equilibrium in macro economy is accomplished at the expense of the interests of the rural areas and the pace of development of rural reform. There exist some kinds of conflicts between the rural economy and macro stability, and the discrepancy between long-term objectives and short-term interests accounts for a series of difficult choices during China's economic transformation period.

Fundamentally speaking, the difficulty in coordinating the rural economy and overall equilibrium arises from the former planned economy system. In the past China stressed giving priority to the development of heavy industry. Consequently, it was inevitable that high accumulation was maintained only at the cost of low levels of income. To achieve this, it was essential to force down the price of farm products, and of raw materials for foodstuffs and most light industrial products. In this sense, the system of unified and fixed state purchase and marketing at low mandatory prices was the cornerstone of the overall planned economy. Now that rural reform has gone beyond the stage of solving the problem of food and clothing and is proceeding toward the goal of marketization, the original foundation with its mechanism of macro equilibrium will be shaken to its very roots. However, in some aspects of reform cities with dominant state-owned economies are lagging behind the rural areas dominated by non-state economies. Commerce and industry with low degrees of marketization cannot easily absorb farm products based on higher degrees of marketization. Since the mid-1980s, the state policies have been turning round and round in the maze of disequilibrium of urban and rural reform. The dilemma may be described as: By speeding up the process of marketization of farm products the urban system will suffer; by slowing down the pace of rural reform the present level of income and enthusiasm of farmers can hardly be sustained. Even more difficult is the situation in which the whole set of policy instruments that used to maintain the macro equilibrium for the former economic system has been distorted or become ineffective in the process of reform. In the transitional period of economic transition, when the contradiction of interests between the urban and the rural areas becomes prominent, the state is in a dilemma as it can neither withdraw to the original unimpaired system of centralized purchasing and marketing that segregated the urban and rural areas, nor can it take a step forward to achieve sensible adjustment through the market mechanism. The situation of "not being close to anything" poses a question with regard to how to carry out effective macro-control policies and operational means to cater to the needs of agricultural development during the transitional period from a planned economy to a market economy. The complexity of the issue resides in how to bring about macro stability and to find a solution for equilibrium in such a predicament under the constraint of the nonsynchronous process of urban and rural reform. This is the major question pending discussion that is closely related to the overall situation of reform.

III. Deepening the Economic Restructuring of Rural China in Accordance with the Objective of Accelerating the Process of Marketization

The fundamental solution to the problems related to agriculture, to the rural areas and to the rural population of China lies in accelerating and deepening reform. The rural economic restructuring of China in the 1990s is confronted with many special situations and problems. Practice in recent years has indicated that rural economic reform is in a critical period of either progression or retrogression, and the role of rural economic reform has become more and more striking in the overall situation of national economic reform.

To make a breakthrough in economic reform it is critical to aim at the acceleration of marketization and to deepen the reform of the rural land-use system in order to recreate a micro foundation for the rural market economy. On the other hand, it is essential to reform the purchasing and marketing system of grain and cotton and to establish a means of macro control that conforms to the needs of the rural market economy.

1. Deepening the Reform of the System of Rural Property Rights by Taking the Long-Term Land-Use Right as the Focal Point of Work, and Correctly Handling the Relations Between the Rural and Urban Areas

Land is the basis of the rural economy, and innovation in

designing a system of land-use right is indispensable to the deepening of rural reform. Without clearly defining the land-use right, any attempt at reform would only accomplish half the results with twice the work. Only by creatively reforming and designing the property rights of land can the enthusiasm of farmers be re-stimulated and a reliable foundation for solving other problems at the present stage in rural areas be established.

Upon the introduction of the responsibility system two major remaining problems related to land are as follows: One is the problem of equivocal relations of property rights, which adversely affects farming households in terms of the stability of policy and long-term investment expectation; the other is the small-scale farming of fragmented land, which is detrimental to the technical advancement of large-scale agriculture. Consequently, the requirement for further reform of the land system is to bring about a system that ensures long-term land-use rights for farming households through defining property rights, and establishing a land-transfer market on this basis.

In recent years some measures have been adopted in reforming the property rights system of land in China, and a series of explorations have been undertaken which have brought about tremendous progress and breakthroughs.

(1) Extending the terms of land contracts. In 1993 the Chinese government formulated a policy which stipulated that, upon the maturity of the original contract for arable land for a term of 15 years, the term of contract should be extended for another 30 years without change. To avoid frequent changes in the contracting of farmland and to prevent the operational scale of farmland from being repeatedly disintegrated piecemeal into smaller and smaller plots, a measure has been introduced to the effect that plots of land should not increase in size with the increase of population and there should be no decrease in plot size with the decrease in the birthrate. Needless to say, the extension of the term in contracting farmland will have a major impact on stabilizing and perfecting the operational system of land-use right. However, one issue pending consideration is how to genuinely realize the land-use right on a long-term or permanent

basis. The policies of the state stipulate that the land-use right for farmers will remain unchanged for 30 years, which is not as good as validating the land-use right on a long-term basis for farmers through legislation, and the significance of which lies firstly in the explicit defining and protecting, in the form of laws and decrees, the varied rights and interests of farmers on a long-term basis related to the use of land as a micro-economic unit. Land-use right may be transferred and leased by the farming household as the owner of land, and may be handed down to one's inheritors. Such a system of land-use right on a long-term basis under the protection of law will effectively prevent the land from progressive fragmentation.

(2) Paid transfer of land-use right. As early as in 1984 the Amendment to the Constitution and the Amendment to the Rules for the Management of Land stipulated that land-use right may be legally transferred. State policies in recent years have repeatedly reaffirmed that, under the prerequisite of upholding the collective ownership of land, the use of land remains unchanged, and paid land-use right according to law is permitted and encouraged with the consent of the contracting parties. However, the paid transfer of land-use right has in fact been developing rather slowly, as to date only 1% of the land-use right has been transferred and the market for land yet to develop. The circulation of land-use right in rural areas must depend upon the availability of relevant policies and the land-use right on a long term basis, in addition to the need for the formulation of a set of concrete measures and rules for the circulation of land.

(3) Scale management. As early as in the mid-1980s, China advocated that management of land on a moderate scale should be implemented in areas where conditions are suitable. In 1993 the state explicitly prescribed with regard for scale land management: In a small number of places where the secondary and tertiary industries are comparatively well developed and where most of the laborers have been transferred to the non-agricultural sectors with stable incomes, it is proper to proceed from the actual realities, fully respecting the wishes of the farmers, to carry out necessary readjustment of the contracted land for the purpose of

executing management on a moderate scale. Scale land management is closely associated with the practice of rural land-use right on a long-term basis and the effective circulation of land-use right. To carry out the management of land on the basis of efficiency requires the support of the reform of the system of land rights.

(4) The development of rural shareholding cooperatives. Rural shareholding cooperatives are another new mode of resources operation created by the farmers of China after the introduction of the household responsibility system. It integrates the characteristics and aims of both the shareholding and collective systems. It is a mode of operation in which the farmers contribute their shares on a cooperative and joint-management basis in accordance with the principle of mutually shared profits and risk. The system of shareholding cooperatives was first initiated in the mid-1980s. By the late 1980s and early 1990s the system had developed on a nationwide scale, and by 1994 the rural shareholding cooperative system covered about 10% of the nation—in some regions the rate was over 50%. The state has also formulated policies to promote this system.

At present there are mainly four forms of rural shareholding cooperative economy: the shareholding cooperative-oriented reform of collectively owned village and township enterprises, the reform of privately owned enterprises based on shareholding cooperation, shareholding cooperative reform of the original community-based collective economic organizations and the diversified specialized rural economic associations, including rural cooperatives derived from the shareholding cooperative system.

The major significance of the emergence of shareholding cooperatives lies in the major breakthrough in the reform of the rural property right system, that is, the promotion of farmland on a shareholding basis.

The so-called land on a shareholding basis means that farming households are encouraged to convert the long-term land-use right into shares to participate in various cooperative organizations, in business fields related to agricultural development, in scale operations, etc., and to obtain periodically shareholders'

211

earnings in accordance with the proportion of shares. Through introducing the form of "land on a share-holding basis" pushing forward adequate scale operations and various types of share-holding economic cooperation is a realistic choice for the transformation of the operational mode of land and for the reestablishment of the basic rural operational system. Farmers can obtain stable returns by becoming shareholders in land, which helps solve the psychological conflict of farmers described as the "nostalgia for the land" and making the land more adaptable to different situations. Consequently, the smooth circulation of land and the transfer of surplus rural laborers is achieved. At the same time, farmers possessing rights to the long-term use of land may obtain loans by mortgaging their land-use rights, thus finding investment resources for farmers.

Land-use right on a long-term basis and land on a share-holding basis are the major content and realistic choice in the in-depth reform of rural land-use rights and the major orientation for the reform of rural land property rights during the economic transition period.

2. Reforming and Improving the Means of Macro Control Based on the Objective of Accelerating the Marketization of Farm Product Prices

Since the beginning of the 1990s China has accelerated the marketization of the prices of farm products. By 1993, 98% of the counties and cities across the nation had already removed controls from the purchasing prices of grain. However, due to the ensuing rise in the market prices of grain, the government had no alternative but to resort to some administrative control measures. But because of several reversals and due to some basic problems which have not yet been straightened out, the framework of a new economic structure and operational mechanism has not yet been established. Since the beginning of 1995 China has introduced the gubernatorial responsibility system for the grain supply. All provincial governments should be totally responsible for the production, purchasing and marketing of grain, its interprovincial circulation, market management and reserves.

In bringing about the marketization of the prices of farm products one of the key problems in the transitional period of rural economic restructuring in China is how to properly exercise effective macro control. A proper solution to this problem will promote the smooth economic transition and help establish a sound economic system for the rural market economy. To this end, it is necessary to aim at accelerating the pricing marketization of farm products, at reforming the macro-control system and at improving the means of macro regulation.

—It is necessary to transform the system in which the state directly manages and monopolizes the agricultural means of production (AMP), as well as any practice that allows the manipulation of the supply of AMP and the level of pricing. Instead, it is essential to carry out the system of competitive management to ensure sufficient supplies of AMP and to stabilize prices. AMP enterprises should join the market to develop competition by transforming the mechanism based on the separation of government administration from enterprise management and on a basis of autonomous management.

—It is necessary to totally reform the system of purchasing and marketing of farm products and exercise liberalized management to ensure the direct entry of farm products into the market. It is essential to abandon the practice of purchasing by state mandatory order or by contract, and to thoroughly decontrol the output and management of farm products so as to ensure the effective formation of a market for them. It is also necessary to abandon the system of prices being set uniformly by the state to safeguard the marketization of farm product prices and to ensure that the mechanism for the price regulation of farm produce functions effectively. In addition, we need to set up a special reserve system for major farm products, which should be purchased directly from the market based on market prices. It is necessary to alter the situation of market monopoly by the state-owned departments in charge of the management of farm products and to encourage the circulation of multiple elements in multiple forms through multiple channels. It is especially necessary to encourage the farmers to directly enter the market in an organized way to participate in competitive management.

—The state policy-oriented macro-control system must be changed to totally segregate policy-oriented business from managerial business. The state reserve regulatory system of major farm products should be segregated from the present managerial department of farm products and a reserve regulatory system directly under the State Council should be established for the purpose of regulating the national farm products market in a unified way. Risk funds for major farm products should be established to cope with the shortage of major farm products arising from natural disasters, war or other calamities. A unified national market for farm products should be established as soon as possible to eliminate regional segregation and blockades, and to transform the practice of allocating and transferring farm products through state mandatory planning into one of automatic regulation through the market mechanism and to establish a new relationship based on complementarity of advantages, regulation of surpluses and shortages and regional equilibrium so as to lay a market foundation for the national policy-oriented regulation and control.

—In regulating and controlling the market for farm products the state should avoid resorting to traditional means of administration and prevent any restoration of the outdated system and policies. Fluctuations in the prices of farm products are normal in a market economy and are reflections of the law of the market. It is senseless to panic when there is some fluctuation in the market and rashly resort to administrative intervention. It is necessary to make the best use of the situation in regulating market fluctuation, mandatory measures should not be resorted to. Efforts should be made to avoid any retrogression with regard to the macro-control system and macro policy implementation.

—In the process of promoting the marketization of farm product prices, a corresponding control system for the rural macro economy should be established so as to utilize the means of economic policy to regulate and control the rural market economy. It is necessary to utilize financial policies to increase capital investment in agriculture and to strengthen the policy-oriented regulation of farm products in the market. It is necessary to resort to taxation to strengthen the protection of agriculture and the income of farmers on the one hand and to alleviate the burden on the farmers on the other. It is proper to establish a rural financial control system to use policy-oriented means for financial regulation and to ensure investment in agriculture. It is necessary to utilize rational price policies to stabilize the prices of farm products by stabilizing production. Target prices or minimum protective prices should be set to guide the prices of farm produce, to stimulate production and to raise the income levels of farmers. A futures market for farm products should be developed to establish a mechanism to ensure the stable production and marketing of farm products.

—It is necessary to formulate policies for the import and export of farm products, to display the comparative advantages of agriculture in China and to regulate the relationship between demand and supply in the domestic market for farm products.

3. Rational Coordination of the Relations Between the Urban and Rural Areas and Between Industry and Agriculture Based on the Objective of Accelerating Rural Marketization

(1) It is essential to spur urban marketization by means of rural marketization for the promotion of the coordinated development of the urban and rural economies.

In the traditional economic system, macro control by the state had generally protected the interests of the cities at the expense of the interests of the farmers. But with the unfolding of the economic restructuring in an overall manner, the contradictions between the urban and the rural economies have been greatly alleviated. In recent years, with the building of small cities and another round of migration of millions of rural laborers, pressure on the land has been eased. However, the experience of the past two years has indicated that the deep-rooted problems relating to the relationship between the urban and the rural economies have not yet been fundamentally solved. Some of the macro policies and means adopted by the government for the rural economy are still on a mandatory basis, resulting in a strong tendency favoring the cities. The establishment of a socialist market economy calls for the elimination of the division between the urban and rural areas to give impetus to the most effective utilization and allocation of rural resources and factors of production in the dynamic development of the national economy for the accomplishment of the ultimate integration of the urban and rural economies. At present, as the overall economic system is undergoing a transition from the planned economy to a market economy system, in deepening the reform of the rural economy, priority should be given to promoting the marketization of the rural economy so as to vigorously promote the development of the marketization of the urban economy. This is because:

a) Agriculture is the foundation of the stability and development of the whole national economy; without the further development of the rural economy it is impossible to create the conditions and environment for the transition of the whole economic system. But the development of the rural economy can only rely upon the overall reform of the rural economy and its marketization;

b) The adjustment of the rural industrial structure brought along by rural marketization, the transfer of rural surplus labor, the expansion of rural markets, the increase of rural purchasing power, etc., will all contribute either to the formation of a competitive situation or to the creation of opportunities for development, consequently promoting the reform of the urban economy;

c) The fundamental transition of the rural economic system will provide experience for the reform of the urban economic restructuring, which may be drawn on for the reform of the more advanced aspects of the urban economy; and

d) China still remains a traditional agricultural society, with over 80% of its population residing in the rural areas. This is a huge market, the cultivation and formation of which will be a long process. Only through accelerating the development of the rural economy can the development of the overall market economy be achieved. In spurring urban marketization through rural urbanization and promoting the coordinated development of the urban and the rural areas, attention should be paid to the following issues:

—It is necessary to eliminate the segregation between the urban and the rural economies and to establish a market for the circulation of commodities and factors of production. It is especially necessary to promote the rational mobility and effective integration of capital, labor, land, technologies, etc.

—It is necessary to reform the current administrative system of household residential registration that separates urban and rural residents, and to establish a unitary system for household registration mainly based on a unified national administration of personal IDs to allow surplus rural labor to seek employment through the labor market.

—It is essential to optimize the rural industrial structure. In vigorously developing primary industry in rural areas it is necessary to encourage the development and to give vigorous support to the rural processing industry that effectively utilizes agriculture as well as resources from rural areas to provide rational guidance to the development of VTEs and to bring about the complementary of advantages between the rural and urban industrial structures.

—It is necessary to accelerate the process of rural urbanization and to create conditions for the integration of the rural and urban economies.

(2) In accelerating the process of marketization attention should be paid to assisting and protecting the weak sectors of agriculture for the coordination of industry and agriculture and their sustained development.

In a market economy agriculture needs the assistance and protection of the government. This is also conducive to the development of industry as well as the overall development of the national economy. In developing the national economy agriculture is the parent of industrialization; should there be a shortage in the supply of farm products industrialization would be bogged down. If the foundation of agriculture is shaky it will be difficult to sustain the stable development of the overall economy.

Therefore, it is necessary to proceed from the basic national reality and to fully understand the overall significance of developing agriculture. Under no circumstances should agriculture be neglected when the economic situation is good. Judging from the overall situation of economic development, as agriculture develops and the incomes of the farmers go up, urban industrialization will have a reliable foundation and the urban market become brisk. Only thus can stagflation be prevented and the sustained development of the national economy maintained. Protection of and support for agriculture are based on the development of the role of the market mechanism, which should aim at making up the deficiencies in the market's self-regulation rather than negating or replacing the role of the market. In the coordinated development of industry and agriculture it is necessary to carry out the development strategy of industry while giving adequate support to agriculture. It is necessary to vigorously narrow down the price scissors to stabilize the price of agricultural means of production. It is also necessary to increase the investment in agriculture and exercise preferential policies for the development of agriculture.

(3) In accelerating the process of rural marketization it is necessary to establish a regional equilibrium of farm products that conforms to the conditions of the market economy through a complete mechanism. At the same time, we must push forward the development of the regional economies through displaying their comparative advantages and with essential support from the state.

The inter-regional equilibrium of major farm products of China is realized through state-planned allocation. Since rural economic restructuring started, however, the former regional equilibrium relation has not yet been fundamentally altered. Consequently, some local breakdowns in and impingements on equilibrium relations occasionally occur in the market economy, and panic transactions in wool and fiber are examples of this. Price fluctuations in 1993 and 1994 were to a great extent caused by breakdowns in traditional regional equilibriums. Serious inequilibrium exists in the regional economic development of China, especially in the development of farm products between different regions. This problem is impossible to be solved totally through the self-regulation of each region. Therefore, it is necessary to speed up the establishment of a national unified macro market and accelerate the unified mechanism of the market on a national basis. In speeding up the establishment of rural marketization it is necessary to make a thorough breakthrough in the regional equilibrium relations of farm products, to eliminate regional blockades and to get rid of regional protectionism for the purpose of establishing a unified and comprehensive macro-market on the national basis so as to lay a sound market foundation for the establishment of an effective mechanism of macro control. In the past few years the regional differences in the rural economy in China have been increasingly aggravated, and the differences in development in terms of speed between rural economies of all provinces and regions are more than double. The inequilibrium in regional development affects the further development of the rural economy. It is also detrimental to the stability of society. To tackle the regional contradictions in the rural economy and to promote the coordinated development of regional rural economies are important tasks for strengthening and improving macro control in the process of accelerating the process of rural marketization. In developing the rural economy two aspects merit our attention: One is the necessity to fully display the comparative advantages of rural resources and factors of production in the rural areas in the process of establishing a national unified market for the purpose of developing agriculture with comparative benefits; the other is that the state should give necessary support and assistance to underdeveloped regions.

(Read at *Conference on Economic and Corporate Restructuring: Experiences and Challenges of the Decade*, Maastricht, the Netherlands, September 7, 1995.)

The Establishment of a New Social Security System During China's Economic Transition

China is in the midst of a transition from a planned economy to a market economy. The establishment of a new social security system should be tailored to this transition. To this end, it is possible to establish a social security system on a reliable foundation which fully plays the role of promoting and safeguarding economic and social development. The principle for the reform of the social security system in China has already been set down. However, in-depth studies need to be carried out with regard to some specific issues of operation, and the successful experience of other countries should be taken into account.

I. Personal Accounts

In the reform of China's old-age pension insurance system it is necessary to maintain its strong point of social mutual aid while gradually perfecting the system of unified planning of retirement to counter the drawback of egalitarianism. It is desirable to introduce a system of accumulated funds for the implementation of a structural old-age pension insurance system that incorporates social mutual aid on a unified planning basis and compulsory budgetary savings. Basic social insurance under social unified planning should be based on cash collection and cash payment, and accounts should be established for both enterprise supplementary insurance and personal savings insurance. The strong incentive mechanism of the insurance money accumulated in personal accounts which are owned by the insurees will be conducive to strengthening the awareness of self-security on the part of the insurees and enhance their initiative in making the payments. It will also help the management agency to improve the quality of management and of service, thus making the old-age pension insurance system a security system characterized by a high degree of openness, supervision and restraint.

Studies show that personal old-age pension insurance money accumulated in personal accounts will be converted into supplementary endowment annuities which are calculated based on average life span and which are paid on a monthly basis until the insuree expires. In this way, supplementary endowment annuity may be mutually regulated among insurees of different life spans (should the insuree expire or emigrate before retiring, accumulated savings in the personal account of the insuree shall be paid in a lump sum to the said insureee or lineal relative or designated beneficiary). Such a practice in fact introduces the principle of social equity.

The ownership of personal accounts by individual insurees is not an ordinary property right, as it can only be obtained through specific means under specific circumstance and conditions. Apart from cases like death or emigration, the insurance money in personal accounts is converted into supplement endowment annuity upon retirement and withdrawn on a monthly basis.

It is proposed in some quarters to set up a basic insurance fund embodying the principle of rational bearing of expenses by the state, the collective and the individual. In fact, both social unified planning and personal accounts are based on different sources of fund raising and ways of providing established in accordance with the actual conditions, such as economic capability of the state, enterprise and individual. Therefore, a separate account should be set up for each, and it is not appropriate to exercise reciprocal regulation between them. In fact, basic social insurance, enterprise supplementary insurance and personal savings will gradually increase their proportions in old-age insurance and, with the development of enterprise supplementary insurance and personal savings insurance, the function of self-protection of the insuree will be greatly strengthened. The state and enterprise will no longer take all-round responsibility for old-age security.

Consequently, the burden of social security on the state and enterprises will be greatly alleviated, resulting in a gradual rationalization of the share of responsibility among the state, enterprises and individuals.

Reform of the old-age insurance system should be based on the principle that takes both the immediate and the long-term interests into account, that is, not only to persist in and perfect the advantages of social mutual aid of the current old-age pension insurance system, but also to overcome the disadvantage in the unified planning system of the "big pot"; not only to draw on and introduce the self-security mechanism of the personal account system, but also to strive to avoid the weakness of the self-security mechanism that lacks the advantage of social aid. It is necessary to incorporate the advantages of both Chinese and foreign practices on the one hand and tradition and innovation on the other to develop a new type of old-age pension insurance system that is socialized and standardized by taking both fairness and efficiency into consideration and unifying rights and duties.

II. Provision of Insurance Money

Based on the principle of unification of rights and duties, the right to receive insurance money should be linked to the duty of paying insurance premiums. The latter should be based on the salary grade. Only thus can the living standard of the retired insuree not be affected adversely by a wide margin.

Dividends should be linked to the inflation index as time progresses.

Such a practice has many advantages. For example: (1) It is a long-term incentive that reflects the principle of "reaping no more than what one has sown," which promotes the increase of labor productivity; (2) It increases the awareness of social security of employees and develops an inner drive to spur both the enterprise and individual to make full payment of insurance premiums in time; (3) Based on the mode of calculation in terms of the index of average premium payment/salary, the degree of openness will be greatly increased with regard to the operation of the old-age pension insurance system in terms of the payment of premiums and the receipt of dividends, which in turn raises higher demands on the management of social insurance and service quality, and which provides a convenient means for the public supervision of and the participation of the insurees in management; and (4) The mode of calculation based on the inflation index eliminates the impact of devaluation by inflation on old-age pensions and protects the interests of the insurees, which increases the confidence of the latter in the new system, consequently promoting the smooth implementation of the reform of the social security system.

In order to achieve efficiency while taking fairness into consideration, it is possible to further perfect the method of calculation in terms of index-averaged premium payments and salary receipts. For example, it is possible to classify index-averaged premium payments and salary receipts into several grades and to work out several different rates of payment in terms of insurance dividends, that is to divide the index-averaged premium payments and salary receipts into several portions, the higher portions receiving smaller rates of payment and the lower portions higher rates. In this way it is possible to narrow differences in the incomes of old-age pensioners resulting from the differences in salary incomes.

III. Equalization of Burden for Enterprises

The essential characteristic of social security socialization is the objective need of market economic development. Only increasing the degree of socialization of all security measures can be beneficial to the establishment of a unified market system, to strengthening the quality of social protection with regard to the capability of risk resistance and spreading, and to promoting fair inter-enterprise competition and rational mobility of the labor force. Consequently, in order to break down the barriers between enterprises of different ownership and between employees of different status, it is necessary to carry out unified rate of premium, unified base of calculation, unified measures of security and unified management. All departments under the central government, all local enterprises run by military forces and all institutions that exercise enterprise-mode management shall no longer carry on the traditional methods of "enterprises dealing with all aspects of social security" and "enterprises running communities." Instead, it is necessary to participate in social insurance on a unified basis to facilitate the establishment of a unified market system (including the labor market) and the development of the overall economy.

In the traditional social security system in China, childbirth, old age, illness and death were all taken care of by the enterprises. This was a heavy burden on the state-owned enterprises. Meanwhile, foreign-funded enterprises and private ones grew rapidly, with no such burden. However, the latter provided no protection for the long-term interests of employees. Consequently, the establishment of a new type of social security system will not only help state-owned enterprises to participate in market competition on an equal footing, but also help the foreign-funded and privately owned enterprises in their long-term stable development.

Some people have proposed that as foreign-funded and privately-run enterprises have a shorter history and a smaller burden of old-age and medical insurance, therefore, their rate of basic payment should be lower and setting a unified rate of payment is not rational. In fields like industrial accident insurance the introduction of different rates based on the rate of risk in accordance with different trades or based on the actual rate of risk of the previous year, makes firms strengthen their measures of labor protection and safety in production, leading to a consequent reduction in industrial accidents. But in fields like old-age insurance it is inadvisable to introduce different rates of premiums, as the average age of employees in each work unit in a relative sense will gradually change.

IV. Standard of Social Security

In the reform of the social security system, on the one hand enterprises and their employees argue that the rate of social insurance premium is too high and the burden is becoming too heavy, and they demand that the rate be lowered through reform; on the other hand, social security administrations hold that the rate of insurance premium is too low and can hardly meet the increasing demand for social security, and request that the rate be raised. The standard of the rate of insurance premium in an area depends not only on the actual bearing capacity of local enterprises and employees, but also on the payment of indemnities, administration cost and whether the proportions between the trio is reasonable, particularly the proportion between the dividends and the total number of local retirees. A comparison between the economic development of the country and that of Shanghai, the region with the highest degree of population aging, shows the number of retirees in 1992 in Shanghai to account for 31% of the total, and the rate of old age premium to 28.5% of the total, which included 25.5% paid by enterprises based on the total amount of wages and 3% by individuals based on the total amount of individual wages. Compared to some provinces, the number of retirees accounts for only less than 15% of the in-service staff. Calculated on per capita bases, the burden of old age is less than half of Shanghai's. If the rate were equivalent to that of Shanghai or higher, then it would be necessary to consider whether the rate of premium is on the high side.

Social security is a sort of transference payment. The standard of social security of a community depends upon the level of economic development of that region, which is at the same time constrained by the situation of population growth. In designing the level of social protection in the reform of the social security system it is only proper to adopt the calculation method that incorporates qualitative analysis and quantitative analysis through making an estimation of the development status of the local economy, population and social security by proceeding from reality to establish a rational and proper standard of social security. Especially, in introducing the reform program generally it is inadvisable to increase the financial burden of the state and the enterprises. As to the individual premium, however, it should also take the bearing capacity of the individual into account so as to gradually increase the premium from a lower level to a higher one.

In our current social security system the level of medical insurance is in sharp contrast with the level of economic development. The original free medical care and industrial accident insurance system were in fact parts of a free medical care system exclusively undertaken by the state and the enterprises. As the economy of China is still in a stage of development the exclusive free medical system that covers illness of all sorts does not conform with the actual national conditions and far exceeds the present level of economic development in China. Such a medical security system has incurred excessive expenses in the treatment of minor ailments while lacking sufficient protection for the treatment of major ones. In recent years, though some reform measures have been taken, such as medical expenses linked to personal interests, there is still a long way to go before a genuine medical insurance system is established. Proceeding from the present economic level of development, what the present stage can offer is only medical protection. Based on the insurance principle giving priority to insurance against serious ailments, it is necessary to use this part of the medical insurance fund to protect against major ailments, which is the greatest concern as well as the urgent need of the insurees.

The core of social security is economic protection. The level of social security in an area is ultimately decided by the level of economic development of that particular area, while it is also constrained by the situation of population growth in the said area. China is a big, developing country with a dual structure of industrial society and traditional agricultural society. Great differences exist in terms of regional economic development and the structure of population. It is undesirable as well as impossible to establish in a short time a unified or even singular mode of social security, or to bilaterally seek to accomplish social unified planning on a greater scale, or even on a nationwide scale. It is necessary to encourage all provinces and cities to, based on the unified principle, proceed from their actual circumstances to explore and establish a multi-tier, multi-form social security system that is conducive to the development of the market economy. In the meantime, it is necessary to see that the coordination of the social security system between different regions across the nation, between the old and new systems and between the national and international systems is realized in order to facilitate the formation of a unified market system and to meet the need for the rational mobilization of labor, for the opening up on a wider scope and for the promotion of the smooth transition between the new and the old systems and the security and unity of the society.

Rural social security in China is a major issue. At present, rural social security of a multi-tier and multi-form character should be gradually developed in places where conditions are ripe. The development of social security should proceed from the actual conditions of the rural areas of China to aim at protecting the basic livelihood of the farming population. It is necessary to persist in the principle of relying mainly on helping oneself supplemented by mutual aid, and attention should be paid to the coordination and unity of personnel of diversified categories. At the same time, other forms of insurance should be actively developed by proceeding from local conditions, such as, cooperative medical care, old-age pensions, collective mutual aid, commercial insurance, etc. As to backward and poor areas, the priority of social security should be given to social aid to ensure that the number of impoverished people is reduced as much as possible.

V. Management of Social Security

At present, the reform of the social security system in China is being unfolded and deepened vigorously and rapidly all over the nation. The accomplishment of the reform objective resides in the establishment of a scientific and effective management system.

Our research shows that major tasks in the management of social security include:

1. Vigorous promotion of the socialization of management.

The socialization of production requires the socialization of security; which in turn demands the socialization of management. Socialization is the essential characteristic of social security as well as the major goal of the reform of social security and the inner need of social security management. Therefore, it is necessary to break through the demarcation line that separates different industries and trades, different administrative grades and different components of ownerships, and between employees of different status such as cadres, workers, permanent workers, contract workers, temporary workers, seasonal workers, etc., to exercise unified premium rates based on unified base, methods and management for the purpose of realizing a unified social security management that covers the society as a whole. All enterprises and forms of labor should be regarded as equal in social security to ensure fair competition and the rational mobility of labor.

2. Realization of the separation of indirect management and micro-direct management, and the separate establishment of government functional agencies and business operation organizations. Social security is an important function of a government. Relevant leading departments at the central level, no matter what form of agency is being established, should earnestly make efforts to carry out social security supervision, planning, coordination, reform, etc. Entities that undertake the business of social security and are responsible for the collection and payment of all sorts of insurance funds should do a good job of improving the qualifications of its personnel and the quality of services. Especially, it is important to do well the management of community and its service.

3. Administration of social security should be separated from the operation of social insurance funds to ensure the safety value increment of the funds.

The macro administration department for social security is a government functional department of administration, social security business organs are non-profit institutions of public utilities, and the business organs of social insurance funds are profit-oriented enterprises. The three of them—administration, institution and enterprise—should be strictly defined as they are vastly different in nature and responsibilities. Only thus will it be possible to clearly define their responsibilities, facilitate supervision and enable them to do their duties, increase efficiency and ensure the value increment of insurance funds.

In order to do a good job of operating social insurance funds it is necessary to take the road that incorporates insurance with finance, that is, to act on the principle of incorporating security and efficiency to make investment in those projects with the best prospects of benefits and least risks. This is conducive to the economic development of the localities through indirect and multi-oriented investment modes to realize the increment of value of the insurance funds. The steps to be considered include: (1) the establishment of a social insurance bank to take special charge of the investment business of social insurance funds; (2) the use of social insurance funds to participate in the establishment of local social development banks on a joint stock basis; (3) the invitation of, through bids, non-banking financial institutions to undertake the business of operating social security funds on a commission or contract basis.

4. Establishing and perfecting supervision over social security. The soundness and effectiveness of social security in a region is a major indication of whether the social security system there has reached maturity or not.

First of all, it is necessary to establish and perfect diverse organs of supervision for social security, including boards of directors of business organizations that take care of social security operations, and commissions of foundations for old-age, medical care, unemployment and industrial accident insurance. Organs of supervision should be composed of representatives from four parties: relevant government departments, employees, enterprises and specialists concerned. Working and supervision procedures should be established to ensure proper work supervision.

Second, it is necessary to increase the degree of transparency in terms of the management of social security for the realization of openness and democracy. All job responsibilities of social security organs at all levels and the procedures for handling affairs should be clearly defined and standardized, and be subjected to the examination and supervision of the insurees. Financial statements must be published periodically to facilitate public supervision. Every insuree has the right to information about the payment of premiums, accumulation and receipt of insurance money and other relevant matters. All queries should be promptly and explicitly answered.

5. Accelerating social security legislation to promote the change of the management of social security from administration alone to management according to legal norms.

The urgent need at present is to standardize social security relations through legal forms, which are mainly: (1) the relations of rights and duties between all concerned with social security, such as the state, social security management organs, enterprises (work units) and individual insurees; (2) the relations between social security items and standards, between the establishment and regulation in terms of proportion of payment of premiums and dividends for all items; (3) the relations between establishment and regulation in terms of social security management organs, in setup, authorized strength, functions, responsibilities, expenses and job procedures; (4) collection and payment with regard to social security funds, that is, fund raising, management, payment, investment and operation (including projects, principle, distribution of interest, risk undertaking, etc.) of all social security funds, as well as the proportion of management cost to be taken from all items of income, the scope of expenditure and methods of spending; (5) the supervision relation of social security and the relation in terms of punishment in case of violation of the relevant rules and regulations.

China is a developing country, and economic development is its central task. Only by developing the economy on a high-efficiency basis can the problems of social security be genuinely solved. Therefore, in the reform of the social security system, it is necessary to correctly handle the relation between fairness and efficiency. It should be clearly understood that fairness implies justice and equal opportunity rather than "sharing from same big pot" based on egalitarianism. It is by no means permissible to implement social security that surpasses the current level of economic development. In the market economy it is essential to totally carry out the principle of "giving priority to efficiency while giving consideration to fairness."

(Read at the *International Symposium on the Comparison of Social Security Systems of Asian Countries*, in Haikou, on March 21, 1994)

China's Anti-Poverty Strategy in the Period of Economic Transition

As early as in 1945, when the United Nations was created "elimination of poverty" was written into its charter. However, in the several decades since then poverty has not only remained a problem in developing countries but has also become a problem that perplexes the entire world. In the last 20 years or so the number of people in developing countries who live under the poverty line has increased by 40%. In the 1980s the impoverished population in the world grew by 2% a year, along with worldwide steady economic growth. Now the world has a population of 1.3 billion who live under the poverty line. The Summit Meeting on Social Development convened by the United Nations in Copenhagen in 1992 had the reduction and elimination of poverty as the major topic for discussion, and set 1996 as the international year for eliminating poverty. This is historically unprecedented. However, elimination of poverty is still an arduous task.

Since 1978, when China began to implement its policy of reform and opening to the outside world, its economy has been undergoing a rapid and sustained growth. During this period China's government has been paying close attention to trying to solve the problem of poverty while making extraordinary efforts to push forward its economic development. As a result, its efforts to eliminate poverty have been repaid with great success, and the number of impoverished people in rural areas dropped from 250 million in 1978 to 70 million in 1994. Now China's government has explicitly announced its determination to make more efforts to help the poor in order to fundamentally solve the problem of the 70 million poor people with food and clothing difficulties by the year 2000.

China is now undergoing an overall transition from the traditional planned economic system to a market one, which determines that its poverty problem has not only the characteristics common to those of other developing countries but also some new characteristics of developing countries in economic transition. Though the proportion of impoverished people in its whole population is relatively small, the absolute number is still very large. And when the problem with its present impoverished people is solved there may well crop up new poverty problems with other people. Therefore, to conscientiously explore and implement an anti-poverty strategy that fits China's actual national conditions is of great relevance to its economic and social development throughout the process of economic transition.

I. Implementing an Anti-Poverty Strategy on the Premise of Maintaining Rapid and Sustained Economic Growth

An anti-poverty strategy involves many fields, such as economy, politics and society, and is an important component of China's economic and social development strategy. Due to the fact that both China's productivity and living standards are relatively low, China's anti-poverty drive is an arduous task. However, China is a developing country whose major task and fundamental objective in the next decade or so is to maintain rapid and sustained economic growth, and this will undoubtedly accelerate the process of its poverty elimination. On the other hand, as China is undergoing a profound transition from the traditional economic system towards a market one, its anti-poverty drive has taken on some new characteristics and is facing some new challenges:

First, with the development of reform, opening to the outside world and economic marketization, the economy in coastal areas in the southeast, with better natural conditions, has been booming and the material living standard of the people there has been improved to a very great extent. This has resulted in the phenomenon that the majority of the 70 million rural residents who can neither dress properly nor eat their fill are concentrated in mountainous areas, areas of barren land and other areas with poor living conditions in the central and western regions. Accordingly, it may be concluded that the seriously unbalanced regional economic development in the process of economic transition has increased the difficulty and cost of poverty reduction.

Second, with the development of market-oriented reform and in the process of rapid economic growth, the income gap has been speedily expanding and the disparity between the rich and the poor has become conspicuously great. Moreover, it is very easy for people who have just extricated themselves from poverty to become impoverished again due to some unforeseen factors such as inflation and for those people who live just above the poverty line to become worse off.

Third, competition among enterprises and employees has been intensified in the process of economic marketization. Consequently, traditional contradictions within some state-owned enterprises, such as low efficiency and redundancies, have been exacerbated, leading to a rise in unemployment. Before a new and sound social security system is established ex-employees of state firms more often than not will become the larger part of the poor in urban areas, from being a very small number in the past. And how to help the poor among urban residents is becoming an important question that merits close attention in China's social development.

China is now in a decisive period for achieving a successful economic transition and for maintaining a rapid and sustained economic growth. It is facing two arduous major tasks, both of which should be accomplished by the year 2000: One is to initially establish a socialist market economy system and the other is to fundamentally eliminate poverty in order to realize a coordinated economic and social development. Economic development and social development are in concord with each other in terms of their long-term objective but in conflict on the short-term basis. In the long run, the establishment of a market economy system is sure to be extremely beneficial for economic development. As a result, the overall national power will be enhanced, which in turn will be conducive to the ultimate elimination of poverty. In the short run, due to unequal bases and starting points for competition, increasingly intensifying competition and market norms yet to be standardized put poor areas and poor people at a disadvantage. And the already scarce capital and all kinds of other resources continuously flow to the more-developed regions. At the same time, a large number of talented people driven by aspiration for material interest go to areas where they can earn more. The experience of other countries shows that, in normal market economy conditions, the interests of poor regions and poor people are most easily neglected. Furthermore, helping the poor goes against market rules and can never be done spontaneously.

Therefore, the major issues China is facing in its anti-poverty efforts in the period of economic transition are as follows: How to correctly analyze and identify advantages and disadvantages economic marketization has brought and will bring about for elimination of poverty; what measures should be taken to make best use of advantages and to get rid of disadvantages and how to effectively reduce poverty while striving to maintain a rapid and sustained economic growth, namely, how to correctly coordinate the relationship between economic transition and social development. The first and foremost objective of China's anti-poverty strategy in the period of its economic transition should be to expedite economic growth. Only by maintaining a rapid economic growth can people's living standard and quality of life be steadily improved and can poverty be gradually eliminated. Although economic transition and rapid economic growth cannot automatically lead social development, nor can they automatically solve the social problem of poverty, they are the fundamental basis for the solution of all kinds of social problems, including poverty. Hence, we should try to accelerate the economic transition and maintain a rapid and sustained economic growth to provide a solid and reliable foundation for anti-poverty work. Only on this basis can an effective anti-poverty strategy be formulated and implemented to quickly eliminate poverty and promote social development.

II. Effectively Reducing Poverty by Coordinating the Relationship Between Regional Economies and by Realizing Balanced Development

Since 1978, when the policy of reform and opening to the outside world was adopted, great changes have taken place in China's policies on regional economic development. The first and foremost is the change of the former regional balanced development policy, which laid particular stress on economic construction in inland areas and the adoption of a development mode which inclined toward economic development in the more developed coastal areas. The government promulgated a series of reform measures to lure investment and policies toward the coastal areas. As a result, factors of production have been flowing to the southeastern coastal areas in enormous quantities propelled by comparative interests. This has strengthened the economic vitality of the southeastern coastal areas, and stimulated their economies. The rapid economic growth in a few coastal areas first of all has brought about the overall development of the whole coastal region, whose population makes up about one half of China's total. To some extent, it has also spurred the development of the central and western regions and expedited the development of China's economy as a whole.

At the same time, disparity in economic development among regions has been becoming more and more conspicuous. In the Eighth Five-Year Plan period, the annual average growth rate of China's GDP was 11.7%, that of the eastern region 16% and that of the central and western regions only 9%. Between 1990 and 1994 village and township enterprises in the eastern region developed at an annual average rate of 48%, while those in the western region grew by only 16.5%. The total output value of village and township enterprises in the eastern region was nine times as large as that of the western region. It is obvious that China's regional disparity in wealth is mainly reflected in the disparity between the eastern region and the western region and that the problem of poverty is closely related to the economic gaps between regions. At present, poor people in the central and western regions make up 93% of the total number of China's poor people, and the poor counties there make up 86% of the total number of poor counties in China. Therefore, how to coordinate regional economic development in order to effectively reduce poverty is an important topic for discussion in the period of economic transition.

However, it must be recognized that, in this period the expansion of the gap in economic development and in per-capita income between different regions is an economic and social phenomenon that cannot be completely avoided. Nevertheless, seriously unbalanced regional economic development may lead to polarization of China's population into the extremely poor and the extremely rich, which may have unfavorable social and economic consequences. Therefore, one of the most important tasks in China's anti-poverty strategy should be to accelerate economic growth in backward areas in the western region. This task involves the following five problems: The first is how to give priority to resources development and basic construction projects in the western region over the eastern region; the second is how to finance these projects; the third is how to transfer resources-based manufacturing and labor-intensive industries from the eastern region to the western region; the fourth is how to attract more foreign capital to this region; and the fifth is how to encourage the eastern region to make investments in the western region.

For quite a long period in the future unbalanced development will remain the major contradiction within China's regional economy. Although our aim is to enable all regions to develop together, this does not mean synchronous development. The disparity in economic development between regions in China is a result of many historical and contemporary factors. This is a fact economic development has to face and a situation that cannot be completely changed within a short time. If no difference in development between regions were to be tolerated the development of some regions would be constrained. In the last decade or so China's widely recognized economic accomplishments have been achieved on the principle of fully mobilizing all kinds of usable resources to enable its economy to develop as rapidly as possible, encouraging all areas which are capable of pursuing rapid economic growth to do so, accepting and tolerating a certain degree of disparity in economic development between regions and at the same time trying to limit the disparity to a stable level at which not only a rapid growth of the entire economy can be achieved but also a relative stability of economic and social order can be maintained. Therefore, there is no doubt that to differentially push forward regional economies is a realistic choice in view of China's actual conditions.

Nevertheless, it goes without saying that narrowing the economic gap between regions is an important issue in China's economic and social development. It concerns the overall situation and in some degree determines whether the present sustained, rapid and healthy economic growth and social stability can be maintained or not. It is no exaggeration to say that without the development and prosperity of the central and western regions it will be impossible to make our entire nation prosperous and powerful. Without economic rejuvenation of the central and western regions, there can be no fulfilling the historical mission of hastening the complete elimination of poverty.

Whatever argument one favors, there is no denying that it will be a long process for China to solve the problem of unbalanced regional development, to realize coordinated development of regional economies and finally to eliminate the phenomenon of the relative concentration of poor people in the central and western regions. It took the United States 50 years to basically eliminate economic disparity between regions, Germany and Japan 20 years. As a vast country with unbalanced economic and social development, it may take China longer to realize its transition from unbalanced development to balanced development, and on this basis to narrow the economic disparity between regions.

In the period of economic transition the most outstanding contradiction China's economic development is confronted with is how to carry out the principle of giving priority to efficiency and consideration to fairness at the same time in dealing with the issue of regional development. That is, how to promote the economic development of the central and western regions and narrow the disparity between regions without paying the price of constraining the development of the eastern region and on the premise of maintaining its good development momentum. To be more specific, it is a question of what necessary macro-economic regulatory measures the central government should take and what regional and industrial policies it should lay down in order to guide different regions to give full play to their respective advantages, to promote coordinated economic cooperation between different regions and to create a rational pattern of unbalanced regional development based on regional advantages and market competition. Meanwhile, a mechanism to encourage backward regions to depend on themselves for their own development should be cultivated in order to gradually eliminate the existence of poor areas and poor people.

III. Reducing Poverty Through Narrowing the Income Gap Between Rural Residents and Urban Dwellers

In China 80% of the population live in the rural areas. Therefore, China's economic basis is agriculture, its basis for social stability is in the countryside, and the development of rural areas as well as the prosperity of peasants are connected with the overall situation of China's economic development and social stability. At present, China's poor people are still concentrated in rural areas. Therefore, China's anti-poverty strategy is interwoven with the coordination of the relationship and narrowing of the economic gap between urban and rural areas. According to China's Statistics Bureau, the poverty line for China's rural areas was set in 1994 as an annual income of around RMB 440. On the basis of this, the number of poor people in rural areas dropped from 250 million in 1978 to 70 million in 1994. And the proportion of poor rural residents in the total rural population fell from 31% in 1978 to 7.8% in 1994. It should be claimed that anti-poverty work in China's rural areas has accomplished notable results. However, though rural residents' average per-capita income has been on the increase, the income gap between rural residents and urban residents has been continuously expanding. From 1978 to 1994 the ratio of China's rural residents' average net per-capita income to urban residents' average income for living expenses per capita increased from 1:2.3 to 1:2.6, and the absolute difference between the two incomes skyrocketed from RMB 182 to RMB 1,959. More worryingly, this figure is tending to increase.

In one sense, the problem of poverty in rural areas cannot be fundamentally solved at present largely because it is closely related to the traditional economic system. In China's past economic construction priority was given to the development of heavy industry. Thereupon, it was a must to maintain a high percentage of accumulation at a low income level. In order to maintain a high percentage of accumulation, wages and costs of other industries had to be kept at a low level. The key was to keep the prices of food and other agricultural products which constitute the majority of raw materials for light industry at a low level. It was for this reason that the state monopoly of purchase and marketing of farm produce at low prices was practised as the foundation for the entire traditional planned economy system. When the rural reform surpassed the stage of producing enough for the population as a whole to wear and eat properly and entered the stage of marching toward marketization, the original system, together with its macro-economic balancing mechanism, shook to its very foundations. However, the urban areas, where the state-owned economy occupied the absolutely dominant position, have lagged in reform by a dozen years behind rural areas where the non-state-owned economy is dominant. Consequently, relatively low-level marketized urban industries and commercial businesses simply have no way to smoothly absorb relatively highly marketized agricultural products. In retrospect, it is easy to see that we have been hesitating in pushing forward some reform programs due to the disparity of reform progress between urban areas and rural areas approximately since the middle of the 1980s. The main reason is that we have been facing a hard choice: If the marketization of farm produce is accelerated in order to raise rural residents' incomes, urban residents cannot bear the price hikes; if rural reform is slowed down, peasants' initiative to produce more can hardly be maintained. Under this factual constraint of the disparity in reform advance between rural and urban areas it is extremely difficult to always give priority to rural development and increase rural residents' incomes. In certain given situations, some peasants' interests have to be sacrificed and the pace of rural reforms has to be slowed down somewhat in exchange for a short-term macro-economic balance. The consistency in the long run and the conflict in the short run between peasants' interests and macro-economic stability is the root of the dilemma in making decisions on a series of issues in the period of China's economic transition. Only after this dilemma is solved in a correct manner can the anti-poverty work in rural areas be energetically pushed forward without fear of disturbance in the rear.

The key to coordination of the interest relationship between urban areas and rural areas in the period of China's economic transition is to increase rural residents' incomes and help rural residents and the countryside get rich as soon as possible. It is true that agriculture needs to make contributions to the development of industry at the initial stage of industrialization. However, historical experience has shown that we cannot afford to neglect the interests of rural residents and the countryside for too long. When urban industries have developed to a level at which they have become capable of accumulating capital for further development more of the value created in the rural areas should be retained there in order to create favorable conditions for rural development. It should be kept in mind that the average income of the bottom 20% of rural households is still very low. Among them, some households have only just raised their income levels above the poverty line, and many household incomes are very close to that line. If there are price hikes or serious natural disasters they may easily become impoverished again. Past experience has shown us that 10-20% of the households who raise their income above the poverty line risk landing in poverty again.

In the period of China's economic transition the most important task in implementing an effective anti-poverty strategy is to coordinate the relationship between rural areas and urban areas, to accelerate rural economic development and to raise the income levels of the rural residents. In this respect, topics calling for urgent study are as follows: how to prevent agriculture from shrinking; how to continuously create favorable conditions for agricultural and rural development; and how to correctly adjust the relationship between agricultural and industrial development. At present, more efforts should be made to realize equivalent transformation between industry and agriculture, and later "reverse nursing" of agriculture by industry should be materialized. In this way poverty will finally be eliminated and common prosperity in both rural and urban areas will become a fact.

IV. Reducing Poverty Through a Rational Adjustment of the Distribution of National Income

In the process of China's economic transition the traditional egalitarian distribution pattern which resulted in a lot of poverty has been broken down, and disparity in personal incomes has been increasingly expanding. In 1978 among 15 roughly defined trades employees in the trades of electricity, gas and water supply enjoyed the highest average wages, while those in the social service industries had the lowest. The absolute difference between the highest annual average wage and the lowest was RMB 458. By 1994 employees in the finance and insurance industries enjoyed the highest annual average wages, and those engaged in agriculture, forestry, animal husbandry and fisheries had the lowest. The absolute difference between the highest and lowest annual average wage was RMB 4,109 (at the current prices of that year). Among all the social strata there has cropped up a social stratum whose average income far surpasses the average income level, and the number of households whose assets are valued above RMB 1 million each amounts to 10,000. On the other hand, there are still 70 million poor people in rural areas throughout the country whose average annual income is less than RMB 500. Perhaps, the disparity in personal income in Haikou City is more expressive of this change. In 1986 the top 20% households' average income for living expenses per capita per month was RMB 114.17, that of the bottom 20% was RMB 37.56 and their ratio was 3.04:1. By the year 1995 the top 20% households' average income for living expenses per capita per month grew to RMB 1,180.78, that of the bottom 20% to RMB 211.15 and the ratio soared to 5.91:1. In the past nine years the top 20% households' average income for living expenses per capita per month in Haikou City has increased by 9.34 times, at an average annual growth rate of 29.64%; that of the bottom 20% has increased by only 4.62-fold, at an average annual growth rate of 21.5%. Obviously, the income gap between the rich and the poor is expanding.

Before the adoption of the reform policy China was poor and had an egalitarian distribution pattern, and there seemed to be no contradiction within the distribution system. In the period of economic transition people are generally paying close attention to fairness and performance measurement. This shows that the practice of the market economy is stimulating the initiative of members of society and optimizing the allocation of factors of production, including human resources. On the other hand, China's economic transition has accelerated the polarization of its population into the poor group and rich group, and unfair distribution among members of society in some areas is quite serious. Therefore, how to adjust distribution among members of society in order to reduce existing poverty and prevent new poverty from cropping up in large amounts is an important task in implementing the anti-poverty strategy in the period of economic transition. And to rationally adjust distribution among members of society, a series of issues need to be carefully studied, as follows:

The first is how to strengthen macro control of income distribution. What should be particularly stressed here is that the adjustment of income distribution should mainly depend on the leverage of financial and taxation policies to prevent income disparity from deviating from a moderate margin. In regard to the lever of taxation, the generally practiced income tax system should be fully utilized to adjust the incomes of different social strata. As for financial means, the government can make use of transfer payments to divert the wealth taken from the rich through taxation to the poor. In this way, the income gap will be narrowed and more opportunities for the betterment of the poor will be created. This kind of transfer payment includes subsidies allocated by the central government to poor areas and relief payments from both the central and local governments to poor people whose income level is below the poverty line.

The second issue is how to maintain a moderate disparity in incomes. The level of such an income gap varies from region to region and from period to period. China has a large population and limited financial capacity. The standard for moderate disparity in income mainly depends on the endurance of 40% of the households with the lowest incomes. Therefore, the ultimate objective of maintaining a moderate disparity by adjusting income distribution is to guarantee the basic living expenses for the bottom 40% of the households with the lowest incomes and their right to develop their means of livelihood. To do this, redistribution of newly added national income is far from enough. The government should provide direct financial aid to the social stratum with the lowest income, impoverished rural residents in particular. The purpose of doing this is to promote their capacity to become rich through increase of production, and not simply to give them relief payments or relief in kind.

The third issue is how to consummate the social security system. A social security system covering such schemes as old-age pension insurance, medical care benefits and unemployment insurance is a means of redistribution. As such, it should be aimed at people with low incomes. This practice is conducive to social fairness and stability. As long as the basic needs of the masses of the people are satisfied it will not matter too much how the incomes of the top social strata are distributed; the degree of disparity in their incomes can be even increased. The fourth issue is how to give equal consideration to efficiency and fairness. To guarantee the basic subsistence of the poor and their right to develop their means of livelihood, the incomes of the rich have to be adjusted by the lever of taxation. However, protecting the poor does not mean protecting the lazy. Therefore, the adjustment of the incomes of the rich through redistribution should be limited to an appropriate level at which their enterprising spirit and initiative to further develop their careers are not discouraged. To give equal consideration to both efficiency and fairness will be helpful for the elimination of poverty and realization of common prosperity.

V. Reducing Poverty Through Expansion of Employment

Unemployment and poverty are two important social and economic issues everywhere in the world. As far as China is concerned, during its profound economic transition to reduce unemployment and to expand employment constitute a brand new task of anti-poverty work.

To solve the problem of unemployment, the Chinese government has made enormous efforts. For instance, it regards it as a strategic task to develop and fully utilize human resources, and has laid down a series of relevant policies as follows: developing diversified economic elements to expand employment; adjusting the industrial structure to rationally allocate human resources; vigorously developing vocational education to improve the quality of the labor force; mobilizing the capacity and encouraging the initiative of all walks of life to create labor service enterprises; guiding in a planned way the rural surplus labor force to non-agricultural industries, encouraging inter-regional labor mobility; giving priority to the employment of women and the disabled, and so on. The implementation of all these policies has promoted expansion of employment, provided a reliable foundation for the development of the national economy and kept the unemployment rate in urban areas below 3%.

As China's population base is extremely large, its economic growth cannot yet meet the demand for full employment. Besides, the labor force is continuously increasing in large numbers, and the contradiction between a large labor supply and small labor demand will remain for a long period of time. Moreover, unbalanced employment levels between different regions and structural unemployment constitute very acute problems. In the next few years China's employment work is and will be confronted with pressures from three aspects: First, the quantity of newly added labor force will not shrink and the number of people who reach the age of employment every year will amount to 10 million; second, the surplus rural labor force which is as large as 120 million prefer other jobs to farming; and third, differential arrangements must be made as soon as possible for the placement of over 10 million redundant staff members and workers of state-owned enterprises. So it is clear that China's efforts to reduce poverty by expanding employment is facing a lot of complicated contradictions, such as:

The first is the contradiction between the speed of economic development and expansion of employment. Confronted with the increasing supply of labor, in order to alleviate the social pressure regarding employment, and for the purpose of reducing poverty caused by unemployment, China has to keep its economic growth at a high speed. However, too high a speed of economic growth will bring about other economic and social problems. At present, China's social pressure associated with employment tends to accelerate the speed of economic growth and increase the scale of basic construction investment. Therefore, how to expand employment by maintaining a rapid, sustained and healthy economic growth in the period of economic transition must be carefully studied.

The second is the contradiction between the acceleration of marketization and employment. The traditional planned economy system has resulted in a large hidden redundant labor force within state-owned enterprises. This phenomenon, which has been seriously hindering the improvement of the efficiency of state-owned enterprises, has been a hard nut to crack in the economic system reform. With the progress of the market-oriented reform more staff members and workers in state-owned enterprises will be made redundant. And the placement of this type of labor force is one of the most difficult problems to solve in the reform of state-owned enterprises. In order to invigorate state-owned enterprises painful decisions have to be made to declare bankrupt those enterprises which have been loss-making for a long time, whose assets are less than their debts and whose products have no market. Furthermore, some enterprises with low efficiency have to be sold or leased. All these reform measures will make a lot of staff members and workers unemployed. Without a sound social security system these unemployed people are sure to face the problem of poverty. Therefore, another issue calling for urgent study in the period of transition is how to help state-owned enterprises cultivate new points for growth or identify other methods of strengthening their capacity to absorb their own redundant labor forces. At the same time, the development of tertiary industry and diversified economic elements should be regarded as important measures to absorb the redundant labor force.

The third is the contradiction between the mobility of a large surplus rural labor force to cities and the limited number of available jobs in urban areas. In recent years the floating population, particularly "the tide of peasants looking for jobs in urban areas," has affected all aspects of social life. With the urban unemployment rate on the increase and the larger part of the surplus rural labor force (which is as large as over 100 million) drifting to urban areas, there is fierce competition for employment and the losers in the competition who are urban dwellers become part of the impoverished urban population. Thereupon, how to transfer and absorb the huge surplus rural labor force constitutes another difficult problem in the process of economic transition. In other words, the solution to the problem of poverty to a very large extent depends on how to transfer and make effective use of the surplus rural labor force.

Peasants' migration for jobs is closely related to the problem of unbalanced regional development. The major orientation of the mobility of the rural labor force is not simply from the countryside to rural areas or from agriculture to non-agricultural sectors but is from backward regions to more developed areas.

247

What influence this type of migration will exert on the inter-regional income balance also calls for careful study.

To implement an anti-poverty strategy in order to accelerate reduction of poverty in the period of China's economic transition is an aspect of systems engineering that requires arduous efforts in many fields. In order to keep their promise of "eliminating absolute poverty by the end of the century," the Chinese government and the Chinese people have been making unremitting efforts. For example, in order to help over 30 million young dropouts to go back to school, "Project Hope" has been launched. In order to guarantee a smooth transition of the traditional planned economy system toward a market one, the "Re-employment Project" aims at finding new jobs for the unemployed and keeping the unemployment rate below 5%. In order to help mothers who are in straitened circumstances, the China Population Welfare Foundation has developed "Happiness Project"; and in order to promote the competence of poor areas and poor people to depend on themselves for their own development, the government has announced a call to help the poor with science and technology. At the same time, it has been continuously increasing investment in education, trying to improve the quality of the population and shaping the social security system as various measures to effectively reduce poverty. We have reason to be fully confident that, with the rapid and sustained growth of its economy, China will surely be able to eliminate poverty at a rapid pace.

(Read at the *Senior Policy Forum on Social Reform and Social Development in the Asia-Pacific Region*, Haikou, February 6, 1996.)

China: Transition from Unbalanced Development to Balanced Development

I. The Chinese Economy Is Growing Rapidly but with Unbalanced Development

1. China takes the lead in adjusting regional development policy in its reform and opening to the outside world

In 1978 China began its reform and opening to the outside world, which has drawn worldwide attention. It has adjusted its regional economic development policy, putting stress on the coastal areas.

To speed up the country's modernization, the central government encourages some people, enterprises and areas to get rich first through fully developing their superiority in funds, technology, talents and geographical positions. This means that the primary beneficiaries of China's preferential policies have been the coastal regions. Five special economic zones were set up, which have taken the lead in opening 14 cities along the coast. These areas have developed their economic latent energy, importing advanced technology and attracting foreign capital energetically, and developing a market-oriented economy. Thus, production elements such as capital and talents have flowed rapidly to the southeastern coastal areas under the stimulus of profit, strengthening the regional economy. As the growth rate in the coastal areas has been over 10% for years, China has had one of the fastest economic growth rates in the world since 1978.

2. The regional preferential development policy embodies the principle of giving priority to efficiency, dictated by Chinese national conditions

The problem of regional development involves balancing efficiency and fairness. China gives priority to efficiency while giving consideration to fairness at the same time.

In China per-capita average possession of resources is very small. The resource structure is irrational and its overall quality is low. This situation dictates that China's economic development must first concentrate on raising the efficiency of resource utilization, and priority must be given to the regions with the best development environments. Of course, this policy must make sure that the poorer areas are not discriminated against. China has always implemented compensatory and encouragement policies toward the backward regions.

3. One of the main reasons why China's reforms can achieve good results is that the country is correctly dealing with the regional differences while first developing the coastal regions' economy

The coastal areas possess a good economic development foundation due to geographical, resource, climatic and historical reasons. The country's limited capital can produce good results only by being first invested in these regions, the development of which can influence the other areas.

The differences in economic development are the results of many historical and concrete factors and cannot be eradicated in a short period of time. However, the central government has tried to encourage all the regions to give full play to their advantages and promote economic cooperation so that eventually the poor parts of the country too can develop their economies.

II. Coordinating the Development Between Regions Is Crucial to China's Social and Economic Stability

1. With the rapid development of the Chinese economy, the gaps between regions, especially between the coastal areas and the inland, are becoming accentuated

A committee of the Chinese Academy of Sciences, in accordance with the World Bank's usual practice, compared the per capita GDP, which reflects the economic development of a region, and divided the country into four kinds of development areas: low income, medium and low income, medium and high income and high income. Low-income areas are those areas where the per capita GDP is 75% lower than the country's average per capita GDP; medium- and low-income areas are those areas where the per capita GDP is between 75% and 100% of the country's average per capita GDP; medium- and high-level income and high-level income areas are the areas where the per capita GDP is 100% to 150% of the country's average and even above 150%.

This can be illustrated as follows:

Table 1   Per Capita GDP for All Areas of the Country (1991)

Order	Areas	Per Capita GDP (RMB)	Percentage of National Average Level
Low-Income Areas			
1	Guizhou	890	50.6
2	Anhui	1,052	59.8
3	Guangxi	1,058	60.2
4	Gansu	1,138	64.7
5	Henan	1,141	64.9
6	Yunnan	1,147	65.2
7	Sichuan	1,180	67.1
8	Jiangxi	1,212	68.9
9	Hunan	1,280	72.8
10	Shaanxi	1,292	73.5
Medium- and Low-Income Areas			
11	Tibet	1,388	79.0
12	Ningxia	1,451	82.5
13	Inner Mongolia	1,466	83.4
14	Shanxi	1,467	83.4

251

15	Hebei	1,545	87.9
16	Hubei	1,584	90.1
17	Qinghai	1,592	90.6
18	Hainan	1,645	93.6
19	Jilin	1,718	97.7
Medium- and High-Income Areas			
20	Fujian	1,803	102.6
21	Shandong	1,876	106.7
22	Xinjiang	2,047	116.4
23	Heilongjiang	2,099	119.4
24	Jiangsu	2,143	121.9
25	Zhejiang	2,310	131.4
High-Income Areas			
26	Liaoning	2,707	154.0
27	Guangdong	2,823	160.6
28	Tianjin	3,944	224.3
29	Beijing	5,781	328.8
30	Shanghai	6,675	379.7
Average		1,758	100.0

The gaps in the average per capita GDP between the low-income and high-income areas are enormous, as can be seen from the table. Compared with relevant statistics from 1978, when the country began to open to the outside world, the gaps in the average per capita GDP have become wider. For example, in 1978 the average per capita GDP gap between Shanghai and Guizhou was RMB 2,332, and it reached RMB 5,785 in 1991. The average per capita gap between Shanghai and Guangdong Province in 1991 was RMB 3,852, while in 1978 it was RMB 2,131.

Because of the local advantageous geographical conditions and comparatively good economic foundation, the peasants in the eastern coastal areas earned an average per capita net income of RMB 1,221 in 1993, an increase of 21.8% over 1992. Among the six provinces, autonomous regions and municipalities where the growth of average per capita net income surpassed 20%, five are located in the eastern areas. They are Shanghai City, Zhejiang,

Fujian and Guangdong provinces and the Guangxi Zhuang Autonomous Region. The average per capita net income of peasants in central China was RMB 802 in 1993, an increase of 15.4% over 1992. Except for Anhui Province, whose increase surpassed 20%, and Heilongjiang Province, whose growth rate was lower than 10%, the growth rate of the other provinces was above 10%. In the western China area the peasants' per capita net income was RMB 661, an increase of 9.3% over 1992. The ratio of peasants' average per capita net income between the eastern area and the central and western area was 1:0.66:0.54 in 1993 from 1:0.69:0.66 in 1992.

Also, income gaps between residents of cities and towns exist. According to statistics, the average per capita incomes for the eastern, central and western cities in 1993 were RMB 2,878, RMB 1,886.8 and RMB 2,045.1, respectively, increases of 31.9%, 24.9% and 22.4% over 1992, respectively.

(2) The financial contracting system has encouraged the initiative of the localities to develop their economies, but at the same time weakened the macro control of the central government over the economy, which leads to even larger differences between different regions.

Since the reform and opening up started China has formalized the system reform of the distribution relations between the central government and the localities, which has gone through three phases:

In the first period, 1980-1984, the system of allowing the regions to administer their own revenues and expenditures was implemented. Except for Beijing, Shanghai and Tianjin, the country implemented the contract system in three aspects:

A. The financial scope of revenue and expenditure was divided between the central government and the localities;

B. The basic contracted revenue, expenditure, and responsibility were defined; and

C. The contracting period was changed to five years from one year for each contract.

In the second period, 1985-1987, the country's financial revenue was divided into three parts: the central government-fixed financial revenue, the local government-fixed financial revenue and the revenue shared between the central government and the localities. The basic expenditure was defined according to the local revenue, and the distribution proportion was defined by adding up the local fixed revenue and the revenue shared between the central government and the localities.

In the third period, 1988-1993, different financial contracting systems were implemented according to the situations in different regions.

The above three periods of reform played a very active role in promoting local initiatives and strengthening the local economic power by giving more autonomous financial rights, helping to solve some problems such as debt, breaking up the highly centralized financial system, and supporting price and enterprise reform.

But they also produced some new contradictions:

(1) The country's financial power is uncoordinated. The proportion of the central financial revenue has shrunk and the central government lacks the financial power to subsidize the poor regions.

Currently, in the key market economy countries the financial revenues accruing to the central government account for over 50% of the total financial revenue. But China is different. One of the main problems of the financial contracting system is that the financial revenue distribution benefits the localities, and the proportion taken by the central government is becoming less and less.

After several changes of financial system the country's revenue percentage in the GDP dropped to 16.6% in 1992 from 21.7% in 1979. The percentage of the central government's financial revenue accounted for 45.0% of the country's financial revenue in 1992, while in 1981 it was 57.6%. The country's financial deficit increased to over RMB 23.74 billion in 1992 from just over two billion in the early 1980s. With the increase in the financial deficit, the country's debt inevitably increased. At the end of 1992 the country's financial debt reached RMB 153.8 billion. With uncoordinated financial power, the central government can not give enough support to the poor regions, and its macro control has slackened.

(2) The informal system leads to unbalanced development.

(3) The regional gaps must be narrowed during the period when the economy is transformed from a planned one to a market one in order to reduce social instability.

The widening income gap is inevitable along with economic development. Some suggest that this problem should be left until the beginning of the next century, others that the problems related to the development of poor regions should be solved first, and the development between all the regions should be balanced. The former represent the regional interests, while the latter represent the interests of the poor regions.

For a big country like China, one thing that cannot be ignored, is an economic gap that can lead to an imbalance in political power. With the increasing weakening of the central financial power which can be used to realize the nation's macro-economic control, the central government's practical control over the localities will be weakened economically and politically, which will put the economy out of control and lead to political chaos. Also, the migration of large numbers of laborers will bring a series of social problems. So, the question of reducing the regional gaps must be put on the agenda during the economic transition period, creating an advantageous macro environment for the stable transition of the economy.

III. Balanced Development of the Reform and Opening Up

1. Developing the reform of the financial and taxation systems and narrowing regional gaps.

A new tax system was inaugurated on January 1, 1994. Two items of the new tax system are favorable for the central government to strengthen its macro-control ability. One is that the central government's financial percentage must be increased annually. This will gradually strengthen the central government's macro-control ability. About 80% of its financial revenue comes from value-added tax, business tax and consumption tax. The new system stipulates that 75% of value-added tax and 100% of consumption tax must be paid into the central treasury. The central government returns 30% of the extra levies to the localities and keeps 70% for itself, which greatly raises its macro-control ability.

In later economic development two elements may narrow the extant regional divergence in China. The first is that the new tax system lowers enterprises tax in the central and western regions compared to the coastal regions. This will encourage faster economic development in such areas. At the same time, the different tax levels in different areas will stimulate the flow of production elements among regions. In recent years the rapid economic development along the coast has brought the problems of over-concentration of processing enterprises and skyrocketing labor costs. There is a possibility that capital from the coastal areas will flow to the central and western areas. Since 1994, coastal enterprises have been setting up enterprises in inland provinces. And partly because of the tax reform, capital, technology and skills have been flowing to the central and western areas. Second, following the tax reform, the investment patterns of the localities in different areas will also show some divergence. With the quick economic development in the coastal areas, the central government will receive a larger tax amount from there. Though from a macro-management point of view this is necessary, the investment concept of the coastal areas will change. And the localities in the central and western areas, though they have to pay higher product taxes, the financial resources and material resources that can be used flexibly there will also be increased. Resources taxes (except for marine oil) are kept by the localities with the central government adjusting the amounts so as to narrow the income gap between regions.

2. Enlarging the transfer payment ability of the central government

The new tax system enables the central government to expand its income range and increase its income quantity, and can influence economic life by utilizing its own income and expenditure. On the other hand, it can coordinate the relationship among localities by transferring the income collected from the faster-developing economic areas to the areas with slower development. That is to say, the new tax system should form a financial distribution mechanism from the central government to the local governments. There are three main aims of transferring payment:

First, to strengthen construction of public welfare facilities in backward areas, including schools, hospitals, etc.

Second, to strengthen the construction of infrastructure. The financial income of some provinces, especially the predominantly agricultural ones, increases slowly and the financial input to infrastructure is less than elsewhere. The central government should support them by transfer payments, as the strengthening of infrastructure in such areas will create better conditions for their economic development.

Third, transfer payments help to keep people's daily lives stable in the conditions of market-oriented economic competition, thus promoting social unity.

The transfer payment system is an important viewpoint in today's market-economy public financial theory, and an important way of distinguishing the financial rights of the central government and the localities. Before its reform and opening up to the world started, China's taxation system was haphazard. In its finance and taxation system reform China used the successful experience of other market-oriented countries for reference to set up the transfer payment system and coordinate the relationship between the central government and the localities.

3. Strengthening lateral connections, opening wider and ensuring equal development opportunities

To change the resource superiority of the poor areas into a commodities superiority, market economy should be developed, lateral economic connections should be strengthened and the policy of opening to the outside world should be pursued. There are long border lines and more ports of entry in the poor areas, and such advantageous conditions should be utilized full to develop trade with periphery countries, and to import foreign capital, technology, talents and management experience. At the same time, we should actively export labor power and technology, and run joint ventures and enterprises with Chinese capital in foreign countries. Communications between eastern and western China should be strengthened. We should also encourage the prosperous provinces, cities and regions to develop enterprises in poor areas using preferential measures.

With its further opening, China is moving its development focus from special economic zones and open cities and regions to the areas along the borders and rivers, and inland provincial capitals. This will promote coordinated regional development. Of course, due to the differences in conditions, the scale of utilizing foreign capital, opening degree, and extent of pushing market reform are all different. Nevertheless, the momentum of opening up and marketization must be maintained.

4. Speeding up market reform and growing national united market to bring about a balanced regional development

In order to set up a socialist market economy China's overall economic system reform is led by the market, and this will be followed by a national united market. Full growth of varied markets is the basic condition for market economic development. Only when such resources as personnel, property, technology and capital flow freely in a united market can we distribute resources properly, and fully utilize all kinds of economic resources, develop the advantages of the regions, to bring about the maximum economic benefits. The full growth of a united market requires that the economy is not restricted by administrative subordination relations and that resources flow unconfined by administrative regions. To reach the two goals mentioned above, first, direct interference in micro-economic activity by the government should be reduced steadily. Second, the economic laws and policies in all areas should be unified. In the course of promoting the formation of the national united market the central government plays an important role.

At the moment, a big united market in China has not been formed, and enlargement of income differences between the central, western and eastern areas is inevitable. To solve the problem of income gap, the macro policy environment should be managed well. Conditions should be actively created to set up a market system with national unity, linking comparative economic advantages via the price system with comparative resources advantages. Under such a market system there is no artificial reduction or increase in prices, products and elements can flow freely, and accurate information is available for all areas to estimate and utilize their own comparative advantages. Economic development will be faster as a result of this. With this economic development, creating products and offering markets for other regions will give momentum to the latter's development. After the big national united market has been set up, the more flourishing the eastern economy is the greater the market demand in the west. Also, as the prices for resources rise, the incomes of the people in the western regions will increase too, and the problem of the big income divergence among regions will be gradually erased.

(Read at the *Workshop on Equity: Intergovernment Fiscal Relations and Development,* Australia, April 11, 1995.)

Development of China's Special Economic Zones in the Economic Transition

Fifteen years have passed since the establishment of China's first special economic zone (SEZ). Over these years the SEZs have carried out arduous explorations, resulting in good achievements and making great contributions to the country's economic system reform, opening up and economic development by adequately performing the roles of "windows," "laboratories" and "pioneers." This proves that the central government's decision to build SEZs, as initiated by Deng Xiaoping, was correct and far-sighted.

Now the development of the Chinese SEZs has come to a critical point in the present domestic and international situations. As President Jiang Zemin has demanded, the SEZs should continue to experiment to guide and hasten the establishment of the socialist market economy. The SEZs, while maintaining their own momentum through further reforms and opening up, should also make new efforts in cooperation with other parts of the country for common development and prosperity; Shenzhen and Zhuhai in particular should try to make greater contributions to the restitution of national sovereignty over Hong Kong and Macao and to the maintenance of long-term prosperity in these regions. In the present domestic and international situations, how will the SEZs align themselves with the new reality, what new development targets shall we set for them, what new advantages should they exploit, and what strategy should they follow in line with international practice? This has become a big issue affecting the Chinese reforms and opening up as a whole.

I. What New Role Will the SEZs Play in China's Reform and Opening Up in Conditions of Equal Competition?

One basic principle of the socialist market economy is equal competition. In the transformation toward a market economy various parts of the country have taken adequate steps in the forming of a nationwide economic environment of equal competition. This poses a practical problem as to whether it is still necessary to keep the original SEZs policies. In other words, what will be the new role of the SEZs in the general framework of China's reforms and opening-up course?

SEZ policy should stress greater flexibility in the reform and opening up and greater independence for business management.

The SEZs should offer exemplary guidance for the national reforms as a whole. The question now is, in the quickened national transformation towards a market economy, is this task equally as important as before, or should it be abandoned? Two things need to be clarified before answering this question. First, the transformation in China is a very long period, during which the underlying relations in terms of benefit and contradiction will be more perplexed with the deepening of the reforms so that the pioneering experiences of the SEZs will be of great help. Second, the present and future economic, social and administrative experiments, as well as the development of democracy and the legal system, on the part of the SEZs will be of exemplary importance to the nation's ongoing reforms and economic system transformation. In this sense, it can be concluded that the quickening of the national transformation toward a market economy will make the tasks of the SEZs heavier and more significant, and that, therefore, it is quite necessary, and even more pressing, to have the SEZs policies continue intact.

A starting point in the SEZs policy is to put the SEZs in a leading position to enter the world market for international equal competition. This was a basic consideration of the state from the very beginning, and it has proved to be correct, for China's opening to the outside world can only be multi-layered and the country can join its economy with that of the world only gradually. China is a large, diversified country, with different parts bearing different fruits in the course of opening up. Having established a solid foundation for opening up and endowed with regional advantages, the SEZs will serve as a good link between the inland areas and the outside world. Besides, they have been functioning as "windows" through which to observe the progress of our country's opening-up policies. In fact, foreign investors from various countries have become used to taking the SEZs as a barometer of China's policies, and any change in this respect can affect the country's image and the confidence of foreign investors.

Is it necessary to keep the SEZs, or will there be important changes in the SEZ policies when China re-enters GATT?

Chinese re-entry into GATT and joining the WTO is no negation of the existence of the SEZs, because, first, the favorable policies and the more opening-up system of the SEZs suit GATT's aim of establishing worldwide free trade by lowering duties and reducing non-tariff barriers; second, nothing in GATT treaties forbids the running of the SEZs (or free trade areas) in its member countries—the principles of non-discrimination and transparency have nothing against the SEZs; and third, there is a tendency of increase in the number of the existing 1,000 and more SEZs in the world today which are run by some full members of GATT.

Nowadays the world economy is showing a trend toward free trade and regional economic unity. The '94 Bogor Manifesto of the Asia-Pacific Organization of Economic Cooperation set the goal of free, open trade and investment in the Asia-Pacific region not later than the year 2020. The establishment of the North American Free Trade Area, and the prospect of an economic coordination area between the mainland of China, Hong Kong, Macao and Taiwan in the direction of regional economic unity, etc., are simply manifestations of this world trend. The SEZs, as advanced models in the opening China, will certainly function as a bridge to link the country with the unified big world market.

The development of the SEZs should be viewed against the world economy, and this makes us map out higher goals for the SEZs, to hasten their entry to the higher level of world competition, which is the only choice if China is to build a market economy and enter the world market at an earlier date.

Therefore, the central problem is not whether the SEZs are compatible with equal competition. In the present domestic and international situations the problem is how to identify the new role of the SEZs in the framework of China's reforms and opening up, and what ways and strategies to follow in line with international practices.

II. What Is the Influence of the SEZs on the Stability of China's Macro Economy?

Macro-economic stability is a precondition for a smooth transformation to a market economy in the country. The SEZs take the lead in the market-oriented reforms and exert influence upon the national market and macro-economic control. Therefore, an objective approach to the influence of the SEZs on the stability of China's macro economy is of great importance for the development of the SEZs themselves.

First, what is the SEZs' influence upon the national price growth? Generally, the SEZs' are not important factors in price growth in the inland areas. The SEZs have existed for over 10 years, yet there was no evidence that inflation or price hikes in the country have been caused by the SEZs. The nationwide price hikes in 1994 impacted mainly on foodstuffs, and the causes were many and various. The SEZs bore little blame in this respect. First, the grain market system reforms started by the SEZs and the coastal open areas resulted in the spread of the same reforms all over the country without triggering off food price rises. Hainan Province loosened its food price control as early as in 1990, and the prices even dropped occasionally. Second, acreage reduction over recent years in some coastal areas like Guangdong Province is admittedly responsible for food price hikes in some way, but the impact is limited. From the short-term point of view, increasing farm acreage in the SEZs and the coastal areas might ease the shortage of food and help to stabilize the food market, but from a long-term point of view it is better to let different areas choose their own industrial structures on the basis of their own resources and seek complementary advantages in accordance with the law of the market economy. Regional blockades, however, will cause prices to go up. Allowing the SEZs and the coastal areas to import some foodstuffs to balance the market prices is an additional good way to ensure the stability of the national market.

Second, what is the influence of foreign investment upon inflation? Foreign investment is of vital importance to the SEZs; without a large quantity of foreign investment development of the SEZs would be almost impossible. In contrast to the recent recession of the world economy, China's sustained high-rate development offers a very good chance for a lot of foreign investment to flow in. It is true that this is followed by a comparative increase in the supply of home and foreign currencies, thus creating a certain pressure of inflation, but one should see that foreign capital is only a small proportion in the total social investment as compared with the 60-70% directly invested by the state. Foreign investment in the SEZs had reached only 18.4% of that in the whole country by the end of 1994, and its influence on inflation was negligible. The key to macro control over foreign capital inflow lies in its restriction in speculative fields to prevent vehement economic fluctuations, whereas investment in productive fields, especially in export-oriented lines, should be greatly encouraged. The main problem of the SEZs is still how to attract more, not less, foreign investment, and this is important for the stability and development of the national macro economy.

Third, how can effective macro control be exercised in the SEZs? A market economy cannot do without effective macro control, and the SEZs are no exceptions. For a unified effective macro control is an important condition of the national macro-economic stability. Yet the point is, as the strength of macro control is measured by the advance of economic development it is necessary to allow localities to adopt different practical methods within the framework of the unified macro control. In other words, macro control in the SEZs should target their rapid economic growth. This is very important. The macro control in the SEZs should aim to contribute to the national macro control, e.g. to contribute to the state revenues with their rapid development, to cooperate in complementary advantages with the inland areas to promote inland development and national stability, and to help build a better national macro-control system through their bold experiments in reforms. In short, specific measures of macro control in the SEZs should be flexible, conducive to the SEZs' development and conducive to the ultimate goal of the central macro control. With this in view, therefore, the principal SEZ policies should be given more life rather than curtailed. Even if it is necessary to make some adjustment, a gradual process is required to prevent negative shocks.

III. What Is the Function of the SEZs in the Change from Regional Non-Equilibrium to Equilibrium in China's Development?

Now China is proceeding from regional non-equilibrium to equilibrium development. Non-equilibrium as a chronic phenomenon has incurred problems that are inviting more and more attention from various sides, and accordingly asking for re-examination of the function of the SEZs.

First, what role have the SEZs played in the non-equilibrium development of our country's economy? In the process of China's economic transformation non-equilibrium is to some extent the materialization in regional development of the efficiency priority principle and the economic growth theory, i.e. with optimal spatial distribution of limited resources, give prior development to advantageous areas for maximum results in the national economy, and then, with the strengthening of forces of these growing areas and through the conductive medium of the market economy, to radiate development in the peripheral areas. In the course of its reforms China started with weighted policies to form a series of economic growth areas in the SEZs and the coastal regions. The rapid growth of these places has shown exemplary functions and is beginning to spur economic development in other areas. Deng Xiaoping has pointed out: "Let some areas with better conditions take the first step to develop, while others grow more slowly. Then let the former bring along the latter to eventual common prosperity." The SEZs, as the first areas to develop, have now begun to bring along the inland areas, and this function is expected to be more and more prominent in the coming days. This is good for the further development of the SEZs, good for the principle of "priority of efficiency with maintenance of fairness and equality" and good for solving the problems arising from the non-equilibrium development in our country. This is the most fundamental point to be grasped in examining the role of the SEZs.

Second, what function will the SEZs have in the building of a unified national big market? In the progress from non-equilibrium to equilibrium development of the Chinese economy it is important to break regional blockades so as to build a unified national big market, and to strengthen inter-regional economic links and cooperation. A unified big market will facilitate the free flow of products and factors of production so as to achieve an optimal distribution of resources and to give full play to the comparative advantages of various regions. From a complementary angle the SEZs at a certain stage of development will have to undergo adjustment in industrial structure by means of substitution, upgrading or transfer to places of low cost and rich resources. In the building of a unified big market both the SEZs and the inland areas will find themselves in complementary positions toward each other. This will be beneficial for the inland areas, for there will be an inflow of capital and management personnel from the SEZs, closer cooperation with the SEZs and a quickening of the pace of entry to the world market. This complementarity will become more prominent and stronger with the building of the unified national big market. The further the SEZs develop, the greater their demand for the resources and markets of the western part of China, and the same is true with the inland's needs for capital, technology, management and international market information from the SEZs. Therefore, in the building of the unified big market the SEZs and the inland areas will increasingly turn out to be mutually-dependent cooperators rather than conflicting rivals.

Further growth of the SEZs will also contribute to the inland development through other channels, e.g. turning over revenues to the central government, part of which will eventually go to local construction in the inland areas; forming economic links with these areas to guide, help and bring them along; and offering to aid or train personnel for their development. Naturally, with the growth of the Chinese regional economy it will be possible for the inland regions to set up various special economic areas of their own, like Shanghai's Pudong Development Area and the Tianjin Economic and Technical Development Area. The emergence of these special zones will add to the economic ties between the SEZs and the non-SEZ areas.

IV. Aligning the SEZs with a New Target of Development in Line with International Practices, and How to Hit This Target

No doubt, further development of China's SEZs should be carried out in line with international practice. Special economic areas in foreign countries, or free trade areas as they are sometimes called, usually take the form of non-tariff zones under customs supervision. With China's imminent re-entry to GATT, accompanied by a more extensive opening up of the country, the SEZs should find a new target of development in accordance with international practice, so as to maintain and strengthen their positive functions outside tariff boundaries, though when to begin is another question.

The five SEZs are ready for the shift outside tariffs. The SEZs have the advantages that they are nearer to Hong Kong,

Macao, Taiwan and Southeast Asian regions, and so find it easy to join the international market; they have better infrastructure facilities for life and production as a result of years of construction and a solid industrial foundation with modern electronics, textiles, light industry, mechanics, chemicals, building materials and food processing as the mainstays. And finally, they have comparatively mature legal, management, resource utility and market development systems.

Further development of the SEZs in line with international practices should be of different modes. There are different modes of special economic areas in the world today, like free harbors, free trade zones, export processing areas, and science and technology parks, to name but a few. Which mode to choose depends on the characteristics and practical conditions of the SEZs in our country. Each of the five SEZs has its own features and advantages.

There will be a transformational process toward the new target, and efforts should be made to bring the SEZs closer to the standards of outside-tariff SEZs.

For this purpose the SEZs should quicken their pace of reform to achieve a thorough economy system transformation. Based on their own advantages, existing or potential, the SEZs should also try to raise their competitiveness to a higher level and create new advantages of their own. For example, Hainan should make the best use of its resources to develop a comprehensive economy of tropical agriculture, tourism and processing industries, while Shenzhen should concentrate on export processing on the basis of its established industrial system. The outside-tariff SEZs will all join the world economy in the end. At the present stage, however, Shenzhen and Zhuhai should forge closer links with Hong Kong and Macao for economic unity. Xiamen should pursue ties with Taiwan, Hainan with Southeast Asia, and Shantou with overseas Chinese business people.

Of course such questions as what new target to set for the SEZs, when to set it and how to reach it involve major decision making and are dependent on the judgment and determination of the policymakers. Now, the SEZs in China have come to a critical point of advance or retreat. Our determination is not to retreat but to advance, and not to dampen but enliven the SEZ policies.

(Published in *the Road of China's Reform*, October 1, 1995)

The Status and Role of China's Special Economic Zones in the New Situation

I. New Role for the SEZs

(1) In the new pattern of nationwide reform and opening up, the mission of experimentation delegated to the SEZs is even more challenging and demanding. Through the explorations of the past 15 years the SEZs have contributed much positive experience in several aspects with regard to the reform and opening up, and to the establishment and development of the market economy. They should fully utilize their advantages as pioneers in restructuring and carry out in-depth explorations for the national reform and opening up, and the growth of the market economy so as to contribute fresh experience and to play better leading roles as "pace setters." SEZs should be pioneers for the whole country in broadening its scope of opening up and approaching internationalization.

(2) SEZs play a significant role in linking the coastal with the inland regions, promoting the balance in regional development and realizing the equilibrium in the national macro economy. The development of the SEZs and that of the inland regions do not constitute a contradictory relationship, rather there are relations of reciprocal promotion. The development of the SEZs has already made important contributions to the development of the inland areas. Yu Guangyuan has stressed that it is essential to overcome erroneous ways of thinking, that is, to unduly overrate the difference between the eastern part of China and the western part. The development of the SEZs has played the role of assisting rather than counteracting the interior regions. The further development of the SEZs is the only way for the development of other areas to be spurred on. It is imperative to solve the

problem of disproportionate development between the eastern regions and the western ones. However it is by no means wise to develop the western regions at the expense of the SEZs. At the same time, the SEZs will also make greater contributions in bringing about a national macro-economic balance, such as turning over more and more profits to the central financial authorities, making more and more investment in interior provinces and training and dispatching more and more professionals there.

(3) In the reunification of the country the role that the SEZs play cannot be played by any other regions; the SEZs are in the front line in the reunification of the country. The two SEZs of Shenzhen and Zhuhai will be integrated into a close joint economic entity upon the return of Hong Kong and Macao to China, and the Xiamen SEZ will play an ever-increasing role in developing trade and contacts across the Taiwan Straits.

II. In the New Situation It is Necessary for the SEZs to Base Themselves on Reality and Strive for New Heights

1. It is necessary for the SEZs to reach new heights and develop further through deepening the reform and expanding the scope of opening up

(1) The basic SEZ policy is that the reform of the SEZs should have greater flexibility. The development of the SEZs in future requires that they carry out active explorations as advanced models. Some people have pointed out that the survival of the SEZs resides in whether or not they pioneer the reform experiments.

(2) Through over a decade of reform, the SEZs have already established the primary framework for a socialist market economy. However, a considerable discrepancy still exists between the current system of SEZs and the established practice of the world market economy. The reform already carried out in the SEZs is only an initial restructuring; to take new steps in reform requires that the SEZs intensify the reform in depth and dynamics,

endeavor to solve the deep-rooted contradictions and problems and spur the complete transformation to the new system.

(3) The mission of reform for the SEZs in future centers on the following guidelines: Carrying out in-depth reform in the economic system, such as by accelerating the establishment of a modern enterprise system, speeding up the process of the cultivation and development of the market system, expediting the conversion of governmental functions and stepping up participation in international economic cooperation so as to dovetail with international practice. At the same time, it is necessary to quicken the pace of administrative reform, strengthen the construction of the democratic and legal systems and carry out social reform.

2. Each SEZ should display its respective advantages based on specific different situations and requirements

(1) All SEZs have their own distinctive situations and characteristics. For instance, some SEZs already possess good economic foundations and industrial foundations, while other SEZs have rather weak economic foundations. Some SEZs have resources advantages, while others have location advantages. All SEZs have their own universality and individuality. Therefore it is necessary to focus on the individual characteristics of each SEZ to allow it to display its distinctive advantages by developing the strong points and minimizing the weak points.

(2) Each SEZ should display its own industrial advantages. In accordance with the local conditions and characteristics, it is necessary for each SEZ to set its own goal of industrial development, adjust its industrial structure and provide guidance to industrial development as a whole. It is necessary to develop superior industry and to speed up the process of the upgrading of industry and to advance technology- and capital-intensive industries so as to strengthen competitiveness in the international market.

3. In winning new advantages for SEZs it is necessary to adapt to the need for further development as required by the macro-economic policy so as to develop new propulsion

(1) Fundamentally speaking, the development of SEZs over the past ten years is attributed to the special preferential policies and regional autonomous power granted by the state to the SEZs based on the policy of macro economy and overall economic framework. For the further development of SEZs, it is still necessary to depend on the support from the state in terms of macro-economic policy and overall economic framework so as to guarantee that SEZs can win new advantages.

(2) It is necessary to give the local government more decision-making power in terms of macro-economic system, with the prerequisite of no change in the existing fundamental policies.

4. To gain new advantages SEZs should strengthen the construction of the basic environment

Through strengthening basic infrastructure construction, it is necessary to improve the investment environment and strengthen SEZs' power to attract foreign capital.

III. It Is Necessary to Carry Out Research and Follow International Experience to Promote the Transition of SEZs in China

(1) The economic zones of different types of all countries and regions are the products of global economic development and their many successful experiences merit our study and assimilation. The economic zones around the world have common characteristics and established international usages, such as the establishment of free ports, free trade zones, etc. They are all within the national territory but outside customs boundaries. For China's SEZs it is necessary to proceed from the reality of the country and to make an earnest study of international practice and of the experiences related to the development of economic zones around the world.

(2) The economic zones around the world have their common characteristics as well as their respective modes. For instance, there are free ports, free trade zones, export processing zones,

science and technology areas, etc. China's SEZs should make a study of the different modes of economic zones around the world and create China's own mode based on the country's actual conditions.

(3) It is necessary to pay attention to the study of the liberalization of world trade and global regional economic integration as well as the opportunities and challenges which face China's SEZs. China should seize the opportunity and adopt more liberal policies, and should accelerate the process of adapting to the needs of global economic integration so as to dovetail with the international economy as soon as possible.

(Read at the closing meeting of the *International Symposium Development in China's Special Economic Zones*, Haikou, April 14, 1995.)

China's Economic Transition and Economic Cooperation in the Asia-Pacific Region

The economic rise of the Asia-Pacific region creates important international conditions for the sustained growth of China's economy, which, in turn, is also an important factor in economic growth in the Asia-Pacific region.

The reform and opening-up policies have brought about tremendous changes in China. They constitute two of the most important factors in China's march forward to the world and for the strengthening of economic cooperation in the Asia-Pacific region. Therefore, we must attach great importance to China's reform and opening-up policies when we conduct in-depth research on how to further promote the economic cooperation between China and other parts of the Asia-Pacific region. Nowadays, many developing countries in the region are facing the pressing issues of how to accelerate their economic development while accelerating market-oriented reform and implementing opening policies. Therefore, China's acceleration of its reform and widening of its opening-up will play an important role in the promotion of economic cooperation in the region. At the same time, the general development trend of the Asia-Pacific economies will speed up China's pace of reform and opening up. At present, China is at a key stage in its economic transition and is making even greater efforts to promote its reform and opening up. This will have an important influence on economic cooperation in the Asia-Pacific region.

I. Evaluating the Importance of the Acceleration of China's Market-oriented Reform on Economic Cooperation in the Asia-Pacific Region

The initial development of China's market economy has created very important and favorable conditions for developing economic cooperation with other parts of the Asia-Pacific region. Meanwhile, we have to be aware that China is still confronted with a series of major problems to be solved in the period of its economic transition.

—Promoting the participation of China's enterprises in economic cooperation and competition in the Asia-Pacific region while strategically restructuring the national economy. To accelerate the reform of state-owned enterprises will not only bring the leading role of the national economy into full play but will also effectively attract foreign investment, which will in turn facilitate the adjustment of China's economic structure and strengthen the cooperation and competitiveness of China's enterprises with enterprises of other places in the region.

—Integrating China's market with the Asia-Pacific regional market by establishing an open and unified national market system with fair competition. Liberalization of trade and investment depends upon the degree of marketization as well as the size of the target market. The size of China's market has a great attraction for foreign investors. Nevertheless, to speed up the realization of fair competition in the process of setting up the financial market, commodity market and other markets in accordance with the actual economic development is of great significance for promoting economic cooperation between China and other parts of the Asia-Pacific region.

—Maintaining China's macro-economic stability while accelerating its macro-economic system reform in order to provide the most important economic conditions for China's economic cooperation with the Asia-Pacific region. In order to avoid macro-economic ups and downs or disorders in the period of economic transition, the most important thing is to accelerate the reform of the macro-economic system and to integrate organically market mechanisms with macro-economic regulations. It is in this respect that we are still facing a rather tough task.

Developing countries, including countries with transitional economies, in the Asia-Pacific region constitute the main body of the economic cooperation in this region. To promote the market-oriented reform of these countries is very important for maintaining sustained economic growth in the region. It is in this sense that we can say that without economic reform and opening up there would be no sustained economic growth in the region. And it can be predicted that further development of the market-oriented reform in this region will greatly enhance economic cooperation, to which China's market-oriented reform in particular will make its due contributions.

II. Judging the Importance of the Role of China's Opening-up to the Promotion of Economic Cooperation in the Asia-Pacific Region

Modern economies are open economies. China's economic opening up has promoted economic cooperation in the Asia-Pacific region. At the same time, it has also intensified the economic competition in this region. At present, however, how to expand and upgrade China's opening up to the outside world constitutes a very important issue.

—Evaluating the role of China's regional opening up in promoting economic cooperation in the Asia-Pacific region. Being a big country with rather unbalanced economic development, China has adopted a region-by-region and stage-by-stage approach to its opening up. In order to adapt to the trend of economic regionalization and conglomeration in the Asia-Pacific region, China's coastal and border areas have taken the lead in participating in the economic cooperation in this region, which has played and is still playing an important role both in facilitating China's overall opening up and in promoting the economic cooperation in Asia-Pacific region as a whole. Therefore, in view of its particular national conditions, China should continue to permit and encourage its coastal and border areas to further open to the outside world so as to enable them to play even better roles in this respect.

—Evaluating the unique role of the SEZs in promoting China's participation in economic cooperation in the Asia-pacific region. In the past decade or so, China's SEZs have played an important role in pushing forward China's opening to the outside world. In consideration of the prevailing trend of liberalization of trade and investment in the Asia-Pacific region, China should enhance its SEZs' role of bridging and linking its economic cooperation with other economies in the region. For instance, when conditions mature some SEZs can be built up into free trade zones. As such, they will be able to carry out economic cooperation with other areas in the Asia-Pacific region and take the lead in participating in Asia-Pacific regional economic integration. Some SEZs can develop closer economic and trade relations with Hong Kong and Taiwan and make greater contributions to the economic prosperity and stability of Hong Kong as well as the promotion of economic cooperation between the mainland of China and Taiwan. SEZs have a significant and indispensable role to play in promoting China's economic cooperation with Hong Kong, Macao and Taiwan as well as in facilitating the formation of a grand South-China economic ring. Therefore, the position and importance of SEZs in promoting China's economic cooperation with the region can hardly be over-emphasized.

—The importance of foreign investment policies in promoting China's economic cooperation with other parts of the Asia-Pacific region. Most of the foreign investment flowing into China is from the Asia-pacific region. Therefore, China's policies concerning foreign investment have a very important impact on its economic cooperation with other parts of this region, as well as on the progress of its own economic growth. Therefore, in the period of its economic transition, China should try to keep its foreign investment policies as stable as possible and create the conditions to enable it to give the same treatment to foreign investors as is extended to Chinese nationals. In order to adapt to the general trend of the economic development in the Asia-Pacific region, China has taken a series of important measures to expand its opening to the outside world, such as greatly reducing its customs tariffs, gradually opening its markets and upgrading the liberalization of foreign trade. Undoubtedly, the further expansion of its opening to the outside world will make very important contributions to the promotion of economic cooperation in the Asia-Pacific region.

III. Promoting Economic Cooperation in the Asia-Pacific Region Through International Exchanges in Market-oriented Reform and Economic and Social Development Policies

Many developing countries in the Asia-Pacific region, while undergoing rapid economic growth, are confronted with a series of new problems in their social and economic development. The solution to these problems requires that these countries should strengthen their exchanges in market-oriented reform and their economic and social development policies. Their learning from and drawing on each other's experiences in market-oriented reform and effective social and economic policies are important factors for the promotion of economic cooperation in the Asia-Pacific region.

The current reform in countries with transitional economies in the Asia-pacific region has an inestimable role to play in this regard. Therefore, to push ahead with exchanges and cooperation between these countries in economic reform is extremely important not only for the economic growth of countries with transitional economies but also for economic cooperation in the Asia-Pacific region. Government officials at ministerial level from nine Asian countries with transitional economies have proposed establishing a "cooperation network of Asian countries with transitional economies" so as to strengthen exchanges and cooperation between them in economic reform. They also suggested that the center of the network be established in China.

China's policy of reform and opening to the outside world first advocated by Deng Xiaoping is both a driving force for China's economic development and an important foundation for promoting China's economic cooperation with other parts of the Asia-Pacific region. Summing up China's successful experience in its reform and opening to the outside world and quickening its pace is very important not only for China's further social and economic development but also for economic cooperation in the Asia-Pacific region as a whole.

(Read at the *International Symposium on the Pacific and China,* Haikou, May 3, 1996.)

Economic Transition and the Formation and Development of the Chinese Economic Coordination System

As China's opening up and reform continue to develop and the economic links between the mainland, Hong Kong, Macao and Taiwan further strengthen, the conception of the formation of a Chinese economic coordination system between the mainland and Hong Kong, Macao and Taiwan has gained acceptance and a common understanding has been reached among an increasing number of specialists and academics in line with the trend toward world economic integration, regionalization and grouping.

Since it is a system, all parties to it should be linked together, so that they can influence, stimulate and coordinate with each other. It should have a certain amount of compactness, and considerable scale and harmony as an economic coordinating system, with its own path, forms and methods of coordination.

This economic coordination system has many layers. The first one is coordination of bilateral or multilateral trade and investment systems, such as bilateral or multilateral trade coordination plans, industrial coordination plans and industrial cooperation agreements. This kind of coordination can be launched by related enterprises or formed by non-governmental bodies. Cooperation plans can be worked out among enterprises in different regions on a competitive basis. They can take the form of cooperation agreements among enterprise groups or coordination plans embracing an entire industry or related industries.

The second layer involves bilateral or multilateral industrial policy and structure coordination and harmonization on the basis of a market economy, including industrial division of labor and coordination, readjustment of investment structure and coordination of trade policy. This kind of policy coordination and harmonization cannot be accomplished by enterprises alone. They must get help from civil bodies that have official backing or from semi-official organizations with the participation of enterprises.

The third layer involves the exchange and coordination of bilateral or multilateral overall long-term development strategy and tactics. It can be accomplished only by official or semi-official organizations or with the help of civil bodies having official backing.

Viewed from the general trend in the development of the world economy and the present state of regional economic development, the main basis for the strengthening of regional economic cooperation is the principles and mechanism of the market economy. This is because, first, the basis of economic coordination is built on economic supplementary relations formed during competition. If there is no competition there can be no cooperation. Economic cooperation can only be promoted in conditions of competition, so that the advantage of the one can supplement that of the other, and vice versa. Second, to turn the advantages of all parties into relations of mutual supplement, an important basis is the market economy mechanism. In the condition of the existence of basically different economic systems, no large-scale economic cooperation relation can really be established. Hong Kong has instituted a highly open market economy mode. An effective market economy mechanism has been formed in Taiwan over the past few decades. The mainland of China is at present accelerating her transition from a planned economy to a market economy. The past 15 years have witnessed great success in China's economic restructuring and opening up. Meanwhile, due to the policy of the Chinese government of "one country, two systems," the problem of returning Hong Kong and Macao to Chinese sovereignty has been solved. For Taiwan "peaceful unification and one country, two systems" have also laid the foundation of gradual relaxation and improvement of relations on both sides of the Taiwan Straits. Consequently relations of economic cooperation between the mainland and Hong Kong, Macao and Taiwan have become vigorous. Manufacturing industries in

Hong Kong and Taiwan, in particular, have invested on a large scale in southern China. There has gradually emerged a type of coordination for systematic trans-regional manufacturing division of labor. Thus an embryonic Chinese economic coordination system has been formed between the mainland (especially the coastal regions of south China), Hong Kong, Macao and Taiwan. Since 1992 the Chinese government has affirmed the restructuring of the socialist market economy as its reform target, laying the foundation for forming a unified economic system. A mutual economic operating mechanism will be gradually linked up among the participants, which will remove the biggest barriers to the establishment of the Chinese economic coordination system. It should be pointed out that the affirmation of this reform target has deep and far-reaching significance for the economic cooperation and development between the mainland and Hong Kong, Macao and Taiwan.

At present, the mainland of China is stepping up its pace of reform. Starting from the reform of the property right system, a modern enterprise system is being established at great speed. Also, starting from the enforcement of the new taxation system and reform of the banking and investment systems, a macro readjustment and control system is being set up geared to the market economy. With the reform of land use and the setting up of a rural shareholding cooperative economy as priorities, rural reform is getting under way at accelerating speed. A comparatively complete market mechanism is being set up with the central theme of developing the market for the means of production. Great efforts are being made to push forward the reform of the social security system in compliance with the requirements of the market economy. A framework for all-round openness is being consolidated and developed, with more regions being opened up, foreign trade accelerated, and foreign capital and technology attracted to China. The competitive capacity of the Chinese national economy in the international market is being enhanced. All these reform measures will undoubtedly stimulate the formation and development of a Chinese economic coordination system in an effective way.

It is predictable that following the accelerated growth of the mainland market economy, various reform and opening-up measures will become more conducive to the development of economic exchanges and cooperation between the mainland and Hong Kong, Macao and Taiwan, including investment, trade, technology, management and scientific research, as well as coordination and cooperation in production, operations and services. This will be facilitated by the return to Chinese sovereignty of Hong Kong in 1997 and Macao in 1999. In fact, a type of common market may come into existence, but, as to what level and stage the economic coordination system will assume depends on the joint efforts of the Chinese people on both sides of the Taiwan Straits.

For the moment and for some time to come the Chinese economic coordination system will play a big role in the process of accelerated establishment of a socialist market economy on the mainland. There are many things that we can do, but the most important tasks are as the follows.

I. Promote Competition and Cooperation of Enterprises on the Mainland and Taiwan as the Main Body of the Chinese Economic Coordination System

The Chinese economic coordination system will have to undergo different phases and levels of development—from the preliminary to the mature and well developed stages. Due to certain qualitative changes twists and turns may take place throughout the course of development. But the course itself is unchangeable because no one can alter the major trend of strengthening competition and cooperation among enterprises.

Viewed from the existing basis of economic exchanges and cooperation between the mainland, Hong Kong, Macao and Taiwan and from the angle of actual possibilities, the Chinese economic coordination system is likely to be formed in the near future among enterprises through directly signing coordination plans, or comparatively long-term systematic coordination can be formed among enterprises with considerable scale initiated by civil bodies or semi-official bodies with the participation of enterprises. Such an economic coordination system is preliminary and low-leveled. But it can soon push forward to a high-level development. The preliminary coordination system will easily and quickly be developed to high-level coordination due to its superior division of labor and cooperation within the system, and strengthened external competitive ability.

Enterprises will be the mainstay of the Chinese economic coordination system in the course both of its formation and its development after formation. The practice in the past decade or so in economic exchanges and cooperation between the mainland and Hong Kong, Macao and Taiwan demonstrates that the cooperation of enterprises has all along played an important role. Enterprise cooperation possesses the features of the civilian type, and is scattered and local in nature. In business operations the enterprises mainly devote themselves to trade and direct investment. Investment takes the form of joint venture, cooperation, sole investment, contracted joint operation and area development. Investment fields originally covered processing and manufacturing industry, and have been extended to infrastructure, basic industry and teriary industry. Obviously the degree, scale, period, form and validity of cooperation between the mainland and Hong Kong, Macao and Taiwan directly influence the formation and establishment of the Chinese economic coordination systems.

There is a sound basis for further cooperation between enterprises on the mainland, and in Hong Kong, Macao and Taiwan.

(1) From 1979 to the first half of 1993 China approved a total of 134,000 foreign-invested enterprises, with an actual investment of 43.75 billion U.S. dollars. Among these, Hong Kong and Macao investment came to 70%. The actual investment by Taiwan enterprises reached around 7%. Meanwhile, about 80% of manufacturing industry in Hong Kong has moved to the mainland. In particular, Hong Kong businessmen have moved to the coastal areas of south China, investing and setting up factories there. A total of over 1,000 Taiwan enterprises have invested on the mainland, forming a trans-regional division of labor. Over 1,000

mainland enterprises have invested in Hong Kong. By the end of 1991 their investment amounted to 16 billion U.S. dollars. In particular, in 1992, when China stepped up its pace of reform and opening up, affirming the market economy as her economic goal, a tendency arose for strengthening cooperation between the mainland and Hong Kong, Macao and Taiwan. In the meantime, Hong Kong, Macao and Taiwan investment on the mainland became large in scale, and extensive in scope. In addition, the periods of cooperation were longer. On the existing basis of cooperation there will be a new leap forward in cooperation between the mainland and Hong Kong Macao and Taiwan.

(2) There is a strong desire to push forward the cooperation based between enterprises on the mainland, and in Hong Kong, Macao and Taiwan for economic interest. First, the enterprises possess advantages with which to supplement each other economically. For instance, enterprises in Hong Kong, Macao and Taiwan have advanced scientific and technical as well as management experiences. As an international financial center, Hong Kong has advanced foreign marketing and financial systems, and Taiwan has a big foreign exchange reserve. All these are urgently required by the development of mainland enterprises. The mainland has considerable advantages in resources, raw materials and labor, as well as land. These are needed by Hong Kong, Macao and Taiwan enterprises. The integration of mutual advantages will form an ideal economic mutual supplementary relationship. Second, Hong Kong, Macao and Taiwan at present face the problem of transfer of industrial structure. They are in need of extensive development of knowledge- and technology-intensive industries. By the transfer of labor-intensive industries to the mainland there will be an industrial upgrading in Hong Kong, Macao and Taiwan. Third, in the new situation of regionalization and economic groupings, and as trade protectionism becomes rife, enterprises face intensified international competition and the challenge and pressure of the dwindling international markets. This leads them to focus on the mainland market, seeking cooperation and coordination with enterprises on the mainland to cope with the changes in the world economic situation. Fourth, due to

historical, cultural, language and geographical factors as well as the improvement of the economic conditions on the mainland, particularly in the coastal areas of south China, adequate conditions are in place for closer cooperation between enterprises on the mainland and those in Hong Kong, Macao and Taiwan.

Cooperation among enterprises is linked to competition among them. In a market economy there is first and foremost a competitive relationship among enterprises; the efficient ones survive and the inefficient ones drop out of the race. This is a law of nature in market competition. For the sake of survival and development, enterprises seek competitive superiority by means of a certain amount of cooperation. Competition leads to cooperation. Cooperation promotes competition. By this means enterprises push each other forward, and thus they grow and develop continuously. This process promotes the development of the economy.

Naturally there is a competitive relationship between enterprises on the mainland and those in Hong Kong, Macao and Taiwan. This kind of competition will promote cooperation among them. By using their advantages and supplementing each other's deficiencies, international competitiveness can be enhanced. At the same time, this kind of competition can help mainland enterprises, particularly state-owned enterprises, to free themselves from the shackles of the traditional economy and adapt themselves to the demands of the market economy, to be linked to the modern market operating mechanism and get onto the track of international practice. The active launching of competition and cooperation among enterprises on the mainland and in Hong Kong, Macao and Taiwan will in the end promote the formation and development of a Chinese economic coordination system.

—On the mainland the reform of state-owned enterprises must be carried out in depth and a modern enterprise system must be quickly set up so that such firms can operate independently, be responsible for their own profits and losses, be self-restraint and develop with their own plans. In this way they will have both the external conditions and internal ability to cooperate and compete with their counterparts in Hong Kong, Macao and Taiwan. State firms will thus become the main body in the formation and development of the Chinese economic coordination system. A share-holding system must be actively implemented to promote cooperation between enterprises on the mainland and in Hong Kong, Macao and Taiwan. This will be conducive to attracting capital from Hong Kong, Macao and Taiwan to the mainland, transforming the operating mechanism of state firms on the mainland, carrying out mass social production with specialized coordination, as well as concentrating technical forces and organizing technical cooperation.

—Measures should be adopted to encourage and actively promote the combination and coordination of enterprises on the mainland with those in Hong Kong, Macao and Taiwan in various forms. The scope and scale of joint operations should be expanded. We should encourage the setting up of trans-regional enterprise groups, trans-continental large companies and overseas companies. By using the superiority of trans-regional groups and the close links between overseas companies and mainland enterprises, large-scale economic coordination among enterprises on the mainland and in Hong Kong, Macao and Taiwan will be promoted.

—Measures must be taken to encourage and promote the direct signing of industrial cooperation plans and trade cooperation plans between enterprises on the mainland and those in Hong Kong, Macao and Taiwan. For instance, enterprises with the same business activities should be encouraged to sign cooperation plans. Coordination plans may be signed among enterprises of the same industry. Cooperation agreements may be signed among enterprises in the same region for industrial division of labor and coordination.

—Enterprise coordination organizations and service organizations should be formed on the mainland, in Hong Kong, Macao and Taiwan, such as enterprise associations, enterprise coordination promotion societies, friendship societies, etc. Civil bodies and semi-official organizations should play a full part in strengthening cooperation among enterprises by opening up, linking up, coordinating, guiding and helping so that the enterprises on the mainland and in Hong Kong, Macao and Taiwan can quickly get on the path to a Chinese economic coordination system.

II. Establishing a Unified Market for the Chinese Economic Coordination System and Broadening Its Economic Cooperation Sphere

Following the accelerated transition to a market economy and the development and maturity of the Chinese economic coordination system, it becomes an inevitable tendency for China's economic development to gradually set up a unified market for the mainland, particularly in the coastal areas of south China, and for Hong Kong, Macao and Taiwan. The unified market is not only a strategy to cope with the changes in the world economic situation but also an objective demand of the development of the Chinese economic coordination system.

As a result of the implementation of the reform and opening up policies on the mainland since the end of the 1970s and for social, economic, historic, cultural and geographical reasons, trade and economic exchanges between the mainland and Hong Kong, Macao and Taiwan have been continuously strengthened.

Economic research reports show that the share of the world's total export volume taken up by Hong Kong and the mainland of China increased from 3.3% in 1986 to 4.9% in 1991. In the increase of the export volume in Asia in the past five years 35.8% came from the mainland of China and Hong Kong. Of the increase of export volume in the world over the past five years 7.1% came from the mainland of China and Hong Kong. This reflects the fact that exports from the mainland of China and the transit trade via Hong Kong play a very important role in the entire world export trade.

Along with the return of Hong Kong and Macao to Chinese sovereignty and progress in China's unification, the setting up of a unified market in the Chinese economic coordination system will promote the common prosperity and progress of the entire Chinese nation.

(1) Circulation of capital. In a unified market capital should flow freely. The leading factor in causing the flow of capital is the function of the market. The essential feature of capital is the pursuit of maximum profit. The role of the market suits this feature of capital. Under the guidance of a unified market the comparative freedom in the flow of capital will bring about a rational readjustment of industrial structure in the region and the effective allocation of resources.

To bring about a free flow of capital several problems have to be solved in the Chinese economic coordination system.

One is the free exchange of currency. The RMB is not an entirely convertible currency. It can be converted into Hong Kong dollars in Hong Kong, and Hong Kong dollars are widely accepted in coastal areas of south China. In China's foreign exchange centers Hong Kong dollars can be changed for RMB. The other is the industrial coordination policy. Between the mainland and Hong Kong, Macao and Taiwan there exists a large degree of mutual complementarity economically. There is also a certain amount of competition. This must be coordinated by means of industrial policy. Within the unified market there must be optimization of the industrial structure and a rational division of labor. Third, mutual financial organizations must be set up on the mainland, and in Hong Kong, Macao and Taiwan. At present, banks with foreign capital, banks with Chinese capital and banks with capital of overseas Chinese, with bases in Hong Kong, have set up branches in the mainland of China. At the same time, Chinese banking and other financial organizations have also set up offices in Hong Kong. The mainland of China encourages Taiwan financial organizations to set up branches on the mainland in the form of joint ventures, enjoying preferential treatment. The setting up of mutual banks and financial organizations will be conducive to the flow of capital in the unified market.

(2) Free flow of goods. This is a basic demand of the unified market. There is a very big volume of trade between the mainland and Hong Kong. But trade between the mainland and Taiwan is

mostly done through Hong Kong. Corresponding measures must be taken to carry out free trade in the Chinese economic coordination system. First of all there must be coordination of trade policies. Trade policies should be readjusted according to the spirit of GATT and the demand of the unified market. Second, direct trade should be carried out between the mainland and Taiwan. Trade on both sides of the Taiwan Straits should be direct, and be mutually supplemented and promoted. At present, however, trade between both sides of the Straits is done via Hong Kong, which acts as a transit port. Costs are increased and time wasted as a result. The quality of goods in some cases is affected in the course of transit. This situation is in urgent need of change.

(3) Exchanges of personnel or mutual migration of labor. Due to the mainland's in-depth reform and opening up and the accelerated pace of moving toward the market economy, free migration or free flow of labor among enterprises and between regions is becoming a reality. The return of Hong Kong and Macao to Chinese sovereignty calls for the free flow of labor and talent between the mainland and Hong Kong and Macao as a generating force in economic development. Taiwan's economic achievement has an important bearing on the mainland, particularly on the province of Hainan in south China. It provides a lesson to be learnt. The mainland is in need of capital from Hong Kong, Macao and Taiwan, as well as their successful experiences in management, advanced technology and talents. The setting up of a unified market will create the conditions for the migration of talents. Several problems must be solved at present. The problem of freedom of movement among ordinary people between the mainland and Taiwan should first be solved. As the return of Hong Kong and Macao to Chinese sovereignty draws near, barriers to the movement of people between the mainland and Hong Kong and Macao will no longer exist. But travel by people from the mainland to Taiwan is very restricted. The movement of technicians and management personnel and other specialists should be permitted between the mainland and Hong Kong, Macao and Taiwan. This will bring about the optimization of allocation of talent resources in the unified market.

III. Building a Legal Basis Which Can Be Adapted to the Market Economy and Promoting Legal Reform to Provide Legal Protection for the Formation and Development of the Chinese Economic Coordination System

Without a legal basis the Chinese economic coordination system cannot be formed or developed smoothly. The concrete meaning and role of the legal basis are as follows:

First, within the Chinese economic coordination system the standardized form of conduct has to be based on law. Without a system and practice based on law there will be serious stumbling blocks and difficulties in mutual economic coordination. Second, the Chinese economic coordination system requires a market economy as a common structural basis to enable it to become an economic operating mechanism. The parties will thus draw near to each other or be linked up with each other. The common economic structural basis must be affirmed by law and should be guaranteed by law. Third, common fundamental principles and regulated behavior must be observed in the economic coordination system. This must be based on law, and the law must be observed in the conduct of affairs. Fourth, if an entirely unified and common standard behavior cannot be formed there should be no major conflicts or differences in the legal entity content and regulated behavior of all parties to the system. Otherwise it will be difficult or even impossible to coordinate and harmonize the economy. Fifth, procedural provisions for all parties to the system must be made to solve legal disputes and legal conflicts, and to facilitate coordination among all parties, related civil bodies and legal arbitration organizations for the solution to concrete problems.

Judging from the situations of the law and legal systems on the mainland, and in Hong Kong, Macao and Taiwan, the Chinese economic coordination system will face a series of legal stumbling blocks and problems in the formation and development of the system. First, the mainland, Taiwan and Hong Kong have different legal systems. The laws on the mainland and Taiwan belong to the continental system, whereas the laws in Hong Kong belong to the Anglo-Saxon legal system. Differences in concepts, meanings and procedures are rather large between these legal systems. Consequently inconveniences and difficulties will arise in the interpretation and application of legal provisions. Second, the stipulations of the law in Taiwan and Hong Kong are based on capitalist private ownership, whereas those of the mainland are based on socialist public ownership. This entails great differences in legal systems and concrete content. Third, due to the influence of the traditional planned economy and various other factors, the legal system on the mainland has not been established completely and is to be perfected, and a legal system and mechanisms compatible with a market economy are lacking, in spite of the fact that much progress has been made in the building of a legal system in recent years. Of the three problems the most crucial is the last. The problem of different legal systems can be solved by studying and comparing them. The difference in basic economic systems will no doubt hamper economic cooperation and the stumbling blocks will greatly reduce and restrict economic cooperation but not affect the general progress of economic coordination, due to the common basis of economic structure and economic operating mechanism. However, unwholesome behavior and weak links in the legal system are wholly incompatible with economic structure and operating mechanism. They will lead to confusion in market regulation and to market disorder. The interests of economic entities cannot be effectively guaranteed. Consequently a healthy legal system and vital legal foundation are very important for the formation and development of the Chinese economic coordination system. In the process of building a market economy on the mainland, attention must be paid to the setting up of a proper legal system and the building of legal institutions.

(1) The mode of behavior of the rule of law must be upheld. Everything must be done in accordance with the norms of law. In the traditional planned economy the norm of behavior was in accordance with mandatory decrees and instructions, and not in

accordance with laws. But since the reform got under way on the mainland efforts have been made to strengthen the building of a legal system. But due to the deep-rooted ways of acting of the old economic system and the influence of the traditional "rule by man" factor, the building of a legal system is no easy task and the mode of behavior according to law has not really been upheld. The market economy target provides ample opportunities to build the legal system on the mainland, as the market economy, in essence, is a legal system economy. Without a wholesome legal system, a market economy cannot be built. Therefore, the custom of traditional rule of man and the practice of behavior according to mandatory orders and decrees must be changed, and the mode of behavior according to the rule of law must be affirmed. The authority of the law must be upheld. The law must be put into force to guarantee that the norm of law becomes the supreme norm of people's behavior. The legal system which operated under the planned economy should be reformed to reflect the demands of the market economy.

(2) Experiences in legislation in Taiwan and Hong Kong should be studied, and their positive features should be absorbed. The market economy on the mainland faces many new situations and problems to be addressed and solved. Hong Kong, Macao and Taiwan have long had market economies and accumulated much experience in this regard. Their legislation deserves study and should be used for reference. Some people have advocated transplanting some Hong Kong and Taiwan laws intact to the mainland. But it would be unfeasible to transplant market economy laws from Hong Kong and Taiwan to the mainland in their entirety due to differences in the legal and economic systems, plus differences in specific situations and conditions. However, laws with common features and of a technical nature may be appropriately transplanted to the mainland in the course of the development of its market economy.

(3) International practices should be consulted on an extensive basis for reference. International economic practices developed quickly after the Second World War. Since they possess the features of wide application, flexibility and practicality, their role

has become more and more important. International economic practices themselves are products of the commodity economy and the market economy. They are the code of conduct for the international market.

The mainland is at present engaged in many tasks: setting up a market economic structure, opening up the country to the outside world, actively taking part in the international division of labor and cooperation, developing international markets, improving the investment environment, absorbing foreign capital, introducing advanced technology and management experience, and solving equitably and rationally legal disputes and problems of law in economic exchanges with foreign countries. It must therefore familiarize itself with international practices and pursue its activities in accordance with them so as to better pursue international economic exchanges and develop the international market.

The best way to remove legal stumbling blocks and conflicts is to conduct mutual economic exchanges and cooperation between the mainland and Hong Kong, Macao and Taiwan by following more closely international practices. The mainland of China promulgated the Law of Economic Contracts Involving Foreign Countries in 1985 and General Rule on Civil Laws in 1986, in which it is explicitly laid down that in cases in which no stipulations have been made in the laws of the People's Republic of China or in international treaties to which China is a party, international practices can be applied. This has provided the legal basis for the application of international practices in economic exchanges between the mainland of China and foreign countries. More importantly, extensive lessons should be drawn from the content of international practices in market economy legislation. Hong Kong, as an international free port, has absorbed international practices in its legislation in considerable number. As for Taiwan, due to its early participation in division of labor and cooperation in the international market, its legislation reflects in some ways international practices. Therefore, to strengthen the economic coordination and exchanges with Hong Kong, Macao and Taiwan, the mainland should similarly absorb and reflect international practices in its legislation. The mainland should adopt prevailing international practices and affirm a common code of conduct with Hong Kong, Macao and Taiwan.

(4) Fully utilizing the legislative power of localities and carrying out experiments in local legislation to promote the early establishment and perfection of a market economy legal system. All provinces, cities and autonomous regions on the mainland have local legislative powers. Without violating national laws and regulations, local laws and regulations can be drawn up by themselves. Hainan, in particular, has been given greater and more flexible legislative power than any other regions in China by the National People's Congress. On the principle of observing national laws and regulations, local regulations can be drawn up in accordance with the concrete conditions of Hainan. Shenzhen City, too, enjoys local legislative power, with the authorization of the National People's Congress. In drawing lessons and absorbing international practices and the laws of Hong Kong and Taiwan, the mainland can put its local legislative power into full play and carry out legislative experiments in localities. It can let special economic zones in particular take the first steps in economic legislation. Then, having gained experience, it can make local economic legislation become national legislation. Being the biggest special economic zone in China, Hainan is most suited to make such legislative experiments. Hainan should fully utilize its greater local legislative power to make the policy advantages of the special economic zones legal advantages. By drawing international practice and absorbing useful points from the laws of Hong Kong and Taiwan, it should be able to set up and perfect market economy legal institutions as early as possible through bold experiments to provide experiences for the whole nation in market economy legislation.

图书在版编目(CIP)数据

中国经济转轨的迫切任务:英文/迟福林著.—北京:
外文出版社,1996.12
ISBN 7－119－01967－8

Ⅰ.中… Ⅱ.迟… Ⅲ.经济体制改革—研究—中国—英文
Ⅳ.F121

中国版本图书馆 CIP 数据核字 (96) 第 16344 号

中国经济转轨的迫切任务

迟福林　著

＊

ⓒ外文出版社

外文出版社出版
(中国北京百万庄路 24 号)
邮政编码 100037
北京外文印刷厂印刷
中国国际图书贸易总公司发行
(中国北京车公庄西路 35 号)
北京邮政信箱第 399 号　邮政编码 100044
1996 年(大 32 开)第 1 版
(英)
ISBN 7－119－01967－8 /F・36(外)
02750
4－E－3146P